ROMAN OFFICERS AND ENGLISH GENTLEMEN

The impact of classical Rome on ancient Britain, as perceived by the late Victorian and Edwardian élites, was a resource of immense contemporary political value. The images it produced helped to define the idea and practice of British imperialism, and the very concept of 'Englishness'. Academics colluded in this process and this created a legacy in Roman archaeology which persists to the present day.

Roman Officers and English Gentlemen is a pioneering work that explores this fascinating relationship. It offers a thorough examination of late Victorian and Edwardian writings on Rome and the ancient Britons and illuminates the historical context and development of Roman archaeology, while simultaneously making an exciting contribution to the current debates on English identity and imperialism.

This landmark study will be essential reading for scholars and students in Roman archaeology, ancient history, colonial studies and historiography.

Richard Hingley is a lecturer in Roman archaeology at the University of Durham.

ROMAN OFFICERS AND ENGLISH GENTLEMEN

The imperial origins of Roman archaeology

Richard Hingley

London and New York

First published 2000
by Routledge
11 New Fetter Lane, London EC4P 4EE

Simultaneously published in the USA and Canada
by Routledge
29 West 35th Street, New York, NY 10001

Routledge is an imprint of the Taylor & Francis Group

© 2000 Richard Hingley

Typeset in Garamond by
Florence Production Ltd, Stoodleigh, Devon
Printed and bound in Great Britain by
TJ International Ltd, Padstow, Cornwall

British Library Cataloguing in Publication Data
A catalogue record for this book is available from
the British Library

Library of Congress Cataloging in Publication Data
Hingley, Richard.
Roman officers and English gentlemen: the imperial origins
of Roman archaeology/Richard Hingley.
p. cm.
Includes bibliographical references and index.
1. Great Britain—Antiquities, Roman.   2. Great Britain
—History—Roman period, 55 B.C.–449 A.D.   3. Great
Britain—Civilization—Roman influences.   4. Excavations
(Archaeology)—Great Britain.   5. Romans—Great Britain.
6. Imperialism.   I. Title.
DA145.H56 2000
936.1–dc21   00–026893

ISBN 0–415–23580–4 (pbk)
ISBN 0–415–23579–0 (hbk)

TO MY FATHER,
RONALD HINGLEY,
WHOSE ACADEMIC WORK
HAS INSPIRED MY OWN

CONTENTS

List of illustrations   ix
Preface   xi
Acknowledgements   xv

1 Imperial discourse: Britain and Rome   1

PART I
Imperialism   17

  2 Republicanism to imperialism: the growth of
    imperial discourse   19

  3 Decline and fall: a political analogy and
    provider of lessons   28

  4 Drawing lessons from Rome regarding
    incorporation and assimilation   38

PART II
Englishness   61

  5 Teutons, Romans and Celts   63

  6 Ancient heroes of the resistance   72

  7 The rise of a theory of mixed racial origins   86

  8 Englishness between the Wars, racial mixing
    and the role of Rome   96

CONTENTS

PART III
Romanisation   **109**

 9 Francis Haverfield and Romanisation   111

10 Romanisation: Haverfield's legacy   130

11 Conclusions: 'Island stories'   156

    Notes   166
    Bibliography   199
    Index   220

ILLUSTRATIONS

Figures

1.1	Francis John Haverfield (1860–1919)	13
4.1	Major General William Roy's map of Rough Castle Roman fort	39
4.2	Ambleside Roman fort	46
4.3	The building of the Wall	58
5.1	The landing of the Romans	66
6.1	The Britons before the propraetor	84
8.1	The Roman signal station at Scarborough	99
9.1	The Romano-British town at Silchester	118
9.2	The Roman 'village' at Woodcuts (Dorset)	120
9.3	The (a) civil and the (b) military districts of Roman Britain	127
10.1	Villas and villages in Dorset, Hampshire and Wiltshire	135

Tables

10.1	Differences between 'Roman' and 'Native'	148
10.2	Numbers of archaeological sites excavated by 5-year period from 1921 to 1995	149
10.3	Numbers and proportions of archaeological sites of differing types excavated by 5-year period from 1921 to 1995	150

PREFACE

Appeals to the past are amongst the commonest of strate-
gies in the interpretation of the present. What animates
such appeals is not only disagreement about what happened
in the past and what the past was, but uncertainty about
whether the past really is past, over and concluded, or
whether it continues, albeit in different forms.

(Edward Said, 1993: 1)

In this book I seek to explain the value of a study of the historical
context of the development of Romano-British studies. I shall
contend that this type of study can help to provide an understanding
of where the subject is now. Although studies of the historical
context of prehistoric archaeology have been popular since at least
the 1950s,[1] Roman archaeologists have rarely indulged in this type
of analysis.[2] Increasingly during the research that I have undertaken,
however, this aim has become secondary to another and I also hope
that this book will contribute to the growing literature on English
identity, and the nature of British imperialism.[3] Recent accounts of
British imperialism and 'Englishness' do not deal in any detail with
the use of the images of Rome and the native resistance to Rome
in the establishment of what I will title 'imperial discourse',[4] but
this book focuses attention on this topic.

  The origin of my interest in the subject matter dates back almost
twenty years. During my research in the early 1980s, I found several
books by English authors who wrote in Edwardian and later times
which drew explicit parallels between the imperial experiences of
England (or Britain) and those of Rome, including a work by the
Roman archaeologist and ancient historian Francis Haverfield. I
found the association intriguing and stimulating and a number of

questions emerged: for instance, why did the English feel a particular association with the classical Romans? Why did some Edwardian English men in the 1900s and 1910s appear particularly fixated by the idea? Moreover, a hermeneutical question: how had matching ideas of British and Roman imperialism interacted and thus impacted upon the early development of Roman archaeology in Britain?[5]

While undertaking research I also discovered and was influenced by several social anthropologists who had drawn attention, in the development of a critical and reflexive anthropology, to the methods by which American social anthropology had served as an arm of American foreign policy.[6] This set me thinking in greater detail about ways in which Roman archaeology in Britain might have served the state during the period of the British Empire.

It appeared to me that, at the same time as the English studied Rome and thus reinterpreted it, they also used Roman history and archaeology to inform their own actions in a complex and at least partly circular process. In Edward Said's terms (above), appeals to the past were used in the interpretation of the present. How have the assumptions that have been made about the association between England and classical Rome influenced the perspectives developed by Roman archaeologists? How has the dominant perspective in Roman archaeology impacted upon the collection of archaeological evidence and therefore affected the data about the Roman period that are available to archaeologists today? How were, and are, Roman archaeologists implicated in the historical processes of colonialism and neo-colonialism?[7]

The original motivation for this book, therefore, grew out of my interest in the intellectual origins of Romano-British archaeology and the context, in particular, of Francis Haverfield's work as 'the founder of Romano-British archaeology'. Looking at Haverfield's work in this context has drawn me deeply into a study of nineteenth- and twentieth-century images of Rome, both popular and academic.

Perhaps such questions arose in my mind as a result of the nature of my education. Although my secondary education was broadly classical, in a way comparable to that of previous generations, the degree of the influence of classical learning had begun to decline by the time I attended secondary school and university in the late 1970s and early 1980s.[8] Likewise, the final vestiges of Britain's empire had almost disappeared by the late 1970s,[9] making me – alongside the Roman archaeologist Martin Millett and others – a member of what might be considered the first English generation after the decline of the Empire.[10] This has perhaps created a rather more critical attitude to British imperialism than might have been the case had I been educated twenty years earlier.

I became distracted from researching this topic for some time in the mid-1980s, but my book on *Rural Settlement in Roman Britain* was published in 1989 and a reviewer in *Antiquity* argued that the book invites us to: 'share in a communal, retrospective guilt not just for the British Empire, . . . but . . . for the Roman imperial presence; and for drawing entirely valid parallels between the advances that both such imperial ventures brought about'.[11] I was rather surprised by this particular set of comments on my book which, while attempting to pay attention to a wide Romano-British social spectrum and to adopt some new approaches to the evidence, did not overtly aim to address the questions of advances toward civilisation or parallels between the two empires.

In fact, the reviewer's comments set me thinking anew and drew my mind back to the accounts of the Edwardian politicians and popular writers that I had discovered some years before. The reviewer, like the earlier writers, appears to draw an explicit association between the imperial missions of Britain and Rome – how else was the reader to be drawn into a 'retrospective guilt for the British Empire' by reading a book about Roman rural settlement in Britain which did not even mention British imperialism? I have always found this association between two very different empires particularly difficult to accept. I feel that no direct comparison exists between ancient and modern imperialism.[12] Instead I feel that it may be helpful to argue that many of the direct associations that have been drawn between the British Empire and the Roman resulted from the former borrowing from the latter; they do not form part of some shared imperial 'mission'. My interest in the subject, therefore, relates more specifically to the association that the English have drawn between themselves and the Romans and the influence of this association on the practice of archaeology.

The review, however, after a period of thought, inspired me to conduct a deeper study of attitudes to Rome among late Victorian, Edwardian and later British writers and the impact of their ideas on the development of Roman archaeology in the twentieth century. This book is a result of that research. I am grateful to the reviewer of my *Rural Settlement in Roman Britain* for the inspiration that he has provided to my research. I am not certain, however, that he will welcome the outcome, as he may be struck by the irony that this book aims to provide some of the critique that he attributed to my earlier publication.

On a more specific level, the critique of my earlier book raises the topic of continuity in British attitudes towards their own Empire. Although attitudes in Britain have changed since the decolonisation of the 1940s to 1960s, it is felt by many in the former colonies that it remains difficult for the average British citizen to take a critical view of the imperial past.[13] During the 1990s, I became increasingly interested in the potential value of so-called 'colonial discourse theory', or 'post-colonial theory' to Roman archaeology.[14] In this book my aim is to explore the context of Roman archaeology with regard to the broader imperial concerns of the British.

During the researching and writing of this book I have continuously struggled to balance a form of doctrinal approach to colonial discourse with a rather more open and less judgmental analysis. I find the judgmental approach particularly useful in providing a critique of past texts and in pointing out alternative ways forward for the discipline. This is likely to have created a context in which some readers with an interest in Roman archaeology will strongly disagree with the approach that I have taken. A more open, less judgmental, approach would deal with variability in texts with more ease.[15] I have attempted to provide a fairly detailed study of the work of some past authors in this book, but I have aimed to avoid losing the analytical coherence that I feel that the post-colonial approach provides.

The motivation for writing this book is also derived partly from the inspiration provided by recent developments in the subject of Roman studies – for instance the welcome inspiration provided by the creation of the Theoretical Roman Archaeology Conference.[16] As such, the book forms part of a general call for a realignment of Roman studies which has been voiced by a number of authors over the past few years.[17]

ACKNOWLEDGEMENTS

I owe a debt of gratitude to Phil Freeman, whose own interest in the work of Mommsen and Haverfield has helped to expand my understanding, as have his comments on my work and his articles.[18] David Miles first encouraged my interest in this subject and I also owe him a large debt of gratitude. Others who have helped me in fundamental ways in developing the ideas explored in this book include Professor David Breeze, Steve Dickinson, Dr Siân Jones, Professor Lawrence Keppie, Professor David Mattingly, Gordon Maxwell, Professor Martin Millett, Dr Mark Pearce, Christina Unwin, Dr Jane Webster and Dr Alex Woolf. I thank them all. Christina Unwin, David Mattingly, Steve Dickinson, Ruth Hingley and two unnamed readers provided considerable assistance with the text at various stages of its evolution. I am extremely grateful to Richard Stoneman for his patience and forbearance. I am also very grateful to the staff of the National Library of Scotland and the libraries of the National Museums of Scotland, Durham University, Historic Scotland and the Ashmolean Museum, Oxford.

1

IMPERIAL DISCOURSE: BRITAIN AND ROME

Summary

This book focuses upon the images provided by the impact of classical Rome upon ancient Britain. The ways in which these images were used during the period from around 1860 to 1930 – the heyday of British imperialism – form the core of the text. The book also considers certain aspects of Roman archaeology in Britain, in particular the development of the subject under Francis Haverfield in the 1900s and 1910s and how aspects of the archaeological interpretation of Roman Britain have continued to reflect the world-view of late Victorians and Edwardians until the present day.

Attention is focused upon the nature of the *imperial discourse* that was current at this time. A study of imperial discourse examines the ways in which various media were used to serve the needs of the British Empire. In this context various Victorian and Edwardian texts concentrated upon the influence of the classical Roman Empire on ancient Britain. I shall argue that, through the creation of imperial discourse, some late Victorian and Edwardian British administrators, politicians and academics used images of the Roman Empire to help them to define the identity and imperial destiny of Britain.[1] It will also be shown that the Roman history of Britain appears to have been particularly significant from this perspective.

In the course of the book I study the interrelated nature of the images of Rome and the Roman Empire which existed in the popular mind, in political and academic works. The aim is to consider two main themes – the ways in which the images provided by Rome operated in the discourse of British imperialism and also the role of the developing subject of Romano-British archaeology. A circular process of interpretation existed in which the past was used to provide lessons for the present and this resulted in the creation of a relevant and useful past. In the context of imperial discourse, archaeological narrative was drawn into the provision of useful lessons for the British Empire. Archaeological knowledge reinforced, supplemented and sometimes contradicted popular imagery.

The organisation of this book

The book has three main Parts. The first Part (Imperialism) studies some of the ways in which images of Roman imperialism were used to help to define and inform British imperial efforts. Part II (Englishness) turns to the ways in which the image of Roman civilisation was used in the definition of English identity. The definition of identity includes both the definition of Englishness and the creation of an image of otherness, which will be titled 'the Celtic subaltern' (see below). The third Part draws the book together by studying the nature of Francis Haverfield's work on Romanisation and the ways in which this related to the imperial concerns of his contemporaries. It also considers the way in which Haverfield's work created a legacy in Romano-British archaeology that has lasted until the end of the twentieth century. The final chapter summarises these three themes and examines the national context of Romano-British archaeology.

Defining imperialism

Classical Rome was attributed with a distinct role in the process of the definition of British imperialism and this is studied in Chapter 2. The image of decline and fall stressed the need for the British to consider morals for the survival of their own empire. A range of late Victorian and early twentieth-century writings focus upon the role of Rome with regard to British administrative, military and frontier policy.

I shall show how the British used the Roman example to assist with their own imperial projects through the creation of a direct form of imperial discourse, which derived lessons from past examples. This imperial discourse drew upon the evidence for the administration of the Roman Empire and the archaeological evidence for the Roman frontier systems in addition to Roman literary texts that addressed military issues. In so doing it helped to draw the archaeological study of Roman monuments into the sphere of imperial discourse. This Victorian and Edwardian tradition also had an influence on archaeological practice in the early to mid-twentieth century. A strong military tradition existed in popular images of Roman Britain throughout the late nineteenth and early twentieth centuries and, within Roman studies, the archaeology and history of the Roman army has remained a clearly defined and fairly distinct area of research. The imperial context of the origins of modern Roman military archaeology helps to explain the way in which military studies have developed during the twentieth century.

Defining 'Englishness'

Curiosity about the history of the British Isles during medieval and post-medieval times was associated with the perceived relationship between various ancient peoples and modern populations.[2] The questions asked of the evidence for the past at this time and the answers that were offered were often motivated by the desire of scholars to examine national identity and destiny.[3] In the process the past was interpreted in terms of a concern to establish historical lines of ancestry. This resulted in the creation of images of origin and identity that are teleological in nature. During the late nineteenth and early twentieth centuries, an interest in national origins continued to hold a fascination for the English. In examining works that were produced by popular writers, politicians and academics at this time, I shall draw upon an idea defined by Raphael Samuel. Samuel has argued that historians (or for that matter ancient historians and archaeologists) however wedded they are to empirical enquiry, will take on, without knowing it, the deep structures of 'mythical thought'.[4] This concept of mythical thought relates to the broader views of society as represented in a wide range of ideas and media, for instance, popular works and political writings. Samuel attributes this adoption of mythical thought to the scholarly wish to establish lines of continuity, or to the symbolic importance attached to the permanence of national life, or to an un-argued and in-explicit but all-pervasive teleology.[5]

The issue of national origins in the late nineteenth and early twentieth centuries came to be focused upon relevant imperial considerations in the search for a useful definition of Englishness which drew upon the idea of the permanence of national life. The Teutonic image of racial origin, which had been dominant for much of the nineteenth century became less powerful in the face of new imperial concerns towards the end of the century. The new representation that developed at this time argued that the English imperial spirit was derived from a mixed genetic inheritance, including ancient Britons, classical Romans, Anglo-Saxons and Danes.

3

This mixed racial origin included the civilising spirit of the Romans. Some late Victorian and Edwardian texts suggest that the classical Romans passed onto the English a civilisation that led fairly directly to the modern state of England. Through the process of conquest, Rome was felt to have introduced civilisation and Christianity to Britain and also to have helped to form the imperial character of the English. English civilisation, religion and imperial spirit are all traced back to the Roman past. This continuity in imperial spirit is defined in such a way that the natives of Roman Britain are often viewed in popular literature to have adopted Roman civilisation and improved upon it in an active effort to create modern England and the British Empire. Incorporated in this distinctly English racial mix was the brave spirit of the ancient Britons who had opposed Rome. In this context, some popular pictures of Roman Britain gave a nationalist view of a civilised distinctly British province – a linear forebear for modern England.

Within the context of Great Britain, the English could be argued to have inherited this distinct Roman character. The Welsh, Irish and Scots had a less direct claim to a Roman inheritance. As a result, a Roman inheritance was used by the English to help to define their relationship to the other people of Great Britain.[6]

Defining Romanisation

Haverfield's interpretation of Romanisation formed an important element in the developing representation of Englishness. It helped to correct an earlier idea that suggested that little of the civilisation of the Romans had passed onto the British – the image of the Celtic subaltern. Concerns about lines of continuity in the national life of England structured academic and popular works and Roman archaeology came to have a distinct value as part of the representation of Englishness.

At the same time, Haverfield's theory of Romanisation was also characterised by certain basic assumptions involving the character of civilisation. It defined a binary opposition between barbaric native 'Celts' and civilised Romans. Romanisation was the process by which the uncivilised Briton (or European) achieved civilisation. This theory of Romanisation reflected aspects of contemporary imperial discourse, particularly images of the progress of civilisation under imperial guidance. Haverfield's work provided the basis for what will be called 'progressive' interpretations of Romanisation. The progressive interpretation carried beliefs about imperial civilisation into the 1970s and beyond.

4

The types of analogies that were drawn between Britain and Rome during the nineteenth and early twentieth centuries deeply influenced the character of Haverfield's studies and also the Roman archaeology that we have inherited. This produced the context for beliefs of a unified civilising mission that united imperial Britain with classical imperial Rome (see Preface). It has also resulted in a tradition in which Britain has often been viewed as distinctly different from the remainder of the Roman Empire.[7]

Classical Rome: a useful imperial image

Before exploring the use of image of imperial Rome in British imperial discourse in greater detail, it is necessary to examine some concepts and terms in greater detail. This book draws upon the idea that the Roman past has been used to help to define the images of imperialism that the British have found to be useful in their own imperial activities. The Roman conquest and occupation of southern Britain during the first four centuries of the first millennium AD drew the classical Romans into the orbit of English domestic history.[8] These events are recorded both in the accounts of classical historians and through the physical evidence of the buildings and structures that were built in Britain during the Roman period of history. Various authors in the recent past have suggested that the classical Romans introduced both civilisation and Christianity to the British Isles.[9] Partly as a result of this direct Roman impact on the domestic history of England, the image of Rome has formed a useful set of historical references (or representation) for the English, as indeed it has for other nations.[10]

A variety of images derived from classical Rome has been adopted (and adapted) in the course of English history because of the assistance they provided and provide with historically specific issues, including those of imperial destiny and national identity. The image itself is, and was, not a simple, coherent or clearly defined historical entity. It included (and includes) a variety of partly independent ideas which have had differing resonances; for instance, the Roman Republic, the Roman Empire, the Holy Roman Empire, the Eternal City of Rome and the Roman papacy.[11] These images have been used in a variety of ways during differing times. A series of dramatic, edifying and entertaining moral tales also stem from classical Roman sources,[12] or could be invented using material that it provided.[13] In fact, part of the value of the image of Rome for the British may well have lain in its flexibility and complexity.[14]

In particular, it is important in the context of this book that Rome has had a role in contributing to the discourse of British imperialism. The focus of the first two-thirds of this book is therefore on the value which the Roman Empire was felt to possess for the definition of aspects of British imperialism during a restricted period in the late nineteenth and early twentieth centuries. This interest often drew upon the archaeological evidence provided by the Roman conquest and occupation of Britain. I shall examine in detail the ways in which ideas of both the impact of the Roman Empire upon Britain and reaction of the native population to the Romans became implicated through the creation of a literary and philosophical imperial discourse.

Imperial discourse

In the early to mid-nineteenth century a critical attitude to imperialism (including Roman imperialism) had existed. The final twenty to thirty years of Queen Victoria's reign, however, have been called 'the Age of New Imperialism'. It was a time when new intellectual and social currents developed to justify and promote European expansion into distant areas of the world. For a period which might be dated perhaps from the publication of J.R Seeley's *The Expansion of England* (1883) down to the Great War, 'Empire' began to appear in school textbooks and elsewhere as a 'slogan' defining the ultimate fulfilment of England's mission.[15] It was also a time at which, in the words of C.C. Eldridge, 'imperial ideology' became part of the language of patriotism in Britain, involving both Liberals and Conservatives.[16] This process of transition from an anti-imperial to a pro-imperial attitude in British society is studied in the next chapter.

In the context of the late Victorian and Edwardian period, I am drawn to the approaches outlined in colonial discourse theory.[17] In this approach, literary works, which were once read as worthy expressions of Western ideals, are now read as evidence of the manner in which such ideas have served in the historical process of colonialism.[18] Colonial discourse theory focuses upon the power of colonial ideology and how rhetoric and representations helped in the historical process of imperialism. David Spurr has suggested that:

> colonial discourse is neither a monolithic system nor a finite set of texts; it may more accurately be described as the name for a series of colonising discourses, each adapted to a specific historical situation, yet having in common certain

elements with the others. This series is marked by internal repetition, but not by all-encompassing totality.[19]

I shall use the concept of imperial discourse[20] rather than that of colonial discourse. The use of the term 'imperial' rather than 'colonial' in the context of this book relates to late Victorian New Imperialism and its use requires some explanation.

The expansionist activities of the British are usually defined as 'imperialism', due to the fact that their occupation of many parts of the world did not always lead to large-scale colonial settlement, although this was the case in some areas (USA, Australia, Canada, etc).[21] 'Imperialism' can signify the practice, theory and attitude of a dominant metropolitan nation or people in establishing control over and ruling another nation or people.[22] In the words of Koebner and Schmidt, the meaning of the term is useful for typifying any system of extended rule from Nineveh to the twentieth-century Soviet Union.[23] 'Colonialism' derives from the classical notion of the colony as a permanent settlement of people who have moved away from their home territory, but has been extended to mean all instances of direct political control of a people by a foreign state, irrespective of the number of settlers present.[24]

Evidently, from these definitions, imperialism and colonialism can mean much the same, but I feel that the term 'imperial' discourse to be more appropriate than 'colonial' discourse in the context of British imperial control, not least because it reflects more correctly the situation than Roman-style colonialism. Many of the lessons which the British derived from the Roman Empire at this time, as we shall see, related to imperial rule, particularly in the context of India, rather than to the management of parts of the Empire which were colonies populated by British settlers.[25]

The imperial discourse that I shall define is characteristic of the writings of a wide range of authors. It was constituted in acts and texts that involved an aggressive patriotism, monarchism, militarism, the worship of national heroes and the cult of personality; and racial ideas associated with theories of progress connected with Darwinian evolution.[26] Recent accounts of the popular culture of this period set works of political and social thought in context.[27] The ideology of empire is apparent in the writings of both popular authors and academics in a variety of texts relating to British history and politics, and also novels and other forms of popular literature. Many texts of this date exhibit a pro-imperial and uncritical view of Britain's role in world politics. It has been suggested that the decline in Christian belief at this time led the educated classes towards the stoicism of the classics and the mysticism of an imperial faith.[28] The virtually all-pervading nature of this imperial discourse has become a significant area of modern study, together with the way in which individuals from a wide range of political and social viewpoints became drawn into adopting pro-imperial attitudes.[29]

The ruling classes developed a number of projects in Edwardian times that were aimed at revitalising the leadership qualities required to maintain the Empire.[30] In addition to a serious focus on administration, education was turned to this purpose and, on the whole, carried a nationalist emphasis as educators, politicians, philosophers and political theorists searched for a more efficient way of building a national sense of ancestry, tradition and destiny.[31] Images provided by ancient Rome were used in this process as a way of defining 'morals' or 'lessons' for the English, as well as a way of identifying and defining national origins.

It would appear that those who produced this discourse were often effectively deceived by their own sentiments and philosophy.[32] In addition, imperial discourse was not solely constituted in state-sponsored imperial propaganda. Writers, publishers and manufacturers took their own commercial decisions based on the positive image that Empire instilled in the minds of the public and which helped to sell their products.[33] We shall also see that jingoism was focused upon a distinct feeling of insecurity about both the present and the future.

In studying this imperial discourse it is also necessary to look both backwards and forwards in time. The imperial discourse which will be considered may represent a development of the late nineteenth and early twentieth centuries, but – like other varieties of colonial discourse – it drew upon earlier roots. Edward Said has written about late nineteenth-century colonial discourse in England and France and has described 'a language whose imagery of growth, fertility, and expansion, whose teleological structure of property and identity, whose ideological distinction between "us" and "them" had already matured elsewhere – in fiction, political science, racial theory, travel writing.'[34]

The images that constituted English imperial discourse in the late nineteenth and early twentieth centuries developed from the fifteenth century onward.[35] As a result, it will be necessary for me to study some of these earlier images in the course of this book in order to set the context for the contribution of classical Rome to the development of imperial discourse in late Victorian and Edwardian society.

From the 1920s onward much of the output of British authors appears less extreme to a modern audience.[36] The British Empire itself, however, continued as a significant institution well into the 1950s and many of the beliefs that formed imperial discourse are perpetuated in works dating from the 1930s through to the 1990s.[37] Aspects of this continuity are explored later in the book.

The classics and imperial discourse

Ashcroft, Griffiths and Tiffin in their study of colonial discourse have suggested that 'The significant feature of imperialism . . . is that, while as a term used to describe the late nineteenth-century policy of European expansion it is quite recent, its historical roots run deep, extending back to Roman times.'[38] The Romans had their own form of imperial discourse[39] and the Roman roots of imperialism and civilisation were considered highly significant by a wide range of writers in the late nineteenth and early twentieth centuries. As a result, the classics (ancient history and archaeology) came to play an important part in the creation of imperial discourse.[40] It is relevant to the use of the image of Rome at this time that classical education, which had developed a significant role after the Renaissance, remained fundamental to gentlemen.[41] The unifying force between the ruling upper and upper-middle classes in the mid- to late nineteenth century was a group of about 150 boys' 'public schools'.[42] These were places at which boys received education and training which helped them to grow up to be 'gentlemen'.[43] Among the most important items of the curriculum was the study of classical (Greek and Roman) language and literature. A close knowledge of the fundamental works of the classics was generally felt to be adequate to qualify a public schoolboy for a university or an administrative career.[44] Symonds, in his study of *Oxford University and Empire*, has considered in detail how the classics contributed to the university education of the British imperial élite during the period from 1870 to 1939 and the special role of Oxford University in this context. The teaching of classics helped to establish the philosophy and national attitudes to the Empire and formed the background to the education of most senior imperial administrators and politicians.[45] The appointees of educational and government posts favoured men well educated in classical languages.[46]

In this context, Stray has argued that classical education had a role in maintaining the solidarity of an élite group and in excluding their inferiors.[47] Representations drawn from the classics were used to frame relationships of inequality, intimately related to structures of power and wealth. The ethos of the gentlemanly male group, united by classical education, was created in public schools and buttressed by the existence of enclaves that supported its prolongation – including universities, Parliament, the Inns of Court and the London Clubs.[48]

Stray has discussed 'classicizing' – the use of classical antiquity to make authoritative sense of the present.[49] In the context of the power of the classics in the creation of imperial discourse, Martin Bernal has explored the way in which classics fulfilled a role in the mission of western imperial powers. His focus has been on the use of the image of classical Greece but he has suggested that:

> Classics has incorporated social and cultural patterns in society as a whole and has reflected them back, to provide powerful support for the notion of Europe possessing a categorical superiority over all other continents, which in turn justifies imperialism or neo-colonialism as *missions civilisatrices*.[50]

During late Victorian and Edwardian times, imperial need partly drove the desire to derive imperial parallels from ancient history and archaeology through this classicising approach. In this process, the classical literary sources were of value in themselves. By defining their own civilisation in opposition to barbarian 'others', classical authors provided a powerful interpretative tool for those who created modern imperial discourse.[51]

This definition of the 'other' is fundamental to the British imperial discourse that is considered below. In the chapter titled Teutons, Roman and Celts, I shall explore the concept of the *'Celtic subaltern'*. The term 'subaltern' has been adopted by a variety of scholars who have derived approaches from colonial discourse theory.[52] The Celtic subalterns can be defined in these terms, not in the guise of the subalterns of the British imperial army, but as those of an inferior rank who are subject to the hegemony of a ruling class. The Celtic others were defined in British imperial discourse through the use of the classical sources which addressed the native population of Roman Britain. The accounts of the natives of Roman Britain that were provided by the classical authors often appeared dismissive.[53] They gave a picture of native peoples of pre-Roman and Rome Britain who appeared more akin to the populations of the backward parts of the British Empire than to the modern English.

In this process of their own self-definition, the English often used classical sources to define self. Some writers in late Victorian and Edwardian England forged a close historical link between Rome and Britain, projecting Britain as the direct heir to Rome. In various late Victorian and Edwardian works, Rome's fundamental role in civilising the Britons is recalled. In some popular works it would even appear that the purpose of Rome in conquering and civilising Britain was to create the historical context for Britain's own imperial mission. It will be argued that this linear conception of a civilising mission that combined both the Roman and the British empires forms a prime example of the creation of a linear national mythical history.

Texts

In my analysis of late Victorian and Edwardian imperial discourse I shall take up Spurr's suggestion that colonial (imperial) discourse theory should address a range of texts that are not usually considered by scholars undertaking work from the 'post-colonial' perspective.[54] From its original adoption by Edward Said, colonial discourse theory has often been applied to works of literature, but it is also possible to apply it to other forms of text[55] – for instance journalism, travel writing, anthropological works, political texts, history, ancient history and archaeology.

Popular and political works

My consideration of imperial discourse in the sections of the book on imperialism and Englishness will be restricted to a range of mainly late Victorian, Edwardian and early twentieth-century texts that contain observations about the relationship between ancient Rome and Britain. The works that will be considered comprise school texts, novels aimed at young people (mainly boys), adult novels, a libretto for an opera, a poem, works of political theory and archaeological texts. Some of these works address the relationship between classical Rome and ancient Britain, but the main emphasis in the works that I have selected in is on the relevance of ancient Rome to contemporary imperial Britain. In fact it would appear that the two themes are difficult to separate in many of the works that are considered.

11

Francis Haverfield and Romano-British archaeology

In the section of the book that deals with Romanisation the focus of attention turns specifically to archaeological texts. In the early to mid-nineteenth century, Roman archaeology in Britain was largely an amateur pursuit conducted by clerics and other gentlemen. It became a professional academic discipline during late Victorian and Edwardian times under the influence of Francis Haverfield (Figure 1.1).[56] The contribution of Haverfield to imperial discourse through the study of Roman Britain is a re-occurring topic in this book.

Francis John Haverfield was born in 1860 at Shipston on Stour in Warwickshire, the son of a vicar.[57] In 1868 he experienced the important discovery of Roman remains in Bath and this perhaps gave a particular sense of reality to his early Latin lessons. He attended Winchester School and New College, Oxford. He secured a 'first' in Moderations but missed his proper class in 'Greats' because of a lack of interest in Philosophy. He became a teacher at Lancing College and this provided him with the opportunity to spend his holidays abroad, studying Roman imperial archaeology.

Much of his early work focused on epigraphy, but he soon turned to the archaeology of Roman Britain and was awarded a Senior Studentship at Christ Church, Oxford, in 1892. In 1907 he was appointed Camden Professor of Ancient History, in succession to his old friend Henry Pelham. He served on various archaeological committees and was the first President of the Roman Society in 1911. He died in 1919 after publishing a long list of articles and books on a variety of topics connected with Rome and particularly with Roman Britain.

Many have seen Haverfield as the founder of modern Romano-British archaeology. Among observations about Haverfield's contribution is that of Sir Ian Richmond, who suggested that Haverfield's passion for detail and gift of sober judgement led him to the 'truth' in matters in which an accumulation of evidence by 1957 had proved him 'abundantly right'.[58] Sheppard Frere observed in 1988 that Haverfield 'was the real founder of the study of the archaeology of Roman Britain in its full sense as an academic discipline'.[59] In recent years, his work has become the focus for a number of differing historiographical studies.[60] I wish to consider Haverfield's work in order to provide an account of his contribution and also to set it in the context of Edwardian views of the relevance of the Roman imperial experience to the British Empire.

F. Haverfield

Figure 1.1 Francis John Haverfield (1860–1919): 'the real founder of the study of the archaeology of Roman Britain in its full sense as an academic discipline' (see text). *Source*: Haverfield and Macdonald, (1924a).

Roman archaeology was one of a range of topics that developed into academic disciplines at this time[61] and it is possible to see developments in archaeology as part of a broader trend in English society. Francis Haverfield argued the value of Roman studies to a broad audience in a number of lectures. It will be suggested that the way that his work contributed to imperial discourse in the Edwardian period is evident in his various 'addresses' which explored parallels between the Roman Empire and the British, through his work on military frontier studies, administration and Romanisation. His theory of 'Romanisation' created a closer area of encounter between England's Roman past and the contemporary population of England by contributing to an evolving image of Englishness. It also had a deep influence on the development of Roman archaeology in the twentieth century.

I should stress that, in the process of studying Haverfield, it is not my intention to seek to condemn either his work or his beliefs. I would accept that his contribution was fundamental to the creation of modern Romano-British archaeology, but archaeologists always seek to update the work of their predecessors and I am intrigued by the reasons that led Haverfield's work to become fundamental in a British context. Haverfield evidently created a more rigorous archaeology of Roman Britain,[62] but I shall suggest that this is not the only reason for his influence on the Edwardian archaeologists and on the twentieth-century archaeological community.

Texts and historical understanding

The process by which the past is drawn upon to help interpret the present can often be considered to be circular in nature. Individuals, in the very process of constructing an image of the past, selectively reinvent it to create useful ideas for the present.[63] One aim of this book is, therefore, to provide an account of the ways in which images of the Roman Empire and of the Roman conquest and the domination of the natives in Britain have been drawn upon in the creation of imperial discourse. It will be argued that works of popular literature, academic works and studies in political theory help to provide an understanding of images of Rome which influenced the development of archaeological theory. Archaeology and ancient history have in turn influenced popular images of Rome and Britain. In fact, the writings and pronouncements of 'specialists', academics and experts, have often been used to legitimise popular and political accounts and archaeologists have often co-operated with (or even on occasions provided motivation for) this practice, as we shall see.[64] It is also true that some thinkers set themselves the task of correcting prevalent representations; we shall see that this was the case with some of Haverfield's work.[65]

The approach taken to the creation of imperial discourse in this book is founded upon the idea that people often use ideas of the past and of origins to help to define their own identity. Relevant aspects of the past in this context are actively selected in the context of the creation of present identity. The perceived imperial mission of Britain during the period from the 1860s to the 1930s focused study of the past upon images that were useful and relevant in the context of the imperial present.

It is evidently incorrect to suggest that all works of this date argue an identical line; individual thinkers had different inspirations and motivations in undertaking the writing of books and articles. In extreme cases, critics of imperialism even countered imperial discourse by attempting to turn some of its claims on their head.[66] The influential nature of imperial politics at this time, however, meant that late Victorian and Edwardian writing is often defined by the repetition of images.

In this context, various images re-occurred in a variety of texts and helped to frame imperial discourse. They did not operate in isolation from the personal motivation of individuals, but were drawn upon in similar ways by numbers of people and reoccur in the various texts. Images that re-occur repeatedly in the text of this book include the following: the decline and fall of the Roman Empire as a parable for the British, the idea that Roman Britain formed an historical parallel for British India, the value of Roman administration and frontier policy to the British, the role of Rome as a civilising power, the significance of Boadicea in British history and a supposed Roman racial inheritance for the English.

Part I

IMPERIALISM

The theme of imperialism considers ways in which images derived from classical Rome were used to help inform British imperial policy during the late nineteenth and early twentieth centuries. Particular attention is paid to the ways in which archaeological monuments were used at this time and upon the contribution of a number of academic ancient historians and archaeologists to the creation of imperial discourse. The initial focus in Chapter 2 is upon how the concept of imperialism grew in significance in the late nineteenth century and upon the contribution of the image of Rome in this context.

2

REPUBLICANISM TO IMPERIALISM

The growth of imperial discourse

Introduction

In this chapter, I shall study the negative image of the Roman Empire that was held by many in the first three-quarters of the nineteenth century. I shall also consider the way in which a new and directly positive view of imperialism and the role of the Roman Empire arose in late Victorian and Edwardian times. This new and positive role for the imperial image was part of the context for the development of the particular form of imperial discourse that is explored in this book. I shall also introduce a range of works of late Victorian and Edwardian date which drew associations between classical Rome and imperial Britain.

Republicanism and anti-imperialism

Society in Britain was inspired by classical associations from the Renaissance onwards and this continued during the nineteenth century.[1] Throughout the first three-quarters of the nineteenth century Hellenic images were used to help to define a range of political concepts, social activities, principles of education and building styles.[2] The Roman model was significant at this time – not only to the old Etonians who controlled Parliament but to politicians, administrators, school teachers[3] and, to a certain extent at least, to the population in general.[4]

The concept of *imperialism* was unacceptable in political terms until the 1870s as a result of Victorian views about the degenerated character of the Roman Empire and also because of the contemporary association of the concept. 'Imperialism' first entered the English language in 1840s, when it was introduced as a term to describe the France of Napoleon III. It was used with reference to a government that glorified its leader, practised despotic rule at home, indulged in ostentatious military display, sought popular acclamation and indulged in an aggressive overseas policy.[5] A clear contrast was drawn at this time between this form of imperialism and the nature of the rule of the British Empire.[6]

Some Victorians drew upon Edward Gibbon in using the image of the Roman Empire to provide an historical lesson of despotic corruption, luxury and indulgence – a direct contrast to the supposed healthy vigour and freedom of the Teutonic English.[7] J.G. Sheppard, for instance, in his *The Fall of Rome and the Rise of the New Nationalities* (1861) considered in detail the legacy which Rome had passed on to Europe – language, law, municipal spirit, ideas of empire, administration, roads, canals, aqueducts, etc. The Roman Empire of Sheppard's account, however, is despotic, corrupt and decadent. In a semi-humorous note he gives rein to his imagination by using Rome under 'Caesarian rule' as a direct contrast to the England of the 1860s. In this note he portrays a situation in which Parliament, all meetings and the 'free press' have been abolished. Government is conducted by a number of the rich and old gentlemen of London who daily receive their orders from Buckingham Palace. However, the 'last heir of the house of Brunswick' has been murdered and the army has sold the crown to Baron Rothschild. Lord Clyde is unhappy with the situation and is on his way at the head of the Indian army to fight for the crown. The Channel fleet has declared for its own commander and is holding the population of London to ransom by preventing the free distribution of corn. Hyde Park has been converted into a gigantic arena, where criminals from Newgate 'set to' with animals from the Zoological Gardens.[8] Sheppard developed the analogy in some detail and it is clear that ancient Rome is seen to represent a direct contrast to Britain in this account; through its own corruption, Rome is seen to reflect back the perfection of Victorian England and the British Empire.

The famous novelist Charles Kingsley, author of *Hereward The Wake* (1866), used Sheppard's observations in his own book *The Roman and the Teuton*, published in 1864. In a chapter titled 'The Dying Empire' Kingsley compared the state of the Roman Empire of the fourth century AD to that of the Chinese or Turkish Empires of his own day and argued the clear superiority of the British Empire over the Roman.[9] He accepted that the Roman Empire of the first and second century AD did bring some wealth and security to each individual country that it 'enslaved', but that after the Antonine emperors all was decline and degradation.[10]

These authors drew upon the ideas of the superiority of contemporary Britain and the British Empire in their discussions of the Romans. John Collingwood Bruce argued in similar terms in his book about Hadrian's Wall, *The Roman Wall*, first published in 1851.[11] In his discussion of the Roman Empire he wrote that:

> Another empire has sprung into being of which Rome dreamt not . . . In this island, where, in Roman days, the painted savage shared the forest with the beast of prey – a lady sits upon her throne of state, wielding a sceptre more potent than Julius or Hadrian ever grasped! Her empire is threefold that of Rome in the hour of its prime. But power is not her brightest diadem. The holiness of the domestic circle irradiated her. Literature, and all the arts of peace, flourish under her sway. Her people bless her.[12]

In the conclusion to his book Bruce returned to the theme of imperial lessons when he suggested:

> We can hardly tarry, even for an hour, in association with the palmy days of the Great Empire, without learning, on the one hand, to emulate the virtues that adorned her prosperity, and on the other, to shun the vices that were punished by her downfall. The sceptre which Rome relinquished, we have taken up. Great is our Honour – great our Responsibility.[13]

Views of this type were expressed by a range of late Victorian and Edwardian authors. These texts invariably turned the imperial parallel to the advantage of Britain in a patriotic manner. Rome's despotism was seen to highlight England's inherited 'freedom'; a freedom which was often felt to have been derived from a supposed Germanic origin (which is studied further in the chapter on Teutons, Romans and Celts).

Imperial Rome, however, also provided a rival set of references for the British to the negative associations of Empire; it represented a recurring reference point for British virtue and also provided an uncomfortable reminder of potential future British imperial decline.[14] Many at this time viewed the Roman Republic as an analogy for the British political system.[15] Rome was of particular importance because it had a relevance to English domestic history – Britain had once been a Roman province. Indeed, the country retained a Christian religious tradition that was closely associated in the minds of its adherents with the spread of the Christian religion within the Roman Empire.[16] The Roman impact on Britain and the supposed Christian inheritance were both fundamental to the use of the image of classical Rome in imperial discourse during the late nineteenth century.

Imperialism

Hostility to the concept of imperialism continued for a short while even after Napoleon III's eclipse in 1870.[17] The attraction of the particular 'discourse of Empire' which was introduced in the last chapter only developed in England after Queen Victoria was made Empress of India in 1876.[18] The use of the idea and images of imperialism from the late 1870s was, therefore, a new development in Britain. A new form of imperial discourse, which drew upon the image of the Roman Empire in a positive fashion, first developed with the heated debate of the Royal Titles Bill, which created Queen Victoria 'Empress of India' in 1876.[19] The trend in British society toward imperial expansion at this time was itself a reaction to the unification of Italy and of Germany[20] and the expansionist activities of Germany and Russia.[21]

Under the influence of the German scholar Theodor Mommsen, an image of Roman Italy arose in the mid- to late nineteenth century that formed a suitable role model for the new states and would-be empires of Germany and Italy.[22] At this time Britain began to respond to this international challenge from these new rivals and Mommsen's seminal work was also adopted as part of British imperial discourse during the late nineteenth century. In the context of political developments in the 1880s, it became increasingly acceptable in Britain to be characterised as an imperialist, as the term lost its alien associations and its meaning had changed.[23] 'Imperialist' came to refer to those who wished to tighten the bonds which united the various parts of the Empire. It also became associated with the acquisition of colonies for economic or political gain, and with the assumed imperial 'mission' of spreading 'civilisation' to others.[24]

The term imperialism changed its meaning in the late nineteenth century from a directly negative image to a largely positive one. As part of this development, the image of the Roman Empire came to be used in the process of the definition of British imperialism.

Classical Rome and the definition of British imperialism

Images derived from the Roman Empire were drawn into imperial discourse. Koebner and Schmidt have described the ways in which the comparison between modern empires and the *imperium Romanum* have often provided a subject for 'rhetorical flourishes', 'sedate reflection' and for praise as well as warning.[25] Imperialism, as well as being constructed on *imperium*, the emblem of antique glory, appealed in late Victorian and Edwardian Britain to the historical consciousness of individual members of the British élite who, as a result of their classical education, were aware fully of the nature of their present.[26]

Even at this time, the image of Rome, in R.F. Betts' terms, was used as 'a magnificent historical reference in an historically-conscious age' but it was not treated to very widespread and popular attention.[27] It has been suggested that popular fascination was vested in the Orient 'or the rank eclectic' and alien living fascinated the public rather than the dead past.[28] Some works of imperial definition show little interest in the Roman example. For instance, the volume *The Empire and the Century: A Series of Essays on Imperial Problems and Possibilities*, written by various authors and published in 1905, has only occasional references to Rome.[29] The Roman example did appeal, however, to a range of classically educated administrators, politicians and school teachers and was used in a variety of ways.

J.R. Seeley, Regius Professor of Modern History in Cambridge, was one of the authors who helped to redefine the value of Roman studies to imperial Britain. He considered the relevance of the Roman imperial image in his immensely successful book *The Expansion of England*, published in 1883. During a discussion of the Mogul Empire, Seeley suggested that:

> not quite every Empire . . . is . . . uninteresting. The Roman Empire, for example is not so. I may say this without fear, because our views of history have grown considerably less exclusive of late years. There was a time no doubt when even the Roman Empire, because it was despotic and in some periods unhappy and half-barbarous, was thought uninteresting. A generation ago it was the reigning opinion that there is nothing good in politics but liberty, and that

accordingly in history all those periods are to be passed over and, as it were, cancelled, in which liberty is not to be found . . . The Roman Republic was held in honour for its freedom; the earlier Roman Empire was studied for the traces of freedom still discernible in it. . . .

We do not now read . . . [history] simply for pleasure, but in order that we may discover the laws of political growth and change . . . We have also learnt that there are many good things in politics beside liberty; for instance there is nationality, there is civilisation. Now it often happens that a Government which allows no liberty is nevertheless most valuable and most favourable to progress towards these other goals.[30]

According to Seeley, the Roman Empire: 'stands out in the very centre of human history, and may be called the foundation of the present civilisation of mankind'.[31] These comments were made seven years after the debate over the Royal Titles Bill and stand in direct contrast to some of the earlier accounts of the Roman Empire discussed above. Seeley's views are particularly central to an understanding of the development of ideas of imperialism in Britain in the late nineteenth century and the role of Rome in this context.

Seeley's comments occurred in the context of changes in British society relating to the creation of a discourse of imperialism, and later authors drew similar conclusions. For instance, W.F. Monypenny, in an article 'The Imperial Ideal', published in 1905, argued that over the previous forty years there had been a change from an interest in 'nation' (the bringing together of 'national fragments' and the extending of 'political privilege' from the few to the many) to concepts of the Empire and imperialism. He suggested that: 'Power and domination rather than freedom and independence are the ideas that appeal to the imagination of the masses; men's thoughts are turned outward rather than inward; the national ideal has given place to the Imperial.'[32] Seeley's reference to Rome as the 'embryo of . . . the modern brotherhood or loose federation of civilised nations'[33] and Monypenny's discussion on imperialism have a European dimension and do not refer exclusively to the British Empire. A wide range of other authors between 1885 and 1930, however, used the image of a glorious Roman imperial past to inform their views on the specifics of Britain's imperial present.

At this time a range of thinkers turned their minds to the analysis of the purpose of the British Empire. The political and social stresses within late Victorian and Edwardian society indicate that the new use of the Roman Empire as a positive rather than a negative analogy was motivated by the need to inform British imperial purpose. Seeley and many of his contemporaries shared this view that political lessons could be derived from the past and applied to the present.[34] Images of 'nationality' and 'civilisation' interested Seeley, Monypenny and others. Many late Victorian and Edwardian speakers and writers drew upon the image of the Roman Empire as a relevant historical reference for the current British generation and some reiterated points raised by Seeley.[35]

Works of imperial comparison

Within the context of the creation of imperial discourse, the Roman imperial parallel developed as a relevant topic of historical interest as the old opposition to ideas of empire became less significant within society. A significant number of writers in the period between 1880 and 1914 drew upon Rome in considering Britain and her empire.[36] These writers include administrators and politicians, such as Lord G.N. Curzon, Lord Cromer (E. Baring), Lord J. Bryce, C.P. Lucas, A. Balfour and E.E. Mills; educationalists and youth workers, such as J.C. Stobart and R.S.S.B. Baden-Powell; children's writers and poets such as A.J. Church, G.A. Henty, R. Kipling and Sir William Watson; academics, such as F. Haverfield, B.W. Henderson, W.T. Arnold and P.C. Sands; and even critics of Empire, such as J.A. Hobson. The Roman image remained significant in a range of works dating to the period from the 1920s and 1930s.[37]

Although, as has been argued above, a range of relevant publications punctuated the whole period from 1890 to 1930, the years between 1905 and 1908 and those from 1910 to 1914 appear to have been particularly significant. Between 1905 and 1908 a number of accounts projected the image of the decline and fall of the Roman Empire directly into the context of the contemporary politics. These include studies by Mills, Baden-Powell, Curzon, Cromer and Balfour. During the years between 1910 and 1914 a range of serious and detailed accounts examined the imperial comparisons in greater detail and looked for 'morals' or 'lessons' from history. Important studies of Britain's relationship to Rome published at this time included three books which focused on the parallel: the Earl of Cromer's *Ancient and Modern Imperialism*, C.P. Lucas' *Greater Rome and Greater Britain* and Lord James Bryce's *The Ancient Roman Empire and the British Empire in India: The Diffusion of Roman and English Law Throughout the World.*[38] Also during this period, Francis Haverfield presented four addresses that drew on the relevance of Rome to Britain.[39] It is significant that a number of the writers who drew the parallel were educated, or taught, at Oxford University (Bryce, Curzon, Haverfield, Fletcher, Hobson and Mills),[40] an establishment which had a special role in the Empire as the supplier of the majority of imperial civil servants and politicians.[41]

Reasons for the drawing of parallels: imperial definition

Why was the Roman reference felt to be fundamental to Britain so long after the end of the Roman occupation of Britain and the Western Empire? Thinkers often articulate images of tradition in order to establish identity in the face of the actual or potential loss of a cherished past[42] and at times of rapid change,[43] and these factors appear to be relevant in the late Victorian and Edwardian context.

The evolution of a modern understanding of Roman imperialism involved a series of separate discourses, which at times are easily distinguished, at other times intertwined. Critical and positive interpretations of Roman imperialism co-exist throughout the nineteenth and twentieth centuries. The parallel between imperial Rome and the British Empire appears, however, to have been increasingly important in the late nineteenth century. The strong oppositions to the idea of imperialism that had existed prior to the late 1870s required that the newly adopted image of British imperialism be discussed and defined.[44] Rapid change in nineteenth-century society and a concern about the future of the British Empire as the dominant force in world politics may have made the Roman analogy particularly important to classically educated politicians and administrators at this time. The value of the image of Rome may have lain partly in its multifaceted nature, ambiguity and complexity. Varying aspects of Rome were drawn upon in different ways.

Much of the writing that will be discussed in this and the following two chapters relates to the definition of the character and nature of British imperialism with regard to the Roman example. Definition often proceeds through the articulation of notions of similarity and difference.[45] Within this process, the image of the Roman Empire was used in an act of definition that involved the identification of both difference and similarities between the two imperial situations.[46] Many if not all of the authors whose work is considered in this book drew contrasts as well as similarities between the two imperial situations.

A range of authors continued the tradition considered above in being highly critical of the autocratic, or despotic, rule of the Roman emperors, and the British political system was felt to be highly superior in this regard.[47] For instance, the Reverent A.J. Church argued in his *Stories from English History; from the Lord Protector to Victoria*, published in 1896, that 'It has been, indeed, a marvellous advance in all that is most to be desired from Claudius, Emperor, to Victoria, Queen and Empress.'[48] In the context of the late nineteenth century and early twentieth, it remained true that Britain's autocratic rule over India required to be examined and explained.[49] It was in the context of British India that the study of the Roman Empire was thought to be particularly relevant by many,[50] as we shall see below.

I wish now to turn to a consideration of some of the ways in which the image of Rome was used in the active definition and manipulation of ideas of empire within the Britain of late Victorian and Edwardian times. The value of the Roman discourse of imperialism to the British was partly the provision of a claim to an historical precedent for imperial action. A circular process occurred, in which interpretations of the Roman past were used to inform the late Victorian and Edwardian present, although in this process the parallels that were drawn were selective and determined by the needs of that present. As a consequence, the present, at least in part, was used to recreate the past in its own image. This was true, as we shall see, not only for popular and political images of Rome, but also with regard to the theory that was created for Roman archaeology and the archaeological sites that were excavated as a consequence.

3

DECLINE AND FALL

A political analogy and provider of lessons

Introduction

In this chapter, I shall turn to the image of decline and fall and the ways in which this image was used in the context of British imperialism, particularly in the Edwardian period. During the late Victorian and Edwardian period a range of writers drew attention to Edward Gibbon's account of the decline and fall of the Roman Empire. Gibbon's work was often drawn upon in the context of the current state of Britain's imperial possessions. This chapter will focus on Edwardian attempts to define the problems faced by the British through a consideration of the comparison of the contemporary British Empire with the decline and fall of Rome.

Some of the Edwardian authors who wrote on decline and fall argued that 'morals' or 'lessons' could be derived from the Roman example. Significant works included those of Lord James Bryce, Sir Charles Lucas, Evelyn Baring (the Earl of Cromer) and Francis Haverfield. Haverfield considered the relationship of the two empires in four addresses and Javed Majeed has recently argued that these addresses point to a genre of work on the Roman and the British Empire that helped in the definition of British imperial thought.[1] Haverfield's addresses indicate that he was in agreement with Cromer and others in feeling that British imperial administrators would profit from a consideration of the ways in which Rome appeared to have successfully controlled her empire.[2]

I shall focus in the following chapter upon the ways in which Roman Empire was used to derive a range of 'morals' or 'lessons' were derived from the fall of the Roman Empire. It was felt that these lessons could be of use to the British in arresting the decline of their own empire. Haverfield's interests included frontier issues ('incorporation'), administration and the 'assimilation' of the native population. In all of these areas Roman archaeology was felt to provide lessons for the British to take to heart. Classical learning and archaeological study were central to all three topics and it will be argued that this indicates the relevance of Roman archaeology to imperial discourse at this time.

Gibbon and decline and fall

Gibbon's *History of the Decline and Fall of the Roman Empire* was first published in 1776–88. Gibbon's work was an historical masterpiece that had a deep influence down the centuries.[3] Gibbon, in the company of many of his contemporaries, stressed the polarity between barbarism and civilisation.[4] For Gibbon the mission of Rome had been to bring civilisation to the pre-historical world of the barbarians. He believed that the Roman Empire provided illumination for the British, but he did not consider one to form a direct analogy for the other.[5] Indeed, while he admired the civilisation which the Roman Empire had spread, he was broadly critical of the concept of Empire in general and the Roman Empire in particular.[6] Gibbon's work provided an historic representation for those who were concerned with Britain's foreign possessions – an analogy that would resonate down the centuries. We have seen in the last chapter that a number of authors in the middle of the nineteenth century continued to draw upon Gibbon in their discussion of the contemporary condition of Britain and the value of the analogy of decline and fall continued into the late nineteenth century and beyond.[7]

Late Victorian and Edwardian images of decline and fall

The demonstrations of patriotic fervour, which characterise imperial discourse in late Victorian and Edwardian times, were not simply reflections of pride and racial arrogance. Rather, they reflected at least in part the view among late Victorians and Edwardians that Britain's position of international dominance was in decline.[8] Indeed, the rush to expand Britain's territorial possessions at this time was itself symptomatic of the growing ambition of other European powers. The image of impending decline, which drew upon Gibbon's pervasive book, perhaps provides part of the context for the relative coherence of some late Victorian and much

Edwardian imperial discourse. The jingoism and the repetition evident in many written works derived from the patriotic need to hold and express strongly sound views at a troublesome time for the nation.

Throughout the nineteenth century Britain had held a fairly secure and unchallenged international position of dominance – in industry, at sea and in its colonial acquisitions.[9] Towards the end of the century there was a growing concern about Britain's position within Europe as Bismarck's Germany came to dominate the continent.[10] There were concerns that Britain might be over-stretching itself because of the scale of its global responsibilities, while the state of the British economy also proved problematical for politicians, industrialists and other patriots.[11] Britain's position of dominance became increasingly at risk as the 'Cold War' with Germany developed during the first fifteen years of the twentieth century.[12] Following on from the disastrous Boer War of 1899 to 1902, and under the growing German threat, there was a serious drive toward greater efficiency in the running of the Empire.[13] The late nineteenth-century crisis was not merely military and economic, as the belief in the inevitability and morality of progress came to be seriously questioned by increasing numbers of people, particularly in the early years of the twentieth century.[14] The concept, however, survived this crisis of confidence, as many turned their minds in the Edwardian period to a consideration of how the spread of 'degeneracy' could be avoided.[15]

It is significant that the truculent mood of much of the British public, administrators and politicians at the turn of the century was in part a response to the growing concern about British military reverses and perceived social and economic decline.[16] The nature of intellectual debate at the turn of the century was deeply influenced by these military and political concerns. It is important to keep these ideas of political and moral insecurity in mind when analysing the imperial discourse that is an evident part of many late Victorian and Edwardian works.

The centenary of Gibbon's death in 1894 brought home disturbing parallels[17] and was drawn upon by late Victorian society. For instance, Cramb, in his lecture on the origins of imperial Britain in 1900, considered the lessons of Rome's decline at several points. He suggested that the current stage of the British Empire corresponded most easily with the period from Titus to Vespasian, when Rome still had 300 years to run.[18] Cramb's consideration of the idea of decline, however, indicates concern over the stability of the British Empire, drawing on the Roman parallel. It is, however, in the context of Edwardian society that the image of decline and fall received particular detailed attention in a range of texts. It became increasingly influential with the coming of the new monarch and the stresses that continued to develop within Edwardian society.[19] In 1903, the poet Sir William Watson drew attention to the disturbing analogy between Britain and Rome in his poem *Rome and Another*.[20] The fall of the Roman Empire was also used for political means by Edwardian Tories and others, as the idea of national decline and decadence perhaps made it inevitable that analogies should be drawn from the fall of the Roman Empire.[21]

One of the more significant of the works produced between 1905 and 1908 was an anonymous pamphlet entitled *The Decline and Fall of the British Empire*, written by Elliott Mills and published in 1905.[22] This was written as a work of future history and its title page describes the book as 'A brief account of those causes which resulted in the destruction of our late Ally, together with a comparison between the British and the Roman Empires. Appointed for use in the National Schools of Japan. Tokio, 2005.' The author was a young Tory pamphleteer, who had just left Oxford University. His book provides a useful summary of Tory anxieties in the middle of the Edwardian period.[23] Mills summarised the purpose of the book as follows:

> Any Empire, which wishes to take a notable part in the history of the World, must realize that other Empires as proudly exultant as herself have passed away. If she wishes to avoid a similar fate, her inhabitants must from childhood be acquainted with the errors of their predecessors if haply they may avoid them.
>
> Had the English people, at the opening of the Twentieth Century, turned to Gibbon's Decline and Fall of the Roman Empire, they might have found in it a not inaccurate description of themselves. This they failed to do, and we know the results.[24]

The fall of the British Empire in Mills' fictional account had happened ten years earlier (supposedly in 1995). India had fallen to Russia, South Africa to Germany, Egypt to the Sultan, Canada had become a protectorate of the USA and Australia of 'the Mikado' of Japan.[25]

Mills runs through a range of reasons for the collapse of the British Empire, drawing a direct comparison with Gibbon's account of the

31

fall of the Roman Empire. As in Ancient Rome, town life, demoralising luxury, physical inertia, gradual decline in physique and health and lack of confidence in the imperial mission were major causes of British decline. Apparently the provision of free meals to school children in 1910 was 'one of the most disastrous acts of false philanthropy' which did so much to ruin England and is linked in Mills' commentary to the provision of free corn to the masses in Imperial Rome.[26]

This exercise in science fiction was very successful, selling over 12,000 copies in six months. Similar ideas of imperial decline were drawn upon by a range of Edwardians, especially General Baden-Powell, who at time of the first publication of *Scouting for Boys* (1908) was Inspector-General of Cavalry. He developed the argument of the connection between classical Rome and modern Britain in his own influential best seller, which includes statements paralleling the decline of the two empires:

> Recent reports on the deterioration of our race ought to act as a warning to be taken in time, before it goes too far.
>   One cause which contributed to the downfall of the Roman Empire was the fact that the soldiers fell away from the standard of their forefathers in bodily strength.[27]

Baden-Powell went on to demonstrate through the use of statistics that the average height, weight and fitness of recruits to the army had fallen in the recent past. One of Baden-Powell's aims in founding the Boy Scout movement was to improve the moral quality of British manhood in order to avoid the fate of the Romans.[28] In the final section of the book, titled 'How the Empire must be held', Baden-Powell observed:

> Remember that the Roman Empire, two thousand years ago, was comparatively just as great as the British Empire of to-day. And though it had defeated any number of attempts against it, it fell at last, chiefly because the young Romans gave up soldiering and manliness altogether . . . they had no patriotism or love for their grand old country, and they went under with a run when a stronger nation attacked them.
>   Well, we have got to see that the same fate does not fall upon our Empire. And it will largely depend upon you, the younger generation of Britons that are now growing up

to be men of the Empire. Don't be disgraced like the young Romans, who lost the Empire of their forefathers by being wishy-washy slackers without any go or patriotism in them.

Play up! Each man in his place, and play the game! Your forefathers worked hard, fought hard, and died hard, to make this Empire for you. Don't let them look down from heaven and see you loafing about with your hands in your pocket, doing nothing to keep it up.[29]

The former British Conservative Prime Minister and Leader of the Opposition in the House of Commons, Arthur Balfour, presented a lecture on 'Decadence' to an audience in Cambridge in 1908. Balfour studied the problem of 'why *should* civilisations . . . wear out and great communities decay?'[30] The short book that was produced as a result of the lecture devotes twenty pages out of fifty-nine to the decline of the Roman Empire. Following the example of Mills, Balfour's book describes the late Roman Empire as a parable of the contemporary state of the British Empire,[31] and was particularly concerned with avoiding an early twentieth-century version of the 'thick darkness' that settled on Western Europe after Rome's fall.[32]

Fletcher and Kipling drew upon a similar idea of decline and fall in their children's history book of 1911:

I fear that Roman Britain went to sleep behind her wall [Hadrian's Wall], recruiting fell off, the strength of the legions became largely a 'paper strength'.

And not only in Britain. The greatest empire that the world has ever seen was slowly dying at the heart, dying of too much power, too much prosperity, too much luxury. What a lesson for us all to-day![33]

The morals and lessons to be derived from Rome

Mills, Baden-Powell and others wished to warn the British through the use of the Roman analogy. J.C. Stobart was an important figure in education and later came to have a role within the British Broadcasting Corporation.[34] Stobart was less certain about the value of Rome as a lesson for the British. His popular *The Grandeur that was Rome* was published in 1912, when he was a lecturer in history at Trinity College, Cambridge, and has been reprinted until the present day. In the introduction to the book he stated that:

The modern reader, especially if he be an Englishman, is a citizen of an empire now extremely self-conscious and somewhat bewildered at its own magnitude. He cannot help drawing analogies from Roman history and seeking in it 'morals' for his own guidance. The Roman Empire bears such an obvious and unique resemblance to the British that the fate of the former must be of enormous interest to the latter.[35]

Stobart could, therefore, see a general value to the British in the study of Roman history and archaeology to provide morals through analogy. He continued by suggesting, however, that the approach of many in treating Rome: 'merely as a subject for autopsies and a source of gloomy vaticinations for the benefit of the British Empire is a preposterous affront to history'.[36] He felt that this had an effect on the development of a negative view of the Roman Empire that was held by many of his contemporaries, for whom the subject represented a long period of political decline.

Despite Stobart's reservations, however, a number of politicians explored the 'morals' or 'lessons' that the history of Rome was felt to provide for the British. Through this process these writers argued, in effect, that Roman studies were of direct value for their own Empire in drawing 'morals', or lessons, for British adults and children.[37] A number of significant works were produced between 1910 and 1914, perhaps partly as a response to some of the earlier stress upon decline and fall.

Sir Charles P. Lucas, the first head of the Dominions Department of the Colonial Office,[38] asked, in his book *Greater Rome and Greater Britain*, published in 1912:

How did the Romans hold their Empire for so long a time? How has the British Empire been held together up to date? And by what means, judging from past experience, and from the signs of the times, are we likely to continue to hold it?[39]

Evelyn Baring, the Earl of Cromer (1841–1917) considered similar issues in his published work. Baring was educated at Woolwich and, although he did not attend university, he was exceptionally well read.[40] He became an administrator with experience in India and Egypt. He devoted his retirement to literary pursuits and was appointed President of the Classical Association for 1909–10.[41]

34

Cromer presented an address on 11 January 1910 to the Classical Association[42] and this address was expanded and published as *Ancient and Modern Imperialism* in 1910.[43]

Cromer suggested at the start of his presentation that:

> I conceive . . . that the main reason why the presidency of the Association was conferred on me was that I might personally testify to the fact that one who can make no pretension to scholarship, and who has been actively engaged all his life in political and administrative work, can appreciate the immense benefits which are to be derived from even a very imperfect acquaintance with classical literature.[44]

Cromer's presentation aimed to draw morals for the British from the Roman past. It was, in the words of Haverfield, a 'very remarkable discussion'[45] and was evidently well received by the public and by academics. The book aroused wide interest and was followed by two meetings in Oxford in 1910. Members of the Classical Association and their friends were invited to these meetings and a number of academics were asked to discuss various aspects of classical literature and society. The second of these meetings was held on 10 May 1910 and attended by Cromer. The five addresses presented to this meeting were later printed in *The Classical Review* for 1910. The first was by Francis Haverfield, who spoke on the Roman Empire and provided a discussion of the value of ancient history in the context of the present imperial situation.[46] Other relevant addresses included E.R. Bevan's contribution on the 'Greeks and barbarians' and D.G. Hogarth's on 'Assimilation'.

Francis Haverfield presented four addresses in the three years after Cromer's address to the Classical Association (between 1910 and 1913). These included his contribution on the Roman Empire to the Classical Association's meeting in 1910,[47] the inaugural Presidential address to the Roman Society (presented at its first annual general meeting in 1911),[48] a lecture to Oxford undergraduates in 1912[49] and an introduction to a talk on the Roman fort at Ambleside (presented to the Cumberland and Westmorland Antiquarian and Archaeological Society in 1913).[50] All four addresses consider the role of Roman studies in providing imperial parallels for the British. Through the use of this parallel the British might aim to avoid experiencing imperial decline and fall.

Haverfield specifically mentioned decline and fall in his 1911 address, when arguing that 'the forces which laid the Roman Empire low concern the modern world very nearly, more nearly indeed than do the reasons for the downfall of any other empire about which we have full knowledge'.[51] Some of these causes were particular to the Roman example, but Haverfield also mentions others, including 'corruption and incompetence in municipal life, the growth of a caste system, the more technical evil of an export of bullion eastward'.[52] He suggested that 'Some of these things come very close home.'[53]

In the published paper that derived from his 1910 lecture to the Classical Association, Haverfield argued that the real value of history is not necessarily that it aids 'us to form political prophecies or draw political analogies'.[54] Its value, he argued, lies in the consideration of various forces with which the contemporary British, like their predecessors, have to deal in their 'everyday politics'.[55] The Roman Empire, therefore, offered general guidance to the British on the character of various current political forces. Haverfield also suggested that young students of ancient history do not always recognise the importance of these forces and that a comparison between Greece and Rome and modern Britain has 'little meaning for them'.[56] He returned to some of these points in a lecture that was presented to Oxford undergraduates in May 1912, when he argued that:

> Greek history sets forth the successes and failures of small states and of 'municipal republics', while Rome exhibits the complex government of an extensive Empire. For the present day the second matters most. Perhaps the world will never see again a domination of city-states . . . But the administration of a great Empire concerns many men today and in a very vital manner. [57]

Haverfield made some rather more specific comments on the value of Roman studies in his address to the Roman Society.[58] Towards the end of the lecture, Haverfield stated that to him Roman history seemed 'at the present day the most instructive of all histories'.[59] He argued a general relevance for Roman studies. It apparently provided few direct parallels or precise precedents but did offer stimulating contrasts and comparisons 'and those glimpses of the might-have-beens which suggest so much to the intelligent reader'.[60] Its republican system offers an analogy to the British political system and 'Its imperial system, alike in its differences and similarities, lights up our own Empire, for example in India, at every turn.'[61]

Haverfield also argued in this address that:

> The methods by which Rome incorporated and denation-
> alised and assimilated more than half its wide dominions,
> and the success of Rome, unintended perhaps but complete,
> in spreading its Graeco-Roman culture over more than a
> third of Europe and a part of Africa, concerns in many ways
> our own age and Empire.[62]

Haverfield therefore identified methods of 'incorporation', 'denationalisation' and 'assimilation' as of interest to the British scholar
in the context of the present. Elsewhere, Haverfield wrote that:

> The greatest work of the imperial age must be sought in
> its imperial administration – in the organisation of its fron-
> tier defences which repulsed the barbarian, and in the
> development of the provinces within those defences . . . In
> the lands that [Rome] had sheltered, Roman civilisation
> had taken firm root.[63]

Therefore, the Roman Empire had established a secure frontier and
also encouraged the growth of civilisation within that frontier. These
were the twin methods by which it controlled its empire and they
were also relevant topics of attention for British people who felt a
concern over the destiny of their own empire. The Roman imperial
parallel appeared of particular value to the British in the context of
averting decline and fall and the topics of imperial defence and the
spread of civilisation became analogies that could be drawn upon.
The next chapter addresses these topics of imperial defence, assimilation and administration in greater detail.

4

DRAWING LESSONS
FROM ROME REGARDING
INCORPORATION AND
ASSIMILATION

Introduction

Francis Haverfield defined the character of the frontier between civilisation and barbarism in the Roman Empire as a topic of relevance
to contemporary society. He also discussed a connected topic – the
progress of barbarians to a state of civilisation under the influence
of the Romans. In this chapter I shall study works by a range of
Victorian and early twentieth-century authors, including Haverfield,
who wrote about these topics.

'Incorporation': the securing of the frontiers

The dominance of classical education encouraged an interest in
Roman military operations and frontier policy from the medieval
period onward in Britain. During the nineteenth century the study
of the military organisation of the Roman Empire was one area in
which the similarity and difference between the two imperial
systems could be explored. The Roman province of Britain often
appears to have been felt to be particular significant in the drawing
of these parallels.

   The lessons provided by the problems faced by the Romans in their
conquest and occupation of Britain and the north-western provinces
were drawn upon by some in the development of British frontier
policy. These lessons helped to inform the experiences of the British
in their control of some parts of their Empire, particularly India.

I wish to consider in some detail the apparent relevance of Roman frontier and administrative policy to the British at this time.

Frontier studies in the eighteenth and nineteenth centuries

Archaeological interest in Roman military frontiers during the late nineteenth and early twentieth centuries drew upon a long tradition of research in Britain and Germany, including the work of various military men.[1] The most significant contribution to Roman military study prior to the mid-nineteenth century was perhaps that of Major General William Roy during the eighteenth-century Hanoverian English military operations in Scotland.[2] Roy mapped a wide range of Roman military earthworks during the 1750s (Figure 4.1). His volume *The Military Antiquities of the Romans in Britain* was published posthumously in 1793 by the Society of Antiquaries of London. This work was of major relevance in the development of archaeological mapping in Britain.[3] A map of the Roman remains

Figure 4.1 Major General William Roy's map of Rough Castle Roman fort (Falkirk, Scotland). Roy's maps of Roman monuments in Scotland were produced in the 1750s and were of major relevance in the development of archaeological mapping in Britain. *Source*: Roy (1793).

of northern Britain engraved in 1775 was not completely super-seded until the publication of the second edition of the Ordnance Survey map of Roman Britain in 1928.[4] Roy's observations drew upon a perceived parallel between the military operations of the Romans and the Hanoverians in Highland Scotland.[5] In this process of self-identification, Roy and other Hanoverian English military men placed themselves in the position of the conquering classical Romans, an association which predates the conscious emulation of Rome in the late nineteenth century.

The parallel was extended by some English officers and visitors at this time to incorporate a connection between the native people of later prehistoric Europe, as described by the classical authors, and the people of the eighteenth-century Highlands of Scotland. Thomas Ashe Lee, an officer in James Wolfe's regiment, had no sympathy with the Highland rebels in 1746. Lee saw the Highlanders as barbarians and compared them unfavourably with the Gauls, defining a partial historical parallel between the activities of the English in Highland Scotland and those of Julius Caesar in Gaul in the first century BC.[6] Other army officers drew on classical authors in a comparable way when considering the natives of Highland Scotland. Duncan Forbes wrote about the state of the Highlands of Scotland (possibly in 1746) and his comments read in a manner which is reminiscent of the observations of Tacitus, Posidonius and Caesar about the Celtic and Germanic tribes of Iron Age Europe.[7]

Samuel Johnson, in his account of his epic journey to the High-lands and the Western Isles of Scotland in 1773, which he under-took in the company of James Boswell, drew upon a connected idea of the survival of uncivilised prehistoric behaviour in the Highlands. He suggested that the Romans had civilised 'other nations' but that Cromwell had 'civilised' the Scots 'by conquest, and introduced by useful violence the arts of peace'.[8] In this statement, the acts of the English in bringing 'civilization' to Scotland are likened to those of the Romans across western and northern Europe.[9]

The historical parallels that were drawn by English men between themselves and the Romans and the contrasting associations which were established between the Scots and the ancient Celts at this time may be seen in the light of classical education and the contem-porary political situation. People at this time self-consciously acted out their lives on an historical stage. Antiquity was familiar through the Latin and Greek authors, who formed the staple element in the education of all gentlemen. Classical ideas about barbarians were derived from the writings of Greek and Roman authors about other peoples outside their own direct contact and were adopted at this time as a model for the contemporary situation.[10]

In political terms, prior to the mid-eighteenth century it had seemed that the European social landscape would always be threatened by barbarians on the periphery of civilisation.[11] During the eighteenth century history provided an aid to the living,[12] and the concept of a monolithic and coherent barbarian society created an idea of linkage between peoples far apart in time.[13] It shall be shown below that a comparable attitude to the 'Celtic' population of Roman Britain in the nineteenth century resulted in the development of the image of what I shall call the 'Celtic subaltern'. In the eighteenth century the idea of the Celtic other was reinforced by an instinctual link between the classically educated scholar and the Roman writer, formed through reading the classical texts and by the fact that Roman authors wrote in the first person and spoke directly to a contemporary audience. In this context, surveying, road-building and the construction of camps and forts were Roman as well as English ways of improving security at or near the margins of state control.[14] This military value is one factor that led to the use of Roman forts, camps and roads to provide inspiration for military strategists over 1500 years after most of the monuments were disused.[15]

During the nineteenth century, Roman military studies continued to develop from their Hanoverian and earlier beginnings. Roman military texts were used for military purposes in medieval and post-medieval England[16] and these continued to have relevance in the Victorian context. J.G. Sheppard in 1861 argued that 'the tactics and campaigns of the ancient generals are as well worth the study of military men as those of Marlborough and Turenne'.[17] The physical archaeological remains of frontiers left behind by the Romans also had a role to play in Victorian society. A range of sites on Hadrian's Wall were 'excavated' in the first half of the century.[18] More intensive antiquarian exploration began in the middle part of the nineteenth century and formed part of a broader study of Roman frontier works in the northern parts of the Roman Empire.[19] In this context Roman military monuments were sometimes used to provided a potential lesson for the imperial administrator and the military planners of the British Empire; as we shall see, this was also the case in the Edwardian context (below). The so-called 'Salt Hedge' or 'Customs Hedge' of British India provides a possible example of the use of a concept derived from the study of Roman military frontiers and frontier policy in the imperial action of the British in India during the mid-nineteenth century.[20]

The Oxford ancient historians H. Pelham and F. Haverfield wrote in 1911 about the 'Customs Line' or 'Customs Hedge'.[21] This frontier work was first established in 1843 and, at its height, stretched almost 2,500 miles across northern India, from the Indus to near a point where the Madras and Bengal boundaries met, 150 miles from the Gulf of Bengal. Its purpose was to enable the raising of duty on salt, but it was abolished in 1878–9. Along the greatest part of its length it was a 'huge material barrier'.[22] It mainly comprised thorny bushes, cactus and trees, supplemented in places by a stone wall or a ditch and mound. Along its length ran a well-made road that was regularly and constantly patrolled. At one time it had as many as 1,700 guard posts[23] and was manned by an army of officers and men around 12,000 strong.[24]

Sir M.E. Grant Duff compared the Customs Hedge to the Great Wall of China,[25] while Pelham and Haverfield considered it to represent an interesting and little known parallel to Roman frontier defences.[26] In the light of the Hanoverian and nineteenth-century interest in the Roman military monuments of northern England and Scotland, it is possible that the inspiration for this British imperial frontier derived from Roman roots. Rather than being seen as a parallel to the Roman frontiers, the idea of the Customs Hedge may actually have been derived from them.[27]

Frontier issues in the late nineteenth and early twentieth century

Vance has suggested that the ways in which the British explored and collated evidence for Roman road-making, building, military administration and domestic life during the late nineteenth and the early twentieth centuries was one of the ways that the complex image of Classical Rome was worked through in Britain.[28] Serious study of Hadrian's Wall and the Roman north continued into late Victorian and Edwardian times.[29] Archaeological excavation also was carried out on the Antonine Wall and other Roman military sites in Scotland, where first the Glasgow Archaeological Society and then the Society of Antiquaries of Scotland undertook major campaigns on a number of sites; these projects led to a considerable increase in knowledge.[30]

It can be suggested that at the same time that the materials collected fed back into an understanding of Britain's place in the Roman Empire they also helped to inform frontier policy in the contemporary British Empire. At this time the image of the frontier, both Roman and modern, was unsophisticated. It derived inspiration from earlier views of frontiers and foreign policy and related to the concept of a distinct physical line that was felt to separate civilisation from barbarism.[31] Frontiers, therefore, served to mark the border between imperial civilisations and the 'others'; these others continued to be defined in opposition to the civilised.

Imperial spirit, the frontier and national identity

A number of Edwardian authors and thinkers studied the relationship between Roman and British frontier policy, often drawing upon archaeological knowledge of Hadrian's Wall and other frontier systems in this process. Rudyard Kipling, in his children's novel *Puck of Pook's Hill*, first published in 1906, interweaves the Roman and the Norman government of Britain, turning the stories in the book into an exposition of admirable conduct for young men faced with the particular demands of empire.[32] The problems of imperial defence are central to the theme of the Roman part of the book, projecting the military problems of late Roman Britain into the context of the frontier of the British Empire, particularly India – a topic of great significance to Kipling. Kipling thus made the defence of the imperial frontier a relevant subject for imaginative reconstruction though a process of historical analogy.[33]

The main characters of the two Roman stories in *Puck of Pook's Hill* are Parnesius and Pertinax. These two soldiers are centurions of Rome, who are burdened with the defence of Hadrian's Wall for three years to save Britain and the Roman Empire for the general Maximus,[34] who later becomes the Emperor of Britain and Gaul. Parnesius is British-born, descended from generations of a Roman family who were first given land for their villa in *Vectis* (the Isle of Wight) by Agricola, while Pertinax is from a good family background in Gaul.[35] These two British residents retained a clear image of their own racial identity, while also feeling a loyalty to Britain and Maximus. The archaeologist A.L.F. Rivet spoke of Kipling's Indian-inspired views of the 'ultra-British Romans' and the 'ultra-Roman Britons' with regard to his characterisation of these figures.[36] The feelings of these members of the Roman population of Britain in *Puck of Pook's Hill*, indicate that their true loyalty lay with Britain. For instance, in one section of the work, Parnesius recalls the words of his father:

> 'There is no hope for Rome,' said the Pater . . . 'She has forsaken her Gods, but if the Gods forgive us here, we may

save Britain. To do that, we must keep the Painted People back. Therefore, I tell you, Parnesius, as a Father . . . your place is among men on the Wall.'[37]

The morals of the Roman section of *Puck* are essentially derived from Kipling's interpretation of the character and actions of his friend Dr Jameson of Jameson Raid fame.[38] The concepts of race and national destiny which are evident in Kipling's text related to Edwardian thought and are out of context in the Roman setting into which the author placed his stories.[39]

British frontier policy and the Roman frontier

The parallel between the respective frontier policies of Britain and Rome was a topic that was considered by a number of Kipling's contemporaries.[40] William Thomas Arnold, Assistant Editor of the *Manchester Guardian* and lecturer at Oxford University, undertook work on the Roman Empire and its provincial administration.[41] He was interested in all imperial questions, drawing a particular analogy between the Roman Empire and the British, and especially the 'Indian dependency' of Britain.[42] He was indeed very much haunted by the tragedy of the fall of the Roman Empire.[43] Sir Ian Hamilton, a successful military man who served in India and elsewhere, visited Arnold in 1903. He recalled that:

> I went to see Mr. Arnold about certain parallels between English and Roman history which were then very much in my mind . . . I wished to give them precision and point by consulting a competent authority concerning the Roman frontier provinces; the methods of keeping the legions up to strength in foreign quarters, and the characters of Augustus and Tiberius.[44]

Hamilton recalled that: 'Directly I arrived we plunged into a discussion concerning the parallel offered by the Roman Empire to our own, and Mr. Arnold gave me some papers he had written on the subject.'[45] It is of interest that Arnold had prepared relevant papers on this historical analogy, since we shall see shortly that, after Arnold's death, Francis Haverfield presented lectures to students at Oxford that addressed comparable topics.

Lord Curzon's detailed study *Frontiers*, published in 1907, explored a range of frontiers from various areas of the world and differing periods of history in a comparative context.[46] Curzon referred to the frontier system of Rome as the 'ancient counterpart and prototype' for the British frontier in India.[47] His study contained a specific consideration of the Roman frontier works in Britain and Germany. In 1908 Balfour considered the burden of securing the Roman frontier in the context of the 'Decadence' of that Empire as a parable for the British.[48] The Romans defended their frontiers from barbarians and thus secured peace, and the British Empire's frontiers also required careful consideration.

Sir Charles Lucas's book *Greater Rome and Greater Britain* drew attention to 'some rough analogy' between Hadrian's Wall and Britain's northern frontier in India.[49] James Bryce considered the search for a 'scientific frontier' in both empires and the comparison between Roman frontier fortifications at Hadrian's Wall and Nauheim in Germany and British outposts in the mountain regions beyond Kashmir, particularly the remote outpost at Chitral.[50] Lucas and Bryce emphasise the Roman frontier in Britain as being the best preserved or most substantial surviving frontier defences. In the light of Kipling's earlier comments in *Puck of Pook's Hill*, Lucas and Bryces' comments perhaps also appealed to the national spirit of Englishmen by referring to a Roman monument in their own country which was manned by the civilised officer of a previous imperial power.[51]

Haverfield developed a distinct interest in Roman frontier policy and Roman military archaeology. His specific interest in the archaeology of Roman frontiers is demonstrated by the work that he undertook on Hadrian's Wall and other Roman military sites in the north.[52] Haverfield was introduced to the Cumberland and Westmorland Antiquarian and Archaeological Society by Henry Pelham.[53] Soon after his return to Oxford in 1892, he began an archaeological study of the western part of Hadrian's Wall which furnished material for his annual 'Report of the Cumberland Excavation Committee' from 1894 to 1903. Further excavation work continued in the Roman north after 1903. He became President of the Cumberland and Westmorland Society in 1915.

Haverfield considered the general relevance of the Roman frontiers to the British in several published works. For instance, in his address to the Roman Society in 1911, Haverfield suggested that a study of the defensive policy of the Roman Empire was of direct relevance to political powers in Western Europe and that 'The man who studies the Roman frontier system, studies not only a great work but one which has given us all modern Western Europe.'[54] Rome therefore, was seen as having had a fundamental role in the creation of modern Europe. Without the frontier between the civilised and the barbarian, modern civilisation could not exist.

Of more specific relevance is the observation that, while under-taking fieldwork in northern England and lecturing and writing about the results, Haverfield was aware of the potential relevance of the subject to the contemporary political and military situation on the frontier of the British Empire. In his lecture to the Cumberland and Westmorland Society on 11 September 1913,[55] in which Haverfield described the excavation of the Roman fort at Borrans Field (Ambleside; Figure 4.2), he stated: 'In Roman times the region [the Lake District] was a tangled chaos of hills in which wild hill-men defied Rome and Roman ways. Rome could not leave them alone.'[56] Haverfield also drew a direct comparison between

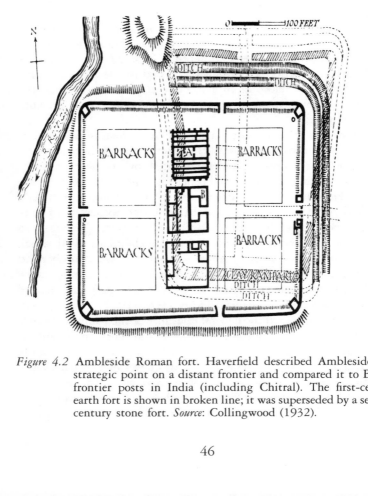

Figure 4.2 Ambleside Roman fort. Haverfield described Ambleside as a strategic point on a distant frontier and compared it to British frontier posts in India (including Chitral). The first-century earth fort is shown in broken line; it was superseded by a second-century stone fort. *Source*: Collingwood (1932).

Ambleside and the British frontier in India when he described the fort as a 'strategic point on a distant frontier, a Chitral or a Gilgit'.[57] He suggested that:

> The lessons to be learnt at Borrans are, first and most, military matters. They concern problems such as we still have to face in guarding our Indian North-west Frontier, and even in making safe our own east coast in Britain.[58]

Elsewhere he drew a comparison between ancient Roman and modern British frontier concerns, in comparing the end of the 'Welsh' struggle against Rome with that of the defeat of the Dervish by the English in Sudan.[59] Frontier issues drew the archaeology of the military areas of northern and western Britain into the context of the contemporary British administrative research.

In the context of the various statements that Haverfield made throughout the decade after 1910, it is evident that he was drawing upon recent history as well as the distant past in developing his views.[60] Haverfield could see the value of Roman military studies in the context of modern imperial frontier issues and, no doubt, discussed these views with friends and colleagues involved in the education of the imperial élite. In addition, in considering Roman military operations, he continued a long tradition in clearly identifying himself and his contemporaries with the Roman army and administration rather than the native 'hill men' of the Lake District, the ancient Welsh 'Dervishes' or Atilla the Hun.

It is evident from a consideration of these accounts that Kipling, Curzon, Cromer, Hamilton, Lucas, Bryce and Haverfield were not necessarily suggesting a direct parallel between the frontier systems of the two empires. It is also clear from their works, however, that the Roman frontier in Germany and Britain, but particularly Hadrian's Wall, were felt to provide an example to the British in their imperial actions. The fact that Edwardian authors drew attention to the defence policy of the Roman Empire in a comparative context, therefore, indicates one purpose that it was felt Roman studies could fulfil. Classically-educated administrators might apply some of the knowledge derived from their classical education during their careers. In addition, scholars such as Arnold and Haverfield could act as competent authorities in providing informed accounts of Roman frontier policy that would be of value to these administrators and politicians in planning their imperial actions. The mention made by Bryce of Chitral as a relevant parallel to the Roman frontier defence of Britain actually appears to mirror the comments of Haverfield about the same issue in his address about the Roman fort at Ambleside.[61]

The establishment of 'civilisation'

Roman provincial domestic life and law and order related to the other theme defined by Haverfield in his 1911 address to the Roman Society and also in his book *The Romanization of Roman Britain*, that of the establishment of Roman civilisation.[62] This topic had only limited relevance to the English in the early to mid-nineteenth century, although some works of nineteenth-century art approached the topic of the introduction of civilisation by the Romans to ancient Britons.[63] The introduction of Roman civilisation became more vital, however, to the late Victorians and Edwardians.[64] A wide variety of authors expressed an interest in the methods by which the Romans had managed to 'incorporate' and 'assimilate' various provincials into their empire and in the lessons that this might have for the British.[65]

Assimilation

In this context, a parallel was often drawn between the civilising missions of Britain and Rome, particularly in the period between 1905 and 1914. Monypenny in 1905 argued that the words 'empire' and 'imperial' are difficult to analyse in contrast to 'nationality': 'They are at once older and newer, less familiar to our modern minds, and at the same time with a longer history behind them and a larger burden of associations to carry.'[66] He defined a 'mission' that the Roman Empire had fulfilled through its 'elastic' system of administration, common system of law and common citizenship; it became the most powerful 'engine of assimilation that the world has ever seen'.[67] This concept of a similar process of assimilation in the two imperial contexts was linked with certain assumptions about the mission of the British to bring peace, stability and, at least a degree of progress, to the non-white population of their Empire.[68]

Questions of assimilation made studies of cultural change in Roman Britain and the Roman Empire relevant to late Victorian and Edwardian authors. G.A. Henty, for instance, in his novel *Beric the Briton* (1893) considered the progress of Roman civilisation and the ways in which the Britons could be brought civilisation if treated with proper respect.[69] People at this time were interested in how the Romans had passed civilisation to the British and other natives in the Western Empire. Part of the context for the interest in methods of assimilation lay in the contrast that was drawn between the western colonising powers and those colonised 'others' that they experienced during their expansion.[70] These views continued to define themselves on the basis of classical concepts of civilisation and barbarian and also the idea of progress.[71]

If the Roman Empire was a successful assimilator of native people, why could Britain be seen to be failing in some of its imperial possessions? A range of Edwardian authors discussed the topic of what Betts has defined as 'race relations' in detail.[72] The title of Lord Bryce's book, *The Ancient Roman Empire and the British Empire in India: the Diffusion of Roman and English Law throughout the World* (1912), indicates a direct interest in the Roman–British parallel. In this book he considered 'Fusion of Romans and provincials: no similar fusion of English and Indians'.[73] Lucas' book of 1912 contains a chapter on class, colour and race in which he suggests that:

> in the Roman Empire there was a perpetual opening out of citizenship. The tendency was all towards fusion and uniformity and race imposed few or no barriers. In the British Empire . . . the tendency has been to greater diversity rather that to greater uniformity.[74]

Cromer argued that there was no need for the British to feel responsibility for their lack of success in this regard as there was no direct comparison between the problems faced by Britain and Rome in their imperial activities:

> We have failed, not because we are Englishmen, Scotchmen, or Irishmen, but because we are Westerns. We have failed because the conditions of the problem are such as to render any marked success impossible. No other modern European nation has, in any substantial degree, been more successful . . .
>
> The comparative success of the Romans is easily explained. Their task was far more easy than that of any modern Imperial nation.[75]

Not all agreed with Cromer's conclusion on assimilation. Hogarth, in his address on 'Assimilation' to the Classical Association in 1910, suggested that all imperial people have begun with a period of non-assimilation. He suggested that they have then passed on to a second stage characterised by a desire to assimilate and further stages of successful assimilation and the production of a more or less complete social uniformity. He concluded that the British Empire was still in the first stage or the opening of the second, while Rome attained its 'conspicuous success' in assimilation during the third. He concluded, in contrast to Cromer, that if Britain reached the third stage there would be a basis for a comparison between the British Empire and the Roman, but not before.[76]

Haverfield made similar observations to those of Bryce and Cromer in his 1905 lecture on the Romanisation of Roman Britain and his address of 1910 to the Classical Association. He argued that the Romans did not assimilate others with ease in all situations. In fact, an obstacle to assimilation might have existed in the contact of the Romans with races whose traditions and civilisation have 'crystallised into definitive form'.[77] This crystallisation might derive from 'political religion', 'national sentiment', or 'memories of the past'. These issues, to Haverfield's mind, obviously influenced both the Roman and the British imperial endeavours, since he also commented upon the problems faced by the British in their attempt to assimilate people in India and elsewhere.[78]

To Haverfield, 'coherence' appears to have represented a far greater bar to assimilation in modern and ancient imperial situations than colour,[79] but racial factors were also of importance. 'Uncivilized Africans or Asiatics' in the modern world are unable to advance because they 'seem sundered for ever from their conquerors by a broad physical distinction',[80] while the 'Hindoos' and Mohammedans of India had too 'coherent' a culture to accept 'civilization'.[81] By contrast to the problem faced by Britain in these areas, in which assimilation was not occurring too readily, Rome in the west had 'found races that were not yet civilised, yet were racially capable of accepting her culture'.[82] This accounted, in Haverfield's writing, for the relative success of Rome. Bryce considered similar issues of assimilation[83] and some cross-fertilisation between Haverfield and Bryce appears to be implied as there is a similarity between Bryce's comments and some of those in Haverfield's 1905 paper.[84]

Majeed has argued that the accounts provided by Bryce and Lucas present the processes of 'assimilation' and 'fusion' in the Roman Empire as already based on the concept of 'race'. This was achieved by arguing that a greater flexibility over racial issues helped the Romans in the process of assimilation; the same is also true of the comments made by Haverfield. As in the case of frontier issues, early twentieth-century concepts of identity were projected back onto the Roman world and helped to create an archaeology of Roman Britain which was of distinct relevance to the imperial concerns of Edwardian society. In fact modern concepts of race have little relevance for an understanding of the Roman Empire, since they did not exist within the world of classical Rome.[85]

Administration: 'Incorporation'

An interest in the incorporation of various native peoples in both empires also required a consideration of any administration parallels.[86] In the context of the British Empire the uncivilised 'others' were often felt to be so primitive and uncivilised or so decentralised that they might always the need the helping hand of the British, although they might achieve some modicum of civilisation, given time. In these cases, at least in the short term, incorporation would not result in direct assimilation. In the minds of some Englishmen, however, Britons could be proud of the achievements that they had made, even if these fell short of total assimilation, or even partial. It is of interest that these images of pride sometimes drew upon the supposed superiority of the British efforts to those of the classical Romans.

W. Lee-Warner, in a book published in 1894, considered the 'protected princes' of Rome and British India as rather different in nature, providing many parallels and not a few contrasts. The provincial administration of Rome was argued by Lee-Warner, however, to be rich in lessons for the Indian official.[87] P.C. Sands, in his *The Client Princes of the Roman Empire under the Republic* (1908), also considered the similarity between the 'Protected Princes' of India and the client kings of the Rome. In drawing upon the work of Lee-Warner, Sands emphasised the contrasts with the British, particularly the Roman failure to interfere with despotic native rule.[88] Sands argued, however, that in allowing their 'protected states' to have far more independence, the Romans showed a direct self-interest in neglecting the welfare of their client's subjects. In contrast to Rome, Britain had acted as a 'protecting power' which had assumed the right to check 'inhuman practices and offences against natural laws or public morality'.[89] According to Sands, Britain's activities in India had initially followed the Roman example and had only changed to a more interventionist stance at a later date because of the 'moral force' to 'secure the happiness of a number of human beings, and almost to enforce government in the interest of the governed'.[90] Sands considered British despotism in India to be justifiable because of the burden of protecting the weak.

On a more general level, according to Fletcher and Kipling, in Sudan and Egypt: 'The justice and mercy, which these countries had not known since the fall of the Roman Empire, is now in full measure given them by the British.'[91] In Sand's and Fletcher and Kipling's account of the Empire, Britain's control of some imperial possessions, while almost despotic in nature, was exercised (in the minds of the authors at least) in the interests of the native population. Britain, however, was failing in the process of assimilating these societies, and this was an area in which the Roman analogy could serve a relevant imperial purpose. This explains why the Roman parallel was so relevant to a range of authors as a way of helping the British to understand how better to assimilate the native people of their empire.

Imperial discourse and the rise of Roman archaeology

In the first four chapters the concept of imperial discourse has been explored and the input of images derived from the Roman Empire has been defined. Through a circular process of interpretation, the past was used to serve the interests of the present. In the process of interpretation the evidence for the past was distorted through its use in creating images which had a particular value within late Victorian and Edwardian imperial discourse.

Classical education created a close association in the minds of many Englishmen between themselves and the ancient Romans. By the same terms, classical concepts also helped to compare the natives of the Empire to the barbarians of the classical sources. The modern study of colonial discourse theory has often focused upon the simplistic ways in which colonial society has defined itself in opposition to 'other'. The manner in which classical society defined the other in relation to self was recruited during the nineteenth and twentieth centuries as a powerful tool in modern imperial self-definition. Classical concepts of civilised and barbarian were reused and adopted in the context of Victorian and Edwardian British imperialism, particularly through their use to help to define issues of frontier policy and assimilation.

Useful ideas derived from imperial Rome and the impact of Rome on Britain came to be used in British society in the late 1870s through to the 1920s. Classical Rome was used quite directly to provide a warning to the British – the necessity of finding a way to arrest impending decline and fall.

The archaeology of Roman Britain and the Roman Empire had a part to play in this process. Archaeologists and ancient historians could provide authoritative information on relevant topics to imperial officials and administrators. Haverfield argued in 1911 that the information provided by the developing discipline of archaeology could provide inspiration to the Empire in helping to maintain the frontier, and in incorporating and assimilating native peoples. Evidence exists to indicate that imperial officials and soldiers sought this advice in person from W.T. Arnold and from the published works of Francis Haverfield. By taking these Roman morals into account the British could try to strengthen their Empire for the difficult times ahead.

The role of Haverfield

In this context, the Roman archaeology that was developed by Haverfield was involved in various ways in the creation of imperial discourse. Haverfield's consideration of the two empires formed part of a genre.[92] His four addresses were delivered just after Lord Cromer's presidential address to the Classical Association in 1910, to which Haverfield had produced a supportive response. The years between 1910 and 1915 also witnessed the publication of Cromer, Lucas and Bryce's books on the Roman and British Empires and these works together with those of Haverfield form part of a body of work on the relevance of the Roman empire to the British.[93]

I have already argued for the imperial value of Haverfield's Roman archaeology several times in print[94] and Philip Freeman has responded by suggesting that it is difficult to discern any political agenda in Haverfield's scholarship. He has argued that Haverfield stressed European rather than British scholarship and showed little concern with imperialism and the benefits of colonial administration in the vast majority of his published works.[95] According to Freeman, the public statements that Haverfield made regarding British and Roman imperialism were usually made to audiences of the general public and contrast with his academic work.

Haverfield's four addresses were aimed at the general public and at students. The 1910 address was presented in Oxford to the Classical Association and associated friends. The First Annual General Meeting of the Roman Society was held on 28 February 1911 and Haverfield presented the inaugural address to the public audience of this new society that called in its advertisement for both the 'patriot and the professor'.[96] His observations on the 'very vital' matter of knowledge of the administration of the Roman Empire to modern people were made to undergraduates in Oxford in 1912.[97] The address to the Cumberland and Westmorland Antiquarian and Archaeological Society in 1913 on the parallels between the Roman frontier in northern Britain and the British frontier in India was made to members of a local archaeological society.[98]

Haverfield's comments to his three public audiences and to Oxford students cannot, however, be ignored. It is perhaps especially in the context of these types of audiences that imperial discourse was likely to strike a popular chord, as it is possible that some ancient historians and classicists might have treated this type of view with less tolerance.[99] Popular support for British imperialism was particularly powerful at this time.

In two of his addresses Haverfield appears to have been talking directly to students who formed prospective imperial administrators. In his 1910 address, he recalled: 'I remember once insisting, through a course of lectures, on various likenesses and unlikenesses of the Roman provinces to British India.'[100] At the end of this lecture, one student came up to him and asked for advice on which province he should choose if he managed to get into the Indian Civil Service. Haverfield acknowledged that Lord Cromer had far better credentials to comment on the actual bearing of ancient history on an understanding of contemporary imperial 'problems' and would be better able to answer this type of question;[101] however, the topic was evidently of interest to him. In his 1912 address to Oxford students, Haverfield stated that: 'Our age has not altogether solved the problems which Empires seem to raise ... it can hardly find men enough who are fit to carry on the routine of government in distant lands.'[102] Haverfield drew on the value of Roman imperial studies with a direct mention of the importance of foreign service.

The 1910 and 1912 addresses demonstrate that Haverfield lectured to students on the relevance of ancient studies to modern imperial politics. Haverfield was a member of Oxford University, the institution that produced the majority of influential imperial administrators, politicians and members of the India Civil Service.[103] We have seen that W.T. Arnold also prepared papers on this topic and presumably also spoke to Oxford students who had an interest in achieving jobs in the Indian Civil Service and other government and administrative jobs. It is likely that many of the students who attended Haverfield's addresses held ambitions to become imperial administrators and, as we have seen, Haverfield evidently did not wish to discourage their aspirations.

My argument is that part of the attraction of Haverfield's addresses and writings to his contemporaries and to later generations (including the present author) lay (and lies) in the context of his archaeological theory. Broadly speaking, Haverfield's work was by the standards of his time a rigorous analysis of the context of Britain within the Roman Empire, but it also contributed significantly to imperial discourse. He could see the value of Roman frontier studies, urban planning and Romanisation in the modern imperial context and discussed these issues with students and his peers in public and no doubt also in private. Haverfield's position as a major academic figure will have provided authority to his words in the minds of the students, administrators and politicians who listened to him.

I wish to argue that we should not view Haverfield's Roman archaeology as politically neutral. His perspective was derived from his own education and upbringing and therefore had an intimate relationship with late Victorian and Edwardian Britain's imperial context. As such, it has directly contributed to imperial discourse and to the historical process of British imperialism because it fitted into a context within a dominant Edwardian and post-Edwardian discourse concerned with the relevance of the Roman Empire to the form and destiny of the British Empire. We should, however, also bear in mind that Haverfield's foreign contacts indicate that he was not a nationalist. The reference in his 1910 address to fact that he did not aim 'to wave flags or to disparage the setting sun'[104] demonstrates a certain distance from the jingoism evident in some other Edwardian accounts. Freeman has clearly indicated Haverfield's European contacts and interest in Roman studies on the Continent[105] and his suggestion that Haverfield's interest focused on Western Europe as a whole is well made.[106] It is even possible to conceive that Haverfield saw Roman studies as, among other things, a way of uniting European scholarship as the 'Cold War' between Britain and Germany gathered momentum.

In addition, Haverfield's wish to encourage the development of Roman archaeology as an academic discipline is presumably of relevance to the imperial discourse that he helped to create. Symonds has considered the way that natural scientists, geographers and anthropologists sought to use the needs of the empire to justify the expansion of research and teaching in their fields of study at this time;[107] this perspective also has value in considering the imperial role of classics and Roman studies. An attempt to make classics relevant in the imperial context helps to explain the appointment of the administrator Lord Cromer as President of the Classical Association in 1909–10, and also the two meetings that were held by the Association in Oxford to discuss Cromer's address in 1910. The report of these meetings recalls that they were held with the hope of making the Classical Association better known in the University.[108] The perceived value of Roman studies is also demonstrated by the fact that the original membership of the Roman Society contained a number of familiar names, including Bryce, Cromer and also Stanley Baldwin (whose contribution to imperial discourse will be considered below in the discussion of Englishness). Many of Haverfield's comments in his four addresses may also be seen in this light, as an attempt to justify Roman archaeology to his contemporaries as a worthy field of study. His 1911 address to the Roman Society, in addition to emphasising the imperial value of Roman archaeology, drew attention to the increasing role of British universities in Roman archaeology.[109] This imperial legacy had an influence on the development of Roman archaeology in Britain, as is evident from a discussion of the history of Roman frontier studies.

Defining frontiers: the influence of imperial discourse on Roman frontier studies

It has been suggested that a knowledge of the work of Roy and others in northern Britain allowed later generations to investigate connections and continuities between Roman and British military administration on the basis of a consideration of the material archaeological evidence.[110] The practical value of Roman frontier studies and their significance in the context of imperial discourse impacted upon the general approach of archaeologists to the frontier policy of the Roman Empire and the consequences of this approach are still evident today.

Carrington has recounted, in his biography of Kipling published in 1955, how *Puck of Pook's Hill* had influenced generations of British men.

In the whole range of Rudyard Kipling's work, no pieces have been more effective in moulding the thoughts of a generation than the three stories of the centurions defending Hadrian's Wall during the decline of the Roman Empire . . . The story of the centurion's task is told as a panegyric of duty and service . . . It strengthened the nerve of many a young soldier in the dark days of 1915 and 1941, and, if that was its intention, it mattered little that Rudyard's Roman soldiers of the fourth century too much resembled subalterns of the Indian army.[111]

Kipling's motivation may perhaps have been to provide a model of imperial duty for British officers in British India, but during the course of the twentieth century the value of his work developed in a wider geographical context.

The process of the misinterpretation of Roman Britain did matter, however, according to the archaeologists R.G. Collingwood and A.L.F. Rivet. Rivet has argued that *Puck of Pook's Hill* presents a highly distorted picture of Roman Britain. The archaeological detail is inaccurate – the description of Hadrian's Wall makes it too high, wide and complex and its function is also misunderstood (Figure 4.3).[112] Another relevant issue is the nature of Kipling's understanding of the Roman Empire and his views of British India as a parallel for Roman Britain. Collingwood observed in a critical fashion that *Puck of Pook's Hill* formed an allegory of British India rather than an accurate portrayal of Roman Britain.[113] Kipling's novel helped to reinforce the views of many of his contemporaries and also of later generations concerning the status of Roman Britain as an historical parallel for British India and also the identity of the British as the imperial heirs to Rome.

Rivet considered the influence on their readers of books such as *Puck of Pook's Hill*. He explored the ways in which the reading of historical novels at an impressionable age left an 'imprint' for ever on their readers.[114] Rivet observed that, apart from the specialist, far more people derive their ideas of history from historical novels than from academic works.[115] He argued that works for children are the more insidious in that the effect that they have is delayed. People who read these accounts at an impressionable age are likely to be deeply influenced by them, especially as they are often used as historical fact by teachers.[116] We cannot, however, assume that the influence of the images created by popular fiction are restricted to children and their teachers, as they also influence academics through the process of their education as children. Although discussion of such issues is rarely addressed in academic accounts of Roman archaeology, Colin Wells has suggested in his book *The German Policy of Augustus* (1972), that an early literary diet of Kipling and others may have predisposed him toward a study of Roman arms.[117] Roman

Figure 4.3 The building of the Wall. Henry Ford's drawing for Fletcher and Kipling's *A School History of England* (1911). This portrayal of Hadrian's Wall makes it too high, wide and complex. Kipling's writings about the Wall also misinterpreted its function.

military studies have represented a fairly discrete and well-contained area of study within British archaeology, with a well-defined body of theory that has been partly derived from the type of nineteenth- and early twentieth-century world-view explored above.

The general approach to frontiers adopted by Haverfield and his contemporaries was based on an Edwardian fascination with frontier issues. For many Victorians and Edwardians, as we have seen, frontiers represented the dividing line between the civilised and the barbarians. This image of a clearly defined division between civilisation and barbarianism itself drew upon a long historical tradition in English and European thought. Many Edwardian gentlemen placed themselves in the position of the civilised Romans, while those outside the Empire were seen in the context of the barbarians; the frontier was the physical boundary to the extent of the influence of the west. An anomalous group of uncivilised native people also existed within the frontier in many parts of both empires: natives who became 'incorporated' and/or 'assimilated'.

The imperial discourse evident in Edwardian and later literature was based upon the creation of a clear frontier between the civilised (us) and the rest (other). In addition, in Kipling's account, a national instinct arises in the Romans of Britain that served to provide imperial morals for their Edwardian successors. The idea of the Roman frontier as a fixed and relatively stable line of military control manned by a civilised society is, however, derived from ideas of the nineteenth-century nation-state and the scramble of Britain, France, Germany and Italy for empire.[118] It remained dominant in archaeological studies until the 1970s. Developments in Roman frontier studies since the late 1970s have been based upon the idea of the frontier as a general zone of social and economic contact and exchange.[119] This approach places greater emphasis on the interaction between the Romans and the native populations of the frontier zone, deriving its focus in part from studies of the American frontier. The imperial legacy therefore led to a strong tradition in Roman frontier work that was not seriously challenged until the 1970s.

Civilian issues

Military studies had a particular value from the perspective of British imperial defence, but civilian issues within the Roman Empire were also relevant. Haverfield's comments about the relevance of the Roman example to contemporary problems of assimilation and incorporation indicate that he felt that a study of civilian settlement in the Roman provinces was relevant from the contemporary imperial perspective. A number of authors in late Victorian and early twentieth-century England explored the way in which the ancient British had behaved under Roman rule. In particular, in a series of publications during Edward VII's reign, Haverfield showed the way in which native Britons were given Roman civilisation and became Romanised. He developed a detailed argument about the processes of assimilation and denationalisation in Roman Britain.

The role of Rome in the assimilation of the ancient Britons to a state of civilisation has remained a topic of importance throughout the twentieth century. These accounts focused upon a linear notion of national history in which the Romans passed their civilisation in a fairly direct manner to the English; images of Rome and civilisation form a recurrent theme in the remainder of this book.

Part II

ENGLISHNESS

In Part II of this book I shall explore some images of English national origin and the ways in which they interacted in the period between around 1870 and 1930. Initially a popular image existed which proposed a Teutonic (Anglo-Saxon) racial origin for the English and this was accompanied by the powerful image that I have titled the 'Celtic Subaltern'. The image of the Celtic subaltern was based upon the idea that the classical Romans in England fulfilled the role which the nineteenth- and twentieth-century English now held within British India. In this equation of the ancient world with the modern, the 'Celts' of Roman Britain were seen to some extent to be in the guise of the native population of British India. They were also seen as the ancestors of the present populations of the northern and western areas of the British Isles.

There appears, however, to have been a growing problem with the drawing of too close an association between Roman Britain and British India in the late nineteenth and early twentieth centuries. This problem may have been associated with the developing wish of some to see the ancient Britons as the ancestors of the current generation of Britons as a whole. Some British writers did not wish to see the past occupants of their own country in the light of the native peoples of India; a certain tension is apparent in relevant works of this date.[1]

The changing spectrum of images of English origin at this time can be argued to have related to broader imperial concerns. It has been suggested that a basic concern between about 1880 and 1920 was that the Teutonic racial myth was too narrowly English. A relevant issue became how to replace this limited ideal with an origin myth that could encompass the United Kingdom and which could be extended to cover the Empire.[2] This repertoire was provided by a distinctly different view of English origins. A number of late Victorian and Edwardian texts claimed that the English strength of character that had led to imperial glory was derived, not from an exclusively Teutonic origin, but from the fusion of a variety of races through time.[3] An image of racial mixing in the English past developed at this time and derived some of its significance from the growing threat posed by modern Germany to British imperialists.[4] This pushed the English to look towards an image of racial origin that was more independent of Germanic roots.

Another image which derived from eighteenth-century and earlier origins dwelt upon the gallant character of the native ancient British ancestors and the idea that these people might in some ways form part of the genetic mix of the current generation of English people. I shall show that William Cowper's poem *Boadicea* (1782) drew upon this idea by associating the ancient British queen with the image of British imperial expansion. Cowper's imperial image was drawn upon regularly during the late nineteenth and early twentieth centuries.

At the same time, the potential of drawing upon a racial inheritance from the ancient Britons also lay in the fact this enabled a conceptual link to be drawn between the modern English and an imperial inheritance from the classical Romans. In the context of a mixed interpretation of racial origins, the English could be argued to represent the inheritors of the imperial torch of the Romans, in racial as well as moral terms. This concept also drew upon the classical education of the British élite.

The idea of a direct Roman contribution to the racial inheritance of the English through the passing on of civilisation from Romans to native Britons developed in late Victorian, Edwardian and later times in a range of works. In particular, Francis Haverfield's interpretation of Romanisation added academic credence to a popular trend that was already gathering momentum. Images of Englishness continued to develop after the First World War. We shall see that the image of a mixed English genetic origin continued at this time to draw upon the idea of Roman racial origins.

These various images of racial identity played a direct part in the discourse of imperialism in late Victorian and Edwardian times. The following chapters in this part of the book focus upon some of the ways that the various images of origin interacted, but emphasis will be placed upon the role of ideas of English origin in the context of the contemporary imperial situation.

5

TEUTONS, ROMANS
AND CELTS

Introduction

The idea that civilisation was inherited from the classical Romans and that of Teutonic racial origin set up a tension in later Victorian and Edwardian thought. Initially, I shall consider a Teutonic myth of origin, which contrasted the healthy vigour of England's northern inheritance with the stale despotism of the Roman Empire. This Teutonic image interacted in complex ways with the alternative idea of a worthy inheritance of civilisation (and Christianity) from the Romans. The image of what I shall title the 'Celtic subaltern' co-existed with both these other images of identity.

An image of Teutonic identity

The development of a strong concept of 'race' in Victorian society coincided with the creation of an ideology of Anglo-Saxon racial origin for the English.[1] The dominant idea, although not uncontested, was that the Romans left Britain and that the ancient Britons were killed off or driven into the west of the country during the Anglo-Saxon invasion, where they had remained to form the modern Welsh and Cornish population. Despite Danish and Norman interference, the English were often viewed as primarily Teutonic. This became a myth of race and destiny that sustained a range of contemporary military ambitions. It was also felt to account for the political complexion of English freedom and was defined in many minds by a strongly discriminatory view of the 'Celts' of Ireland, Scotland and Wales as racially inferior to the Germanic English.[2] The Germanic peoples, in settling England in the post-Roman period, were felt to have brought a love of freedom and respect for the family. It was considered that the constitutional liberties in British society derived from this Germanic root.[3]

A 'literary' movement focusing upon Teutonic identity grew with particular force in the third quarter of the nineteenth century, although it did draw upon earlier roots.[4] We can read about the Teutonic myth and also the relationship of this image to a negative conception of the Roman Empire in the works of three Victorian authors – Thomas Arnold, J.G. Sheppard and Charles Kingsley. Arnold expressed his view on the Teutonic origin of the English in 1841:

> our history clearly begins with the coming of the Saxons; the Britons and Romans had lived in our country, but they were not our fathers ... We, this great English nation, whose race and language are now overrunning the earth from one end to the other – we were born when the white horse of the Saxons had established his domain from the Tweed to the Tamar.[5]

Arnold felt that the English had learned the historical lessons of Greece, Rome and Israel but also had the distinct benefit of the direct inheritance of the racial spirit of the Germans.[6] For J.G. Sheppard in his *The Fall of Rome and the Rise of the New Nationalities*, published in 1861, the Teutonic invasion was the 'true birthdate of English history, and beneath the banner of the white horse inaugurated that Anglo-Saxon empire which has overspread the world'.[7]

We have seen in an earlier chapter that Sheppard acknowledged the institutions that England had inherited from Rome, but at the same time contrasted the despotism of the Roman Empire with the perfection of contemporary England.

Charles Kingsley wrote in 1864 that: 'It was not the mere muscle of the Teuton which enabled him to crush the decrepit and debauched slave-nations, Gaul and Briton, Iberian and African.[8] It was also down to 'purity ... a calm and steady brain, and a free and loyal heart; the energy which springs from health; the self-respect which comes from self-restraint; and the spirit which shrinks from neither God nor man'.[9] Kingsley drew upon the moral righteousness and nobility of the northern peoples and developed an explicit contrast to the decadence and despotism into which Rome and its empire was plunged.[10]

The Teutonic image of English origins survived well into the twentieth century in popular accounts of the history of England.[11]

H.E. Marshall in her highly influential children's book *Our Island Story* (1905), described how after the withdrawal of the Romans the few remaining Britons took up residence in Wales and Cornwall, while the Anglo-Saxons killed their relations and took over 'England'.[12] C.R.L. Fletcher and R. Kipling, in their *A School History of England* (1911), viewed the Saxons as having wiped out the Britons and introduced a 'life with a good deal of freedom in it'.[13] The 'First Englishmen in England' in Elizabeth O'Neil's book *A Nursery History of England* (1912) are Hengist and Horsa.[14] This view also re-emerges in some of the literature that was published during the later twentieth century.[15]

Roman officers and 'Celtic subalterns': Roman Britain as British India

Another clearly defined representation in nineteenth-century England was posited upon the character of Roman Britain as an historical parallel for British India, a parallel that provided a set of historical lessons.[16] Romans and Britons according to this approach were felt to be as distinct as Victorian/Edwardian Englishmen were from Indians (Figure 5.1).[17] It was often felt that the Romans of Britain comprised officers and imperial officials who lived in fortified cities, fortresses and impressive villas. The population of native ancient Britain was thought to cluster, at some remove, around these Roman officials and settlers, in effect in the manner of 'Celtic subalterns'.[18] For some Englishmen at this time, the ancient Britons were felt to be the parents of the Irish, Welsh and Scots and many Victorian scholars felt that the 'departure of the Romans' in the fifth century left the Britons almost as 'Celtic' as their coming had found them'.[19] The uncivilised Celts of England were considered in turn to have been defeated and massacred, or driven into the North and West, by the freedom-loving Teutonic ancestors of the English.

On occasions the image of the Celtic subaltern was drawn in an explicit fashion. For instance, Thackeray, in his account of Ancient Britain under the Roman Empire published in 1843, envisages third-century Britain as comparable to the state of 'Hindostan' when it was first subject to the English.[20] The Britons were encouraged to learn 'eloquence' and 'the Arts', but only to soothe the vanity of the Romans and to divert British attention from 'military pursuits' and too deep a reflection on their own condition.[21] The Roman Empire, according to Thackeray, has a messianic role in spreading Christianity to the West; but despite this: 'the calm eye of the

Figure 5.1 The landing of the Romans. Henry Ford's drawing for Fletcher and Kipling's *A School History of England* (1911). This image shows bright, upright and orderly Roman soldiers and dark and disorganised native Britons. The woad-covered bodies and hair styles of the natives must have brought to mind images of non-white populations of parts of the British Empire.

philosopher, and, much more, of the Christian, detected many latent springs of dissatisfaction and misery.'[22]

S.R. Gardiner's influential children's book *Outline of English History* (1887) suggested that the Romans treated the British very much in the same way that the British in the nineteenth century treated the people of India. The British brought the natives civilisation, built roads and towns and forced them to live at peace but without very much of the civilisation passing on.[23] Some authors could see very little Roman influence on the native population, other authors considered Rome's major legacy to have been negative – the removal of the war-like virtue of the native Britons, which consequently left them powerless to resist the Anglo-Saxon invaders.[24] J.R. Seeley's in *The Expansion of England* (1883) drew upon a slightly different parallel, between Roman Gaul and Spain and British India.[25]

The Reverend Professor A.J. Church,[26] in his children's novel *The Count of the Saxon Shore* (1887), wrote about the departure of the Roman legions in AD 410 and the consequent troubles as Britons reverted to their pre-Roman 'Celtic' ways and as the Britons, Picts and Saxons fought it out. Towards the end of the novel, after the departure of the Romans (including the Count), the Britons had thrown off acquired Roman culture and 'all signs of that subjection'.[27] They had returned to British dress and manners. It was the dream of Ambiorix, one of their leaders, 'to have Britain such as she might have been had Rome never conquered it'.[28] Carna, the British adopted daughter of the Count of the Saxon Shore, stayed behind when he returned to Rome and, after facing and surviving intended sacrifice by druids at Stonehenge, witnessed the burning of the villa on *Vectis* (the Isle of Wight) in which she grew up. This forms a symbolic ending of her old, Roman way of life; she then speaks as 'some mighty inspiration seemed to carry her beyond the present'.[29]

She predicts that the British population will be replaced by a Saxon race, but that: 'God hath great things in store for this dear country of ours . . . for the sea shall be covered with their ships; and they shall rule over the nations from one end of heaven to the other.'[30] Why this should encourage Carna's demoralised comrades is problematic, as she has also had to explain to them that these successful imperialists will not be their descendants, but those of the very Saxons who are currently attacking their country. Carna's words, rather than being directed at her comrades, are meant for a late Victorian audience and presumably draw upon the inspiration of William Cowper's poem about Boadicea (which is discussed on pp. 74–5). Church's novel thus incorporates a dismissive image of the Celt in association with the Teutonic myth of English origin.

As the image of Anglo-Saxon origins became increasingly dominant during the nineteenth century in England, much of the antiquarian activity was directed towards the monuments and records that were left behind by the medieval English. In particular the Middle Ages occupied the mind as a result of its 'religiosity' and of the wish to dwell upon English identity.[31] The parallel between British India and Roman Britain was not always felt to be exact but this did not detract from its value. It often had a deep influence on the ways that archaeological remains were interpreted. The archaeology of the ancient Britons and Roman Britons remained relatively undeveloped until the early part of the twentieth century. The relevance of both Romans and ancient Britons to racial origins and the destiny of the nation appeared limited to many Victorians. The monuments of prehistoric populations often appear to have had limited relevance, while Roman forts, villas and towns were often interpreted as the houses and stations of officers and other settlers from Rome itself.[32]

Bertram Windle in his *Life in Early Britain* (1897), in considering the essentially military character of the Roman occupation of Britain, mentioned forts, military roads, great fortified cities, the Roman Wall and the 'magnificent villas' which were built for Roman officials.[33] The villa in Vectis in A.J. Church's novel of 1887 was the property of the Count of the Saxon Shore, an official who returned to Rome with the Roman army during its withdrawal. Fletcher and Kipling, writing in 1911, saw the villas of Britain as the homes of Roman imperial officials who had been posted to Britain or had settled there, and other authors had similar views. In this view of affairs, by placing Roman officials in the context of British officers in India, a connection was drawn between the contemporary English and the classical Romans. Even if the English were derived from Germanic origins, they had learnt the lessons of civilisation and imperial organisation which were provided by the classical Romans. In contrast to this English racial inheritance, the 'Celtic' population of northern and western Britain derived their inheritance from the pre-Roman population of the British Isles — the Celtic subalterns.

The mission of Roman officials in Britain

In the imperial context, a premonition of national destiny is evident in the attitude of imperial Roman officials in Fletcher and Kipling's account of Roman Britain in their book *A School History of Britain*, published in 1911.[34] The book suggests that the 'spirit of the dear motherland' (Britain) became a passion with the Roman 'gentlemen' who were obliged to stay in Britain because of their duty or business and they came to have 'an equal share of . . . love and devotion' to Britain and Rome'.[35] In particular, Kipling's fictitious centurion in his poem *The Roman Centurion speaks*, which forms part of *A School History of England*, on being ordered back to Rome from Britain where he has served for forty years, wished to stay because 'Here is my heart, my soul, my mind'.[36] Later accounts again draw upon the inspiration provided by Kipling's work.[37]

The pro-British views expressed in Kipling's *Puck of Pook's Hill* (considered in the last chapter) and *The Roman Centurion*, suggest that he felt that some of the Roman imperial officials may actually have remained in Britain after the accepted date of the Roman withdrawal in AD 410. A problem existed, however, with the Teutonic image of origins from the point of view of these portrayals. It suggested that these retired officials could not form part of the genetic stock of the English, since all the pre-Teutonic inhabitants were slaughtered by the Saxon ancestors during the English take-over.

'The Romans of Britain'

Kipling's wish to draw upon Roman racial roots indicates that not all Edwardians held to a strict version of the Teutonic myth of English origin. In fact, an alternative Roman racial origin for aspects of English society is explored in a variety of works of Victorian and Edwardian date.

H.C. Coote, a solicitor with an interest in England's past, wrote two thought-provoking books, *A Neglected Fact in English History* (1864) and *The Romans of Britain* (1878) in which he developed an alternative Roman origin myth for the English. Coote's work had some considerable influence on his own and later generations. His idea is clearly developed in the later book, which was written to attempt to counter arguments raised by scholars who criticised his earlier work.[38]

Coote's argument that a homogeneous English race was a fiction[39] was ahead of its time and is echoed in later Victorian and Edwardian works. Coote drew attention, in a similar manner to Sheppard (whose work has been considered above), to a number of institutions and traditions which united Roman Britain and Victorian England, including law, the '*civitates*', civilisation, art, even 'imperial coinage'.[40] By contrast, for the Anglo-Saxon 'barbarism was his sole inheritance and endowment'.[41]

The Teutonic myth apparently:

> post-dates the English origines and dries up the springs of our early history, the merits and interest of which are by this

supposition lavished upon a race of strangers. It disentitles a large proportion of the Britons of Imperial Rome to the sympathies of the present race of Englishmen, between whom and the Eternal City it leaves a gap without connection or transition. Provincial Britain becomes a lost nation, and four centuries of historical associations, with their momentous consequences are divorced from our annals.[42]

In addition to the analysis in his attack on the Teutonic myth, Coote developed a theory to link the modern English with the classical Romans. He argued that the Roman population of Britain were descendants of the original Roman colonists and that they survived the Anglo-Saxon conquest in the 'ark' of their cities. The Norman, or 'Gallo-Roman', conquest in the eleventh century then relieved the 'depression' that had resulted from the Anglo-Saxon and Danish conquests and subsequent periods of control. With Gallo-Roman support the Romans of England then became 'the creator, under providence, of the medieval and modern greatness of England'.[43]

The lack of any detailed archaeological understanding of the Roman or post-Roman history of Roman towns in Britain perhaps enabled Coote to develop this theory. In due course his idea of a long-term Roman survival in the cities of post-Roman England was disproved by the evidence uncovered by urban archaeology during the twentieth century.[44] Coote's work did, however, have a considerable influence in late Victorian England. It was particularly useful in providing an image of historical continuity for the Christian religion from Roman to post-Roman Britain.[45]

Summary

Coote's influence upon a range of writers in later nineteenth-century England will be considered below. It demonstrates that not all Victorians and Edwardians held to a doctrinal version of the type of Teutonic myth outlined by T. Arnold, Kingsley, Marshall, Fletcher and Kipling and others. A contradiction in thought existed between those who wished to celebrate the Roman inheritance and others for whom the image of the Roman Empire was a more negative one. This is perhaps to be explained by the basic intellectual opposition between, on the one hand, a dislike of the idea of absolute rule and the centralising state and, on the other, a sentimental idealisation of the Roman tradition derived from classical education.[46] This idealisation is also evident in the context of the idea that the

Romans in Britain fulfilled a similar imperial role to the contemporary British in India. Through the use of the idea of the Celtic subaltern, an image of the colonised 'other' could be utilised to help to define and isolate English identity. These Celts appeared to have adopted little of the Roman civilisation and were seen as the ancestors of the contemporary Welsh, Irish and Scots. The English, by contrast, had inherited the freedom of the Teuton and had learnt the positive aspect of the imperial inheritance of the classical Romans through classical education.

The growth of a positive attitude to Roman imperialism in late nineteenth-century Britain was reviewed earlier and this also evidently had an impact in providing the context for an image of Roman racial inheritance. Later chapters will explore a myth of a Roman racial origin for the English that developed in late Victorian, Edwardian and later times. In the next chapter, however, I shall review the role of the valiant ancient Britons who resisted the Roman invasion. This was another of the mix of images of origin which was drawn upon in late Victorian and Edwardian times. Its existence indicates that ideas of English national origin were more complex than the dual opposition between a Teutonic and a Roman myth of origin might suggest.

6

ANCIENT HEROES
OF THE RESISTANCE

Introduction

Norman Vance has suggested that the image of Rome was imbued during the late nineteenth and early twentieth centuries with the problematic idea that the pride of Britain had once been humbled by the Roman army who made most of the island a colony.[1] Children's novels and history textbooks sometimes struggled with the idea of previous phases of 'foreign' (Roman and Norman) domination. Many books focused on medieval and modern England when the country had remained free from conquest.[2] When they deal with the Roman conquest children's authors often struggled with the idea of native British defeat. For instance, W. Locke suggested in his *Stories of the Land we Live in; or England's History in Easy Language*, published in 1878 that:

> I dare say every one of our forefathers, when they saw the Romans come first, were discouraged, and thought all was over with them; they should never be happy any more, their towns and castles taken, many of them killed and their enemies very proud and haughty. But those very things were meant for their good. Their savage customs and barbarous manner of life were thus changed. There we find the first steps on the ladder that has conducted Englishmen to such power and greatness . . . Let us heartily thank God for it.[3]

In addition to showing an embarrassment with a period of former foreign domination, these comments related Britain's late Victorian greatness to its history. A number of children's authors and other writers discussed the Roman impact on Britain for a variety of reasons. In the context of these works it would appear that national pride could be reasserted in a number of ways; for instance, by exploring the active opposition which the ancient Britons had provided to Rome.[4] In the following chapter another source of pride is explored – the image that the English drew upon classical Rome as their imperial successors.

The range of characters discussed in the classical sources include Boadicea, Caratacus and Calgacus. In addition, Victorian authors were not averse to inventing their own heroic figures. I shall argue that these characters could be used in the determination of images of English ancestry.

Caratacus was a son of king Cunobelin, who fought the Romans in the area of present-day Wales. According to the Roman author Tacitus, he was handed over to the Romans by Cartimandua, queen of the Brigantes, taken as a captive to Rome in AD 51 and gave a speech in front of the Emperor Claudius and the Senate, which saved his life. Caratacus' role as a national hero has usually been less problematic than Boadicea's but his fame has perhaps declined to an extent during the twentieth century.

'Boadicea' is an alternative spelling of the Celtic 'Boudica', possibly derived from a Romanised form of the name. Where I quote from the works of a past author, that author's own version of the name will be used. Boudica herself was the wife of a first-century AD king of the tribe called the Iceni. After her husband's death, she rose to fight the Romans in AD 60–61, with the support of certain other tribes, and was discussed in the works of the classical authors Tacitus and Cassius Dio. S. Macdonald has defined a popular national image of Boadicea, which has developed during the last two centuries, as a former queen of England who has often been associated with a sense of victory, patriotism and empire in the English national memory.[5] 'Boudica' in Celtic means 'Victoria', and so on occasions during the reign of Queen Victoria she naturally provided an analogy for the contemporary British Queen.[6] As a national heroine, however, her story has at some times been more complex and problematical – it has, indeed, been developed in different ways in various epochs of English history, making Boadicea a 'multi-faceted historical template'.[7]

For the Scots, Calgacus provided a figure of native resistance. Calgacus has been drawn upon as a national hero far less often that Boadicea and Caratacus, possibly as a result of the range of other heroes available from the wars of independence against the English.

It has been argued above that imperial discourse utilised past imagery in defining its own imperial present and we shall see that this was true of late Victorian and Edwardian representations of Caratacus and Boadicea.

Renaissance

The increase in the availability of classical sources in the sixteenth century brought the attention of the English to a range of individual ancient British characters who had resisted the Roman conquest of the island. Mikalachki has suggested in a recent study of Boadicea that a contradiction existed in early modern English (sixteenth- and seventeenth-century) nationalism. On the one hand there was a longing to establish a respectable historical precedent and continuity for Englishness, while on the other the exorcism of primitive savagery from national history and identity was practised. In fact, this contradiction appears to have a lengthy life in terms of English self-definition. As we have already seen, an image of some form of Roman origin for the English reoccurs in Victorian times,[8] indicating the wish to establish a direct link between contemporary Britons and classical Romans.[9]

In sixteenth- and seventeenth-century accounts of Boadicea two contrasting aspects are evident – the idea of uncontrollable female barbarity and that of the female national icon. These two aspects of Boadicea's image re-emerge in later representations;[10] indeed, they were partly derived from the contrasting approaches to the actions of the queen presented in the classical texts of Tacitus and Dio.[11] Contradictions in the images of ancient Britons also relate to contrasting positive and critical views of primitive society, again an inheritance from the classical sources.[12]

The Boadicea of Cowper and Tennyson: continuing contradictions

In the late eighteenth century a number of poets championed the resistance of the British to Rome. In particular Caratacus and Boadicea were frequently selected as examples of heroic patriotism.[13] The most significant work in the context of my account is William Cowper's poem *Boadicea: an ode*, which was published in 1782 at a time of British territorial expansion and political ambition following the lengthy conflicts of the second half of the eighteenth century, including the American War of Independence.[14]

In this poem a Druid speaks to Boadicea prior to her final battle with the Romans and encourages her to fight by prophesying the fall of Rome. In the Druid's speech before the battle he states that after Rome has perished:

> Then the progeny that springs
>> From the forest of our land,
> Arm'd with thunder, clad with wings
>> Shall a wider world command.
> Regions Caesar never knew
>> Thy posterity shall sway;
> Where his eagle never flew,
>> None invincible as they.[15]

The idea that Boadicea's progeny would command a far greater extent of the world than the Romans could ever conquer coincided with a developing interest in British national heroes at a time of imperial expansion.[16] Boadicea then rushes into the final battle 'with all a monarch's pride' and in her death hurls at the Romans the cry:

> Empire is on us bestow'd,
>> Shame and ruin wait for you.[17]

The clear references here are to the decline and fall of the Roman Empire and the rise of its British successor.

S. Macdonald has argued that Cowper's poem fostered a triumphal asexual image of British heroism,[18] while Mikalachki has suggested that the modern transformation of the queen into a figure of British patriotism marked the eclipse of female rebelliousness as a public concern as female roles became increasingly more domestic during the seventeenth and eighteenth centuries.[19] Unlike some earlier writers, Cowper developed Boadicea as a symbol of English pride.[20] In the context of this book, Cowper's poem helped to project Boadicea into the context of late Victorian and Edwardian imperial discourse by giving her actions a distinct role in the formation of the British Empire.

Native heroes who had resisted the Roman Empire continued to form a reference point for British people in the nineteenth century, despite the view held by many about the assumed Teutonic origin of the English. Caratacus and Boadicea provided inspiration for plays, sculptures and paintings at this time,[21] although Boadicea sometimes had a more problematic role, in line with earlier interpretations of her contribution to British history.[22] In Tennyson's *Boadicea*, published in 1864, the Icenian Queen shows a particularly savage taste for violent battle.[23] David has argued that Boadicea's behaviour is contrasted with the 'moral serenity' and 'middle-class propriety' of Queen Victoria in several works by Tennyson [24] and that, in effect, Tennyson used Queen Victoria to create a curb for the barbaric rage of Boadicea.[25] In the general Victorian context, however, Caratacus and Boadicea joined Arthur and Alfred not as native chieftains but as patriotic heroes, staunch defenders of Britain against the evils that might beset it from outside.[26]

Late Victorian and Edwardian representations

Ancient Britons figured in historical novels – a particularly important source of inspiration for late Victorian and Edwardian children. At this time the British redefined their celebrations of national heroes, including Caratacus and Boadicea,[27] and also invented them as, for instance, in the cases of Beric the Briton, and Carna, step-daughter of the Count of the Saxon Shore (for Carna, see above).[28]

A range of children's history books and works of fiction mention Caratacus and Boadicea and their, ultimately unsuccessful, struggles against the Roman invaders.[29] For instance, in Church's children's novel *The Count of the Saxon Shore* (1887) we learn that in the early fifth century AD, as the Romans were preparing to leave Britain: 'Caradoc [Caratacus] and Boadicea, and other heroes and heroines of British independence, were household words in many families which were yet thoroughly Roman in spirit and manners.'[30]

Caratacus

In 1897–8 Elgar produced his cantata *Caractacus*, to which a libretto was added by H.A. Ackworth. The resulting opera presents the defeat of the native Britons who had resisted Rome. In his speech to the Romans, Caractacus states:

> Do thy worst to me: my people spare
> whom fought for freedom in our land at home.
> Slaves they are not; be wise and teach them there
> Order, and law, and liberty with Rome.[31]

This was followed by a chorus extolling the British Empire under Queen Victoria, stating a direct historical continuity of purpose between the two Empires.[32] In the late Victorian context, however, Caratacus was overshadowed as an imperial figure by Boadicea.

The imperial cult of Boadicea

Cowper's poem had a particularly important role in the development of a late Victorian and twentieth century image of Boadicea. It was learned by thousands of Victorian and twentieth-century school-children and quoted widely in later times, being 'known to every schoolboy' as late as 1962.[33] It also helped to foster a strong image in England of Boadicea as a national heroine, although, as we have already seen from Tennyson's poem, she was not a problem-free figurehead. The image of Boadicea as a national heroine was re-used and redefined in the late nineteenth and early twentieth centuries and elevated into a fairly coherent representation – an image that has been regularly invoked and redefined.

Thomas Thornycroft designed a number of statues of figures from British history, including Boadicea. Between 1856 and 1871 he worked on a massive statue of Boadicea in her chariot with the Prince Consort's encouragement and assistance; he even lent horses to help with the modelling of the statue. In the 1870s it appeared that Thornycroft might receive a commission from the state to complete the execution of his Boadicea group. It was praised in *The Times* newspaper in July 1871 as 'the most successful attempt in historical sculpture of this barren time', but the Government did nothing to aid its completion at this time.[34] The group was not cast in bronze until after it was presented to the nation by Thomas Thornycroft's son, Sir John Isaac Thornycroft in 1896.[35] London County Council raised the money for the casting by direct public subscription. The committee which was set up to help with the casting consisted of well-known members of the legislature, Royal Academicians, London County Councillors, journalists and, apparently, leading Welshmen![36] The statue was placed on Westminster Bridge in 1902 (see below).

A linked image involving the glorification of Boadicea as a national heroine is provided by Marie Trevelyan in her astonishing book *Britain's Greatness Foretold: The Story of Boadicea, the British Warrior-Queen*, published in 1900 and which sported a Union Jack and part of Cowper's poem[37] on its front cover. Trevelyan had had early experience of the Welsh language – in her own words, the language in which Boadicea thought and spoke. She developed a deep interest in the former queen of the Iceni and wrote a poem about her when she was 18, which was later developed into her novel.[38]

The inspiration that drove Trevelyan is evident from her book:

> I felt that there must be a peculiar interest in going to the sources whence sprang the patriotic spirit of a race who, eighteen centuries ago, fought boldly against the Romans – who saw empires and monarchs vanish – who bravely held their own against all the warlike nations of Europe – whose soil is the dust of patriots – whose exhaustless vitality through all ages supplies renowned commanders on land and sea, and whose logs and roll-calls record the names of those who have distinguished themselves at the head of our gallant sailors and soldiers in maintaining the honour of Britain.[39]

She recalled the history of the design and casting of Thornycroft's statue and looked forward to its erection, which would occur two years after the publication of *Britain's Greatness Foretold* – indeed a photograph of the sculpture forms the frontispiece to the volume. Trevelyan also recounted the events of 'the great and unparalleled patriotic revival of 1899–1900',[40] presumably including victories against the Boers in South Africa and also, perhaps, the Tory victory in the General Election.[41]

The events of 1899–1900 are directly reflected in the content of her book. She suggested that, as a result of the Boer War: 'the ancient fires of British valour and patriotism were replenished, and blazed forth with the strong, unwavering light that in the past bewildered the Romans, and in the present astonishes Europe.'[42] Trevelyan used the preface of her book to stress the patriotism of the Welsh people to the cause of Britain and to argue that the war effort had been the result of British, rather than English, work alone. Indeed, she appears to infer that the ancient Britons are the ancestors of the British as a whole, although she places much emphasis on the Welsh as the upholders of ancient British racial claims.

Trevelyan's Boadicea is not the barbarian of Tennyson's work. Trevelyan countered the view of critics who wished to see Boadicea as a 'barbaric queen, surrounded by fierce warriors and *masculine* women.'[43] She recalled how the Iceni had come to terms with the Romans and at the time of the invasion 'had almost entirely forfeited the name of Britons' and afterwards had 'remained unfaithful to the National cause'.[44] She argued that it is likely that the 'refining influences' of Roman civilisation formed an important element in

Boadicea's early training and subsequent position as wife of King Prasutagus.[45] The Boadicea of Trevelyan's novel is stately, civilised and kind. The atrocities mentioned in the classical sources are not discussed in any detail. Boadicea even shows clemency in treating some captured Roman soldiers as 'state-protected prisoners of war'.[46] Although Boadicea is defeated and dies by her own hand the end of the novel, the action finishes in a positive fashion as the grand-daughter of Caratacus, Princess 'Golden Beauty', marries a Roman and becomes a 'Nazarene'.[47]

Perhaps the most remarkable element of this astounding book is the prophesy which is put into the mouth of the 'Arch-druid' Arian-rod by Trevelyan. Arianrod utters this prediction after a range of British military victories over the Romans and the burning of London:

> 'Slumber now!' said the Arch-druid, looking sadly towards the smouldering city of Caerlud [London], 'slumber and take rest, while warring hosts struggle and perish. But the time shall come when Britain shall be avenged! The Romans shall vanish, other invaders shall be laid low, and thou, O city, rising from the dust and ashes of purifying fire, shall ascend and become the fairest queen and mother of cities in a vast empire on which the sun shall never set!'
>
> As Arianrod uttered the prediction which, in ages to come, was brilliantly fulfilled, the rising sun, like an emblem of eternity, bore witness to the prophesy.[48]

Arianrod's prediction drew upon that of the druid in Cowper's poem, which is reprinted in full at the start of Trevelyan's book. Trevelyan wrote that the evidence for the early struggles of British valour is to be found in this Arch-druid's prediction, immortalised by histor-ians and poets 'and rendered familiar to later generations by Cowper's celebrated and deathless ode'.[49]

The prediction, which is replicated at several different stages in the book,[50] has no basis in the classical sources but is treated throughout as an historical fact. The author states at the start of the book that: 'In the past, I beheld Buddig — Victoria — intently listening to the Arch-druid's wonderful Prediction. In the present, I behold our great and good Queen Victoria realising the marvellous fulfilment of the Prophesy'.[51]

The writer Edwin Collins provided an introductory piece for Trevelyan's novel titled 'The Prediction Fulfilled', in which he appeared to be unaware that there was no reliable historic basis for Arianrod's prophesy. He wrote that since the prophecy was made in the first century: 'through all that lapse of time the characteristics of the British race have been tending towards bringing about its fulfilment'.[52] After considering the progress of the Boer War, and other imperial topics, he concluded his piece by arguing:

> Surely it is not inappropriate to preface an imaginative work which portrays an heroic period in Britain's past by the foregoing sketch of some recent historical events, which seem, by their realisation, in solid facts, of a prediction uttered over eighteen centuries ago, to show how close is the relation between the imagination and history.[53]

In the case of Arianrod's prophesy these two authors appear to have projected a work of mythical history as fact.

Thornycroft's statue was finally placed on the Embankment in front of the House of Commons in 1902 by the London County Council – shortly after victory over the Boers and one year after the death of Queen Victoria. Graham Webster has suggested that the statue created a emotive patriotic stir at the thought of the 'virago of a queen' defying a great but alien power and that it was deliberately placed to provide a symbolic defence for the House of Commons from an attack from over the Thames from the south.[54] This representation of Boadicea shows her as a wild and powerful woman;[55] it was apparently particularly popular with children[56] and remains a source of fascination for tourists. On the front (west side) is an inscription which reads:

> Boadicea
> Boudicca
> Queen of the Iceni
> Who died A.D. 61
> After leading her people
> against the Roman invader

While on the south side of the pediment is an inscription that quotes Cowper's poem:

> Regions Caesar never knew
> thy posterity shall sway.

In relation to the context of the cult of Boadicea which developed around the end of the nineteenth century and the start of the twentieth, one location proposed for Thornycroft's statue was a barrow in Parliament Hill Fields 'traditionally' known as Boadicea's grave.[57] London County Council started to excavate this site within ten years of Thomas Thornycroft's death, but the Society of Antiquaries rejected the identification of the mound as the burial place of the Queen and alternative sites for the statue were discussed. In view of the development of the site of Vercingetorix's final battle against the Romans at Alésia in France as a state-sponsored 'memory factory',[58] it is interesting to speculate what might have occurred if the archaeological community had been able to agree a location with London County Council for the site of Boadicea's last stand against the Romans, or for that of her burial. The British might have had their own 'memory factory' devoted to Boadicea to counter the French shrine at Alésia. The state sponsorship that was mooted in the 1870s shows an interest in the cult to Boadicea to match the interest of Napoleon III in Vercingetorix during the 1860s.

These representations of Boadicea recall the words of Marina Warner that: 'Boadicea . . . [was] . . . a real figure colonized to become a symbol of British greatness in a Victorian myth of Empire'[59] Thornycroft and Trevelyan's portrayals of Boadicea drew directly upon Cowper's poem in projecting a nationalistic motivation through the glorification of Boadicea as an upholder of British nationality at a time of foreign oppression. They also drew upon the association that Cowper created between the former Queen and the expansion of the British Empire. Boadicea, in effect, was recruited as an upholder of Britain's imperial might in late Victorian imperial discourse.

A counter-image of barbarity

The image provided by Boadicea throughout history has, however, been multifaceted and complex – late Victorians and Edwardians were not consistently positive in their judgement of her achievements. Although a connection may sometimes have been made between Boadicea and Queen Victoria, this was not a regular occurrence. As we have seen, Tennyson in the mid-nineteenth century developed Boadicea in the guise of a type of anti-Victoria, and in this he was drawing upon earlier images of the first-century British queen. After all, Boadicea led a bloody battle against a civilised, if oppressive, occupying power – a difficult image to apply in the context of the British domination over India.

Her role perhaps appeared particularly problematic to those who felt that English freedom had developed from a Teutonic root. For instance, a negative representation of Boadicea exists in the ancient historian B.W. Henderson's comparison of her sacking of Colchester (Camulodunum) and the 'Indian Mutiny':[60] 'We English, too, have had to face the doom in India, which fell out of a sunny heaven upon amazed Camulodunum, and we too may know how the Romans died.'[61] Apparently, 'Iceni, Trinobantes, Brigantes, the tribes to the number of a hundred and twenty thousand men, swept down upon the defenceless Roman settlers as Indians upon New England home-steads, as cruel and as relentless'.[62] Henderson argued that it would be 'but maudlin sentiment' to 'deplore' the Roman victory over Boadicea. In fact, 'The revenge was one of greater races than the Britons, of time rather than of the avenging sword . . . But the Roman conquest was Britain's first step along the path to her wider Empire'.[63]

Although rather unclear, Henderson appears to have argued that, as a result of the Roman victory over Boadicea and the Anglo-Saxons' victory over the Romans, the seal was set on the future greatness of the English. If so, it would appear that Henderson was drawing upon an image of the Teutonic racial origin of the English at the same time that he used the common association between the Celts of Roman Britain and the Indian population of British India.

Victorian and Edwardian concerns over these negative associations of female barbarism perhaps provide one reason for the failure of Boadicea's cult to develop to quite the same degree as that of the state-sponsored cult of Vercingetorix in France. The continued influence of the Teutonic myth of national origin for the English may provide one further reason for the comparative lack of large-scale support for Boadicea as a developing national symbol. The failure to identify an authentic archaeological site for the establishment of a 'memory factory' for her cult may provide another.

Beric the Briton

Ancient British heroes could on occasions be entirely mythical in character. G.A. Henty wrote more than eighty children's novels with eventual sales of perhaps twenty-five million copies.[64] The settings for these stories range from pre-Christian times to the beginning of the twentieth century.[65] One of his novels, *Beric the Briton: A Story of the Roman Invasion*, was first published in 1893 and is particularly relevant in the context of the creation of an ancient British hero.

In this novel Henty invented a British hero – Beric – who was the fictitious son of a chief of a sub-tribal grouping within the Iceni. Beric is take hostage by the Romans and learns Roman ways through classical education in the household of Caius Muro, a legionary commander resident in Camulodunum (Colchester). Beric's experience of Roman ways does not detract from his distinctly British nationality. He joins Boadicea's rebellion, and after several victories and a glorious role in what proved to be the final defeat of Boadicea's army of ancient Britons by the Romans, retreats to the Fens where he fights a successful rearguard action against the Roman army. He is finally captured only as a result of trickery and taken to Rome. In Rome he becomes a gladiator and saves a Christian maiden in the Colosseum, before becoming a bodyguard to Nero and then leading a rebellion. He finally returns to Britain after being made provincial governor of a large part of the island. There he becomes a Christian, rules wisely, appoints Britons in place of dishonest imperial officials, and establishes a dynasty.[66]

Beric is described as of gigantic stature and his character in the novel is a clear historical projection of the image of a later Victorian English gentleman. His genetic make-up, classical education and conversion to Christianity effectively created in Beric a first-century AD version of an idealised member of the late Victorian British ruling élite (Figure 6.1). He is conscious of his status as a member of the tribal élite of the Iceni, but during the rebellion of Boadicea he is happy to defer to the older and senior leaders of the tribe until called upon for advice or assistance. He is fully consistent and reliable, he has integrity and is fully conscious of his obligations to those who are obliged to him, both Britons and Romans.[67] His followers, like Beric himself, are valiant and stronger and bigger than their Roman adversaries. The success in winning a number of significant victories is largely a result of the physical abilities of the Britons combined with Beric's Roman education and leadership qualities. The eventual defeat of Boadicea is a result of the Romans' far greater efficiency, while the Roman's success against Beric's forces in the Fens results from superior manpower and from the local Fen-dwellers being bribed into giving away Beric's position. Defeat in either case does not result from a lack of patriotic spirit on the part of the Britons. Henty wrote that Beric's contemporaries in Britain were proud of him. When he returned from Italy to Britain:

> The news of his coming had preceded him, and the Iceni flocked to meet him, and gave him an enthusiastic welcome.

Figure 6.1 The Britons before the propraetor. W. Parkinson's drawing for Henty's *Beric the Briton* (1893). This shows a distinctly white and civilised Beric addressing the Roman officer. The two other Britons flanking Beric show the lack of a classical education in their clothes and hairstyles.

> They were proud of him as a national hero; he alone of their chiefs had maintained resistance against the Romans, and his success *had obliterated the humiliation of their great defeat*.[68]

Henty is evidently writing for a late Victorian audience and these comments, at the end of his novel, suggest that patriotic pride could be felt by Victorians in these British ancestors and in their active resistance to a despotic foreign power. This is especially true because Henty felt that the modern population of England was derived in part from this ancient British racial strain (see p. 92).

National defence

Boadicea, Beric and Caratacus, were perhaps partly utilised by some late Victorian and Edwardian writers to obliterate a memory of a period of foreign rule over the country whose inhabitants 'never shall be slaves'. The ancient British population who followed Caratacus, Boadicea and Beric in fighting against Rome were also useful in this regard. Authors often felt that these ancient Britons were brave in their defence of liberty. Fletcher and Kipling suggest that Caesar's account of his invasion of Britain: 'Leaves us with the impression that the spirit of the dear motherland had breathed valour and cunning into the whole British people.'[69] In fact, as the ancient Britons lived in many distinct tribes that only finally united when faced with the powerful Roman army of conquest, any worship of 'motherland' by these people was a modern attribution rather than an ancient British concept. It is clear from these observations that the invocation of ancient British national folk-heroes could counter, or at least moderate, the impact of the idea of Roman domination of these islands[70] and project British national spirit into a modern context of imperial discourse. As such, the image of the ancient British hero fulfilled an important role in the creation of imperial discourse. It also provided an ingredient in the theory of a mixed racial origins for the English which developed in the late nineteenth and early twentieth centuries.

7

THE RISE OF A THEORY OF
MIXED RACIAL ORIGINS

Introduction: problems with the inheritance

The use of individual ancient Britons as national heroes by late Victorian and Edwardian authors drew upon the problematical idea that these people were the ancestors of the current generations of the English. We have seen that in a range of cases these ancestral figures had a particular value because of the role that they were made to fulfil in the discourse of British imperialism. Cowper's poem helped with this identification in drawing Boadicea into the orbit of British imperialism and other ancient Britons were used in comparable ways.

For those late Victorians and Edwardians who did wish to draw upon the idea of an ancient British ancestry, the humbling of Britain by Rome could be countered. This could be achieved not only by stories of the strength of the native opposition, but also by the idea that Britain itself had now become the coloniser of an even larger part of the world than that which had been dominated by Rome.[1] This view of imperial inheritance drew upon a variety of sources, including the Roman history of the British Isles, the nature of classical education and an interpretation of progress derived from Darwinian evolutionary theory. Under this evolutionary theory of progress, Britain could be argued to represent the heir to Rome, but could also be considered to have improved upon this inheritance.

Peter Bowler has suggested, in his book *The Invention of Progress* (1989), that the industrial and political domination which Europe exerted upon the world in the late nineteenth century and the theory of progress supported the claim that Europeans had a moral right to lead other branches of humanity into the light. Many influential late Victorians in Britain claimed that their society was at the pinnacle of social development, with all 'earlier' stages of humanity placed in a linear progression towards this ideal state. These earlier forms of humanity were seen as lower down the scale of social development and it was often felt that they would progress to a modern state through the influence of the British Empire.[2] Although a growing realism developed in Edwardian society, this progressive interpretation of social development remained powerful in British society into the twentieth century.[3]

One image within late Victorian and later society posited an effectively cyclical vision of history, whereby history repeated itself through time; a more common attitude, however, was a more linear version combined with a cyclical image, in which each empire built on the lesson of the past.[4] In this context, the British Empire could be seen as the outcome of history in which, as the successor to Rome, it synthesised and improved upon past examples. For instance, J.A. Cramb (Professor of Modern History, Queen's College, London)[5] in a lecture presented in 1900 as part of a reflection on the significance of the Boer War to the British, argued that

> Rome was the synthesis of the empires of the past, of Hellas, of Egypt, of Assyria. In her purpose their purpose lived . . . In Britain the spirit of Empire receives a new incarnation. The form decays, the *divine* idea remains, the creative spirit gliding from this to that, indestructible. And thus the destiny of empires involves the consideration of the destiny of man.[6]

Britain not only had inherited directly the imperial spirit of Rome, but also had distinctly improved upon it. This linear inheritance of imperial civilisation gave Rome a role of fundamental importance in the development of Europe and Britain.

This emphasis on modern Europe and, in particular, Britain as the heir to Rome is evident in some late Victorian and later literature. J.C. Stobart, in *The Grandeur that was Rome* (1912) stated that:

> The destiny or function of Rome in world-history was nothing more or less than the making of Europe. The modern family of European nations are her sons and daughters . . . For this great purpose it was necessary that the city itself should pass through phases of growth, maturity and decay and some of her daughters have grown up and married foreign husbands and given birth to offsprings.[7]

Roman history therefore had a purpose. Rome was 'the greatest civilising force in all the history of Europe'.[8] It had taught civilisation to much of western Europe, and Britain was considered by many British patriots to be exporting the most enlightened form of this inherited Western civilisation to large parts of the globe. This view of Europe's inheritance from Rome was shared by Francis Haverfield, and in the third edition of his important work, *The Romanization of Roman Britain*, published in 1915, Haverfield argued that:

> Had Rome failed to civilize, had the civilized life found no period in which to grow firm and tenacious, civilization would have perished utterly. The culture of the old world would not have lived on, to form the groundwork of the *best culture* of to-day.[9]

In this context, an historical link was forged between Rome and Britain,[10] projecting Britain as the direct heir to Rome. Britain had a Roman phase of domestic history and in various Edwardian works, Rome's fundamental role in civilising the Britons is recalled in a way that is reminiscent of the earlier comments of Samuel Johnson and others.[11]

According to Fletcher and Kipling in *A School History of England*:

> [A]fter . . . conquest came such peace and good government as Britain had never seen before. The Romans introduced into all their provinces a system of law so fair and so strong . . . Everywhere the weak were protected against the strong; castles were built on the coast . . . fleets patrolled the channel and the North Sea.[12]

Civilisation was introduced; roads, cities and country houses were built. In the minds of some authors, at least, the Romans had passed their civilisation on to Britain so that Britain could in turn pass it on to the people of its Empire.

There was a problem with this linear image of civilisation and progress, however, which related to powerful images of national origin that existed in Victorian society – those of Teutonic racial origin and the image of the Celtic subaltern. The image of the Celtic subaltern indicated that very little of the Roman civilisation had passed to the ancient Britons during the Roman occupation, while the Teutonic image of racial origins suggested that the English were, in any case, descended from the Anglo-Saxons rather than the ancient Britons. What ultimately was the relevance of the ancient Britons and classical Romans to English domestic history?

Linking England and Rome: the image of a mixed island race

A number of authors in the late nineteenth and early twentieth centuries began to develop an image of Englishness that provided an alternative idea of English origins to that of the Teuton. A new representation arose of the English as a mixed island race. This image drew upon a racial inheritance from the range of people who had lived in Britain in the past, including the ancient Britons, Romans, Anglo-Saxons, Danes and Normans. This inheritance could be thought to include two of the images that have already been discussed: the inspiration of the valiant ancient British heroes and the inheritance of the classical imperial torch of Rome.

I shall focus in this part of the book upon the perceived role of Rome in this representation of Englishness. This chapter will consider the period prior to the First World War, while the next chapter examines the 1920s to 1940s.

Struggling toward a theory of Romanisation

In the minds of some authors in late Victorian and Edwardian times, the image of the Celtic subaltern began to crumble as it was conceived that classical Roman civilisation had been passed, at least to a certain extent, on to the British population.[13] Two elements in many of these accounts helped in the development of this interpretation of national origins and both drew upon a similar tradition to the work of Coote (see above). First, was the concept that Rome passed on civilisation to the ancient people of present-day England and, second, that at least some of the descendants of these civilised ancient Britons had survived the Anglo-Saxon invasion to bring this civilisation to the racial mix that formed the modern English nation.

The passing on of classical civilisation to natives within the Roman Empire was defined by the German scholar Theodor Mommsen as 'Romanising'.[14] Haverfield later adopted the term 'Romanization' for the same process.[15] In general, however, the majority of accounts of the 'Romanisation' of society in popular accounts of Roman Britain prior to Haverfield did not provide a clear picture of the way in which this 'civilisation' of the native ancient Briton occurred. As a result I would suggest that the late Victorian and Edwardian works reviewed in this section were 'struggling towards a theory of Romanisation', although few accounts use the term.

J. Rhys, Professor of Celtic at the University of Oxford, in his book *Early Britain: Celtic Britain*, published in 1882 by the Society for Promoting Christian Knowledge, talked about the Roman influence on the native Britons. He noted the spread of Christianity, some knowledge of 'municipal institutions' and also the spread of the Latin tongue. He felt that much of this culture was restricted to the 'Strongholds' of a 'Latinizing party' in York, Lincoln, Colchester and London.[16] The study of inscriptions found in Britain, however, showed that, compared with most other portions of the Empire, Britain had a military character, with little consideration paid to the civil elements.[17]

H.M. Scarth, Prebendary of Wells and Rector of Wrington, Somerset, had a book published in the following year in the same series, *Early Britain: Roman Britain*.[18] Scarth suggested that the Roman 'colonists' intermarried with 'natives' and as a result: 'Roman blood mingled with the population, and Roman blood has flowed ever since in English veins, and we believe ever and anon given proof of its refining influence.'[19] The planting of Roman 'colonies' thus resulted in a great change in the 'habits and manners of the people'.[20] This included the introduction of Christianity, which in later ages was 'revived and rekindled, so as to become permanent'.[21] Despite this Roman influence on the natives of Britain, the natives and the Romans in Scarth's account appear on the whole to have kept a distance from one another and there is certainly no coherent theory of Romanisation in this book.

Other authors explored the topic of the Roman contribution to the civilisation of the English. We have seen in the last chapter that in Henty's account of Beric, the chief attained a high degree of Roman learning through a process of classical education and exposure to Roman order. On his return to Britain as governor of part of the province, Beric established himself at Caistor-by-Norwich and 'set about the erection of a suitable abode',[22] a villa. To some Victorians, at least a few of the imperial officers who lived in villas in the southern British countryside could, therefore, be British in origin. Trevelyan's Boadicea also attains a degree of culture from the Roman example.[23]

Another scholar offered a clear, intellectually acceptable solution to this problem of how the civilisation of the Romans spread to the ancient Britons. Haverfield developed a persuasive interpretation of Romanisation in his *The Romanization of Roman Britain*, first published in 1905 and expanded and republished several times during the 1910s and 1920s. In fact, in Haverfield's view, the British actually became Roman through a process known as 'Romanisation'. In an earlier chapter I discussed some Victorian and Edwardian works (by Windle, Fletcher and Kipling and others) which suggested that the villa-dwellers of Roman Britain were officials from Rome, some of whom developed a loyalty to Britain.[24] In Haverfield's account, however, many of the villa-dwelling élite were argued to have been Romanised native Britons, as suggested by Henty (in his novel about Beric). Haverfield also argued forcefully that the idea of a large body of Roman settlers living in towns, forts and villas amongst a population of largely native Britons was inaccurate and helped to put a nail in the coffin of the image of the Celtic subaltern.[25] It is of interest that, in this argument about Romanisation, Haverfield mirrored the opinion of Henty in his *Beric the Briton*, published over ten years before Haverfield's first work on Romanisation. Even after the publication of Haverfield's important study, however, ill-defined images of Romanisation survived, as the idea of the Celtic subaltern persisted in some sections of society, especially with regard to the north and west of Britain.[26]

Racial survival

A number of the authors whose work has been discussed in the last section also considered that elements of the civilisation of the Romans had been passed through to modern Britain as a result of the survival of some of the population during the Anglo-Saxon invasion. J. Rhys felt it probable that some of the ancient British population had survived the Anglo-Saxon conquest, while H.M. Scarth used the work of Coote[27] to suggest that the 'colonies' of Rome and the culture that it spread to Britain survived the departure of the Romans and the Anglo-Saxon invasion. Scarth argued that: 'There is little doubt that a Romano-British population continued to exist in the island, and that culture, learning and religion were not totally extinct, as is often supposed, after Roman rule had ceased.'[28] Scarth's work suggested a survival of Roman civilisation into the post-Roman period. The existence of Christianity in both Roman Britain and modern Britain, and its supposed survival from one to the other, provided part of the context for Scarth's wish to find evidence for continuity and the same is true of a number of other accounts.[29]

Frederic Seebohm in his *The English Village Community* (1883) referred to the attempts of a range of historians to trace in English constitutional history the development of ancient free Germanic institutions.[30] He also investigated the idea that non-Germanic elements in English economic history may have been more significant than the German inheritance and also referred positively to the work of Coote.[31] He suggests that the 'tribal' system of the pre-Roman 'Celts' in Britain was transformed by Rome but also acted as the historical origin of the medieval manor. The Germanic conquerors probably acted in Britain as they had on the continent and, although they may in some cases have exterminated the old inhabitants, the evidence of the English open-field system is argued to show continuity between the Roman and the English system of land management.[32] The conquered people possibly survived by being made serfs.[33]

A similar attitude to ancient British racial survival is evident in other works. For instance, in the introduction to Henty's *Beric the Briton*, where he writes:

> How far the British population disappeared under the subsequent [Anglo-Saxon] invasion and the still more oppressive yoke of the Danes is uncertain; but as the invaders would naturally desire to retain the people to cultivate the land for them, it is probable that the great mass of the Britons were not exterminated.[34]

As a result:

> It is at any rate pleasant to believe that with the Saxon, Danish and Norman blood in our veins, there is still a large admixture of that of the valiant warriors who fought so bravely against Caesar, and who rose under Boadicea in a desperate effort to shake off the oppressive rule of Rome.[35]

G.E. Green, in his *A Short History of the British Empire for the Use of Junior Forms* (1900), began his account of the British Empire with the Roman Empire and then passed on to later phases of British history. He suggested that Saxons married British women and kept other Britons as slaves and that modern Britain is a 'mixed nation', including British, Teutonic and Norman elements.[36] We have seen in the last chapter that Trevelyan also drew upon the contribution of the ancient Britons to modern British culture.[37]

92

In the Edwardian context, P. Vinogradoff in his seminal *The Growth of the Manor* (1905) argued that a certain mixing of the Germanic and Celtic population probably occurred and that the Celtic 'tribal' system of pre-Roman and Roman Britain probably contributed to the medieval manorial system.[38] T. Rice Holmes in his *Ancient Britain and the Invasion of Julius Caesar* (1907) turned to the issue of the 'Permanence in English history of prehistoric and Celtic elements'. He argued that the descendants of 'neolithic aboriginals', Bronze Age people and the 'Celts' continued to live on, mixing with Saxons and Danes to form the 'British character.'[39] Indeed:

> Everywhere in Britain the pre-Roman stock have, in greater or lesser proportions, survived ... Few Englishmen, Welshmen, or Scotsmen, if their pedigrees could be traced back far enough, would not be found to count among their ancestors men of the type who were buried in long barrows, sturdy warriors of the Bronze Age; and Celts who fought against Caesar or were subdued by Agricola.[40]

Genetic mixing and imperial discourse

These ideas of genetic survival and Roman inheritance had a distinct role in the discourse of imperialism. In his book *The British Empire* (1915), Sir Charles P. Lucas, stated that in the fifth century:

> [A]lthough all vestiges of Roman rule disappeared, the island up to the Highlands of Scotland had been more or less united under one Roman administration. Roman blood must have been intermixed with the native Britons, and it is difficult to suppose that the future England did not derive some strength from the wonderful people who gave us law and roads and government to the greater part of the then known world.[41]

Lucas also suggested that:

> The great point to notice is the many strains which have entered into the English blood. If an amalgam of so many different elements produced such a strong and successful people, it may fairly be argued that the many and great diversities which now exist in the British Empire will, if

wisely handled, be ultimately a source not of weakness but of strength.[42]

The suggestion in the work of Henty, Lucas and others is that the Anglo-Saxon invasion did not lead to the total replacement of ancient Britons and that these Britons form part of the racial mix of current British generations – including also Angles, Saxons, Danes, Normans and others. Lucas' work placed particular emphasis upon the supposed imperial value of the Roman contribution to the racial mix that formed modern England.

Ideas of racial survival and civilisation had a growing role in images of Englishness during the Edwardian period. Together with H.E. Egerton, the first Beit Professor at Oxford University (1905–20), Lucas adopted an almost religious approach to the way in which successive racial virtues of Britons, Romans, Danes, Saxons and Normans had combined in a mix to forge the British Empire.[43] Racial mixing as a source of English racial strength evidently had a distinct role in the ideology of imperial purpose. The idea that the population of England and Britain was genetically mixed served to provide a more open myth of origin, which could act to create a greater sense of unity to the British people. The mixed racial inheritance could play a distinct role in the context of the unity of the populations of the individual parts of the United Kingdom and also of the various white populations of the British Empire. Importantly, the inheritance of the imperial spirit of the classical Romans perhaps gave the English a distinct role in the guidance of the imperial policy of Great Britain.

At the same time as fulfilling a direct role with regard to imperial discourse, it is also probable that the idea of racial strength as a result of genetic mixing derived in part from a need to distance the English from Germanic racial stock. In the late nineteenth and early twentieth centuries Germany was becoming a significant political and military threat to Britain[44] and the English may have been drawn to an origin myth which helped to distance them from the Germans.

Summary

Haverfield's work on Romanisation supplemented ideas which were held by a range of his contemporaries relating to the inheritance of 'civilisation' through the genetic survival of the ancient British in the current English population. If Britons could, in effect, become

Romans through a process of Romanisation and the Anglo-Saxon invasion had permitted a partial genetic survival of the ancient British racial strain, then a direct Roman contribution to modern English character, as envisaged by Coote in the 1860s and 1870s became a distinct possibility. To the popular mind, the English could appear to have a direct Roman origin, with a share of the brave spirit of the ancient Britons. This wish to assume a Roman racial element by the late Victorian and Edwardian ruling élite was amplified by their classical education and interest in the assumed imperial parallel between Britain and Rome. The growing value of the idea of imperialism to the English élite after 1875 made the classical Romans attractive forebears.

We shall see below that the argument set out by Haverfield formed a fundamental part of the theory that has existed for Romano-British archaeology in the twentieth century. His interpretation of Romanisation, nevertheless, can also be seen in another context. The process by which ancient Britons became Roman through Romanisation in the Henty/Haverfield account presumably helped to lessen the impact of the idea of Roman rule over Britain in the minds of members of the late Victorian and Edwardian public. The idea of Romanisation removed the stigma of conquest; through the process of Romanisation, the conquered were empowered to become the conquerors of an even larger part of the world than that which had been dominated by Rome.

I shall now turn to the period after the end of the First World War to show how the idea of Roman genetic inheritance formed part of the evolving representation of 'Englishness' at this time.

8

ENGLISHNESS BETWEEN THE WARS, RACIAL MIXING AND THE ROLE OF ROME

Introduction: 'Englishness'

It has been suggested that the emergence of an image of 'Englishness' had a long history of development, arising out of the strains emerging in English politics in the 1880s and resulting partly from a general crisis in urban society.[1] A cultural response beginning in the 1890s and 1900s spread widely across English art, letters, music and architecture by 1914. A wide range of popular history books, novels and travel books were published between the wars with 'England' in their titles with many drawing upon this set of often backward-looking images in a variety of ways;[2] these works have been studied by a range of modern authors.[3] We should remember that the construction of a monolithic national discourse is never complete. The discourse of Englishness was continually disrupted by supplementary, alternative or directly competing images.[4] I shall not study the complexity within the representation of Englishness at this time but will turn to some of the ideas of national origin that exist within works of this date.

Samuel has discussed the way that the prevalent 'gung-ho' attitude of some of the British to imperialism did not survive the War, as a more introverted note to nationalism was introduced with a focus on the domestic history of England.[5] Several authors have studied the nature of these images of English domestic history.[6] Daniels has suggested that the rather less heroic pose adopted by many spokesmen for England at this time related to the idea that the English were not actually a super-race but a domestic people – 'kindly, tolerant and slightly at odds with the world'.[7] In this context the global reach of European imperialism was accompanied by a countervailing sentiment for cosy rural scenery.[8]

Originating before the First World War, but reaching its peak in the inter-war years, there was also a movement towards outdoor pursuits as the countryside became an accessible source of leisure.[9] Part of this development of an image of Englishness was the idea of a united country focused around an idyllic southern English rural countryside.[10] It has been suggested that this was a cohesive, empowering and inherently conservative story to be told in the face of domestic and imperial insecurity,[11] and is also to be seen as a response to the great loss of life during the First World War. It is important that the image of Englishness also focused attention upon national origins.

Englishness and the Roman inheritance

I shall turn to the writings of some influential authors who addressed the role of Rome and ancient Britons in the origins of Englishness. A range of authors explored images of national origin during the period after the end of the First World War. The focus that was placed upon English origins drew upon some of the ideas developed in late nineteenth- and early twentieth-century texts that were considered above. Rome and the ancient Britons were recruited as part of this discourse, often in the guise of English ancestor figures – individual people and whole races who were perceived as having added strengths to the national character.

How was Britain related to Rome? How had the burden or torch of civilisation been passed between two empires so far apart in time? A strongly linear idea of English national origins continued to develop after the end of the First World War, perhaps in part as a result of the horror of the massive loss of life which it had caused.

The archaeologist and philosopher Robin G. Collingwood's book *Roman Britain* was first published in 1923. With regard to the post-Roman history of Britain, Collingwood followed the suggestions of Rice-Holmes in arguing that the 'great mass of the Britons' must have survived the Anglo-Saxon invasion, when the towns and villas were destroyed.[12] The British race in this context is, according to Collingwood, compounded of not just Saxon, Norman and Danish blood, but also that of the ancient Britons. Collingwood continued by speculating:

> Can we go further and claim for ourselves a real kinship with
> Romanized Britons, as the modern French rightly claim

continuity with the Romanized Gauls? It may seem fantastic, but I cannot resist the impression that the qualities . . . in Romano-British art are qualities especially English, qualities re-expressed in all the great English artists and valued by English people more than others . . .The civilization vanished, but the race remained, and its character, I venture to think, has reassessed itself – mental and physical character alike.[13]

Another work by Collingwood helps to put these suggestions about art into context. In 1925 he wrote a short pamphlet for visitors to the Roman signal station at Scarborough (Yorkshire; Figure 8.1). In this publication he addressed the mixed Teutonic and Roman racial origins of the English. He remarked that the signal station was one of a series erected to aid the defences of Britain against the Saxons. He continued:

[T]o-day we trace our descent to these barbarians and are apt to forget what we owe to Rome. Yet without the civilization which grew up behind these defences, we would not be civilized to-day. Everything that is best in England is the result of a fusion between those Romans and the Saxons.[14]

According to Collingwood:

[T]o this day the English character blends the law-abiding Roman's love of sound government with the self reliance of the seafaring Saxons, and is unintelligible and unimaginable except by people who realise this fact. So close do the lessons of ancient history stand to the problems of modern life.[15]

This suggests that Collingwood felt the Roman racial inheritance to be fundamental to the mixed race that formed the modern English.

Archaeological evidence suggests that Roman civilisation was lost during the Anglo-Saxon invasion; how then did the legacy of this Roman civilisation find its way to the modern English? In his autobiography Collingwood suggested that the passing down of tradition may often have occurred through 'folk memory';[16] it is possible that he felt this to be the context within which the inspiration behind

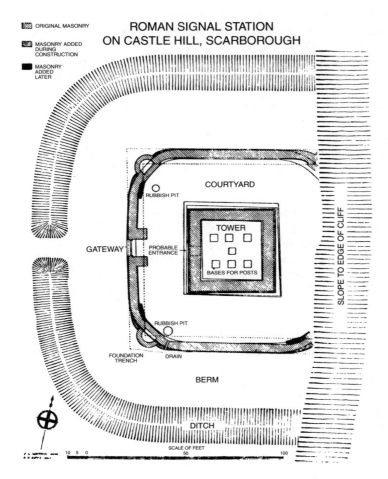

ORIGINAL MASONRY

MASONRY ADDED DURING CONSTRUCTION

MASONRY ADDED LATER

ROMAN SIGNAL STATION
ON CASTLE HILL, SCARBOROUGH

COURTYARD

RUBBISH PIT

TOWER

GATEWAY

PROBABLE ENTRANCE

BASES FOR POSTS

SLOPE TO EDGE OF CLIFF

RUBBISH PIT

FOUNDATION TRENCH   DRAIN

BERM

DITCH

SCALE OF FEET
10 5 0   50   100

Figure 8.1 The Roman signal station at Scarborough. A symbol of the fusion of the Roman and Saxon races which, according to Collingwood, created the modern English nation. *Source*: Collingwood (1932).

Romano-British art had been passed through to the modern English. It is interesting that in his observation on art and signal stations Collingwood stressed the domestic history of *England* rather than that of Britain. Through this device he created a linear conception of English history through the medium of the style of Romano-British and modern English art and civilisation.

Collingwood was in good company in pushing this idea of a mixed racial inheritance for the English.[17] I shall consider the work of five other authors (Windle, Baldwin, Weigall, Hughes and Grose-Hodge) who drew upon a similar basic set of ideas about genetic continuity and racial mixing during the 1920s, 1930s and 1940s. B.C.A. Windle, an English educationalist, published a series of lectures on the Romans in Britain, which had been presented to an audience of the general public at the University of Toronto in Canada. These lectures were published as a book; a text which Collingwood and Myres described as an 'untrustworthy' account of Roman Britain.[18] In this book Windle proposed that:

> The hoards of pagans from across the North Sea who poured into Roman Britain after the departure of the legions . . . neither expelled nor in most parts of the country submerged the 'Keltic crumb', which persisted and, thought in different proportions in different parts of the country, formed the basis of the race which nowadays is commonly called 'Anglo-Saxon' – a term never likely to be abandoned, but very misleading in its ethnological bearings.[19]

Stanley Baldwin, Arthur Weigall and Mary Hughes also drew upon the supposed Roman contribution to the English racial character.

Stanley Baldwin[20] presented two addresses in the mid-1920s which helped to identify the significance of the Roman Empire to the English ruling classes at that time. These addresses were 'On England and the West', presented to the Royal Society of St George at the Hotel Cecil in 1924 and a presidential address to the Classical Association in 1926.[21]

'On England and the West' was presented on 6 May 1924. It is a celebration of Englishness in which Baldwin defined what it is to be English by drawing upon a variety of images, including classical Rome. With reference to Rome, he argued in the final conclusion that:

> It may well be that these traits on which we pride ourselves, which we hope to show and try to show in our own lives, may survive – survive among our people so long as they are a people – and I hope and believe this, that just as to-day more than fifteen centuries since those last of the great Roman legionaries left England, we still speak of the Roman strength, and of the Roman work, and the Roman character, so perhaps in the ten thousandth century, long after the

> Empires of this world as we know them have fallen and
> others have risen and fallen, and risen and fallen again, the
> men who are of this earth may yet speak of those character-
> istics which we prize as the characteristics of the English
> ... [that] ... men in the world of that day may say, 'we
> still have amongst us the gift of that great English race.'[22]

These comments do not indicate a necessary racial connection
between the English and the Romans but do suggest an inheritance
of the 'burden of Empire' – the English were descendants of the
Romans through the inheritance of the imperial ideal. Baldwin was
drawing here on cyclical aspects of the ideas of inherited imperial
mission raised by a number of Victorian and Edwardian writers. He
was also drawing upon another popular Edwardian image – the
probability of the future decline of the English nation.[23]

Baldwin's address of 1926 was presented sixteen years after Lord
Cromer's presidency of the same Association (for Cromer's address
see pp. 34–5). Baldwin was one of the original members of the
Classical Association, which had been founded in 1903. He
presented his Presidential Address on the evening of 8 January 1926
to an audience that overflowed the Elizabethan hall of the Middle
Temple.[24] Baldwin's appointment as President of the Classical
Association in 1926 demonstrates the continued relevance of the
classics to imperial and national policy after the end of the
Edwardian period.[25] In this address Baldwin described the particular help and inspiration that he had derived from the classics in
his life, and particularly in his political career.[26] The address was
intended to explore the value of the classics from the perspective of
the 'common folk' by presenting the view of the 'ordinary man'
exemplified by the British Prime Minister![27]

Baldwin in 1926 considered the nature of the imperial procession
in a way that is reminiscent of the views of several of the late
Victorian and Edwardian authors whose work has been discussed in
the last chapter. He liked to:

> picture the procession of the nations through the ages as a
> great relay race of heroes ... Rome ran her mighty race
> bearing her torch on high. Of those who came before, of
> those who followed after, none ran so far, none so surely.
> And when her course was run the torch came into other
> hands who bore it forward according to the strength and
> guidance that was in them, until after many centuries it

was passed to us, the youngest son. Our race is not yet run. But we shall run more worthily so long as we base our lives on the stern virtues of the Roman character and take to ourselves the warnings that Rome left for our guidance.[28]

In Baldwin's view, Britain was one of a fellowship of European nations, but one that had inherited a particular role as the torch-bearers of imperial civilisation.

Baldwin also studied the topic of the relationship between the English and the Romans more fully. He began with the value of the classics to the present by emphasising that Britain was part of the Roman Empire 'for a period as long as from the Reformation until this present night'.[29] This geographical connection between Britain and Rome was evidently important to him, as it was to a number of earlier writers. Baldwin argued that to be ignorant of the history of the Roman Empire is to be without the sense of perspective in viewing the changes of events that are essential to national life. For Baldwin, this Roman occupation of western Europe, including Britain, appeared to have caused major changes in the nature of the ancient Britons which resulted in England's imperial present. He continued that: 'It was not for nothing that Western Europe was forged on the anvil of Rome, and who can say how much we owe to those long years of Roman law, Roman discipline, Roman faith, and partnership in a common Empire.'[30] Baldwin, in defining the similarity between the English and the Roman characters, identified the strength of the later and its value to the English as lying in the concepts of *pietas* and *gravitas*:

> These were the foundations of a patriotism which alone could carry the burden of Empire, a patriotism innate, a motive force of incalculable power, yet something at its best so holy that it was never paraded, sought no rewards, was taken for granted, and had no single word to express it.[31]

These concepts were introduced to the English gentleman through classical education, but Baldwin chose a more direct genetic link between the Romans and the English. Baldwin felt that this Roman influence during the period of imperial control of Britain had helped to form the character of the English. He argued that:

> During the first four centuries of the present era Roman thoughts and Roman manners imposed themselves upon

our island and made themselves a home here . . . It may well be that subconscious memories of those days and the mingling of blood for four centuries played their part no less than the arrival of the Normans in modifying certain characteristics of our Teutonic invaders and saved us from becoming what Carlyle called 'A gluttonous race of Jutes and Angles, capable of no grand combinations, lumbering about in pot-bellied equanimity; not dreaming of heroic toil, and silence and endurance, such as leads to the higher places of this universe and the golden mountain-tops where dwells the Spirit of the Dawn.'[32]

It is clear that Baldwin was drawing upon many of the same images that had been explored by his Edwardian predecessors. It is likely that Baldwin's claims for the Roman ancestry of the English were derived from ideas outlined by Sir Charles Lucas but developed further into the definition of the English character.

The idea of the Roman ancestry of the English appears to have become a topic of some importance in the 1920s. Arthur Weigall, author of *Wanderings in Roman Britain* (1926) also held views on this topic. He had attended Brasenose College, Oxford, where he was a contemporary of several of the Oxford men whose work was discussed earlier in the book.[33] He became one of a number of Oxford men who taught abroad and had been headmaster of Sydney Grammar School. The individual chapters of the book had first been featured in the *Daily Mail* newspaper and it was a considerable success, passing through at least four impressions in its first year of publication. He expressed a wish to show the close connection between the British of 'the present day' and the Romans.[34] The Romans brought civilisation to the British, but 'the blood of the Romans' had only passed through 45 persons 'in reaching our veins'.[35]

He accepted that after the fall of Rome the arrival of the Anglo-Saxons and Normans added to the mix; however,

The blood of the heterogeneous Romans is in our veins; and, remembering this, let us look with new eyes at the astonishing mass of remains these ancestors of ours have left behind them in this country to tell us of the days when we were proud to call ourselves Romans.[36]

With regard to the Roman invasion:

[I]t is the beginning of the history of our connection with the Eternal City, which ultimately introduced into our blood something of 'the grandeur that was Rome' which has helped to send us forth adventuring and conquering over the whole face of the earth.[37]

This suggestion of a direct genetic connection between the ancient Britons and the current population of England reflects the earlier comments of Henty, Lucas and others that were reviewed in previous chapters.

In this context, Roman monuments came to serve a directly patriotic purpose. Weigall makes one particularly explicit statement about the patriotic worth of Roman monuments stating that our ancient ruins have real purpose:

always before my eyes, as I went from ruin to ruin of Britain's past, there has shone like a fiery sunrise the glory of England to-day and the splendour of the future of the British Empire, if only we can keep inviolate the traditions and ideals of our race.[38]

Weigall aimed above all to propagate among 'our people' a 'sense of the patriotic usefulness of our ancient records which can only be engendered by the realisation of their deep significance to us, and their bearing upon our national character and its interpretation'.[39] By visiting archaeological monuments people would be able to build up a sense of their genetic origins. The Ordnance Survey had published the map *Roman Britain* in 1924 (two years before Weigall's book was published) and the *Daily Mail* had described the publication of the map as 'opening up a new era in motor touring'.[40] The appeal of Weigall's vision to at least a section of the English public is indicated by the success of his book in terms of its sales figures.

The German menace

I have already suggested that a range of motivations may have lain behind attempts by some Edwardians to claim a more mixed genetic make-up for the British than the pure Anglo-Saxon root favoured by many Victorians. This concept of mixed racial origins may be seen in the context of a desire to find an ideology of mixed race that would act to unite the supposed disparate white races of

England, Great Britain and the Empire. It may also, however, reflect a concern over the continuing political threat posed by Germany and the wish to create a clear racial distinction between the English and the Germans. Weigall, in his 1926 book, covered this point comprehensively when he argued that 'we' are the progeny of marriages between Anglo-Saxons and Britons. In addition, the Britons had a good deal of 'heterogeneous Roman blood in their veins';[41] so that the British are a mix of Romans, ancient Britons, Anglo-Saxons, Danes and Normans. Weigall even goes so far as to suggest that the modern Cockney 'is as much Roman as he is anything else'.[42]

The *'wild blood'* of the Anglo-Saxons had, therefore, been diluted and 'The modern Englishman differs from his ancient English ancestor and from his Teutonic kinsman by this happy circumstance that in his veins, amongst many different strains, there also runs the glorious blood of Briton and Roman.'[43] Weigall thereby sets up an interesting polarity between the Teutonic 'wild blood' and the 'glorious blood' of the ancient Britons and Romans which turns some of the Victorian views of Teutonic origin on their heads. It is certainly difficult to avoid reading the contemporary political context into Weigall's thoughts about Teutonic society.

In the wryly humorous but patriotic *About England*, published in 1927, Mary V. Hughes also considered the mixed genetic heritage of the English. The trait of 'masterly inactivity' in the English character has, apparently, been 'absorbed' from the Romans and has been fundamental in enabling the English to build up their Empire.[44] In a chapter titled 'Some of our Conquerors', Hughes considered the 'curious' fact that a 'race' of 'world-wide conquerors' such as the English should have itself been conquered so often in the (distant) past.[45] Like earlier popular authors discussed above,[46] Hughes, in writing for a popular audience, appears to have found the idea of these earlier invaders problematical.

Hughes recorded that the Romans conquered Britain:

> Then the Germans conquered us. Oh, yes. After the Romans had retired according to plan, the various German tribes who visited our shores made themselves so completely at home, that those of us who had not fled to the west accepted their name and language.[47]

Hughes clearly takes the side of the Britons in the context of the Anglo-Saxon conquest and their adoption of Germanic customs;

presumably memories of the Great War may be relevant in this context. Hughes considers the way that the 'Germans' were later followed by 'men of France' (the Normans), who also invaded Britain.

The 'Germans' and 'French' had a mission, however, as is evident from Hughes' use of the term 'plan'. The Germanic peoples introduced 'rather rough manners' but also 'that sturdy self-sufficiency . . . that [has]. . . served us so well.'[48] The Romans, Germans and the French all added to the genetic complexity of the English, which helped them achieve their imperial destiny. The curious fact of invasion therefore helped to create the racial strength of England that had resulted in the creation of the Empire.

The comments of Windle, Baldwin, Hughes and others developed a range of views that were previously expressed by the Edwardian authors. The emphasis on the inclusion of the Romans in a generalised view of the English character nevertheless provided a new emphasis as part of a discourse of Englishness, as the claim for Roman racial inheritance appears to become increasingly extreme. These concepts of Englishness continued to develop well into the twentieth century, although the number of relevant publications appears to have declined over time.

For instance, Humfrey Grose-Hodge, headmaster of Bedford School and formerly a member of the Indian Civil Service, published his book *Roman Panorama: A Background for Today*, in 1944, just before the end of the Second World War. The book was written as a plea for the continuation of classical learning in British education. It also reflected the supposed political value of the classics to the English.[49] Grose-Hodge suggested that although the Roman people had been dead for a long period, fascist Italy did not feel this to be the case. The character of the Roman people, however, had lived on as the 'direct ancestor' of the English,[50] while:

> The Romans were the first people to discover 'how to rule free men', and their domination lasted in one form or another for nearly 1700 years . . . The British Empire, in growth and development so strangely paralleled by the Roman, has carried these principles a step further.[51]

He felt that 'in actions we are Romans'.[52]

Grose-Hodges' claims of Roman ancestry repeat earlier views, but can also be seen in the context of the development of Roman imperial imagery by Mussolini. Benito Mussolini drew directly upon classical Rome in developing his own imperial ambitions and these ambitions were often couched in terms of opposition to Anglo-Saxon imperialism.[53] Grose-Hodge was perhaps seeking to counter Mussolini's efforts by claiming the classical culture of Rome for England. Roman civilisation might still appear attractive to some, but Roman imperialism was less to be admired. In the light of these Italian developments many were reminded of the despotic nature of Roman rule, a topic which had ceased to exercise the British mind as a significant factor during late Victorian times when there was an increased emphasis on the significance of the civilising mission of Rome. During the mid-1930s and 1940s Rome came once more to be seen in the guise of foreign despotism – a threat to national security – rather than in the image of the great civiliser and a provider of imperial morals.[54]

Englishness: a summary

Although the Teutonic myth of English origins did not suddenly cease in the Edwardian period, the image of an English racial inheritance derived from the Romans appears to have become increasingly popular from the 1890s to the 1920s. I have suggested that it became politically useful for the imperial élite to draw upon both the idea of the inheritance of the bravery of the ancient Britons and the civilising of the native Britons by imperial Rome at this time.[55] To carry the inheritance of the ancient Britons and the Romans of Briton into the modern world required at least a partial survival of the Romano-British population during the Anglo-Saxon conquest, hence the decline of the Teutonic myth.

The idea of racial mixing had also become the acceptable archaeological interpretation for the history of Britain during the twentieth century, drawing upon the ideas of Rice-Holmes.[56] The idea of a mixed racial inheritance for the English had a part to play, however, in imperial discourse.

A.L.F. Rivet talked in 1959 of a myth that had developed in the British context as a result of Haverfield's work. Through his work on Romanisation, Haverfield, had changed the prevailing idea of Britain as a province inhabited by 'rich Romans' (usually generals) on the one hand and seething masses of savage blue-painted Britons on the other. This he achieved by pointing out that Briton and Roman were not mutually exclusive concepts. This, according to Rivet, had resulted, through no fault of Haverfield's, in a new myth of Britain as 'a province so thoroughly British that no foreign landowner would dare to show his face in it'.[57] Rivet did not mention which individual pieces of work he is thinking of in this context, but his comments on Kipling's use of the analogy of British India for his interpretation of Roman Britain[58] may provide part of the context for his comments. Kipling's contribution to ideas of the identity of the English has been discussed in Part I of this book; some of the works by other authors which have been reviewed in this chapter may also have been in Rivet's mind when he made his comments.

Many of the texts considered in the last two chapters posit a linear and teleological view of English domestic history. Some accounts appear to suggest that the Romans passed a distinct Romano-British civilisation onto the English which led directly to the modern state of Britain. In this way the English spirit is traced back to the Roman past in such a way that the natives can be seen to have adopted Roman civilisation and improved upon it in an active effort to create modern England. Incorporated in this distinctly English racial mix was the brave spirit of the ancient Britons who had opposed Rome. As Rivet stressed, some popular pictures of Roman Britain gave a nationalist view of a civilised British province – an inherently exclusionist concept. Concerns about lines of continuity in the national life of England structured academic and popular works, and Roman archaeology had a distinct value. Archaeological theories, and the materials collected through archaeological practice, helped to substantiate images of Englishness. I shall argue below that the twentieth-century focus in Romano-British archaeology upon Romanisation has derived part of its motivation from a wish to identify national origins.

Part III

ROMANISATION

In Part II I examined a range of popular and political works which focused upon English identity and race. Part III focuses upon the development of the theory of Romanisation in Britain from 1905 until the 1990s. This theory developed alongside popular images of Englishness – sometimes contradicting them and sometimes providing academic support. In the next chapter Francis Haverfield's initial definition of the theory is explored, while the following chapter studies the way in which Romanisation developed after Haverfield.

9

FRANCIS HAVERFIELD AND ROMANISATION

Introduction

I have already considered Haverfield's contribution to Roman frontier studies and his addresses on the significance of the Roman Empire to British imperial problems. In this chapter I shall consider the contribution of Haverfield to the development of the theory of 'Romanization'. This theory was created to account for the transformation of native society within Roman Britain and the Western Empire into a Roman form. It helped to discredit the image of the Celtic subaltern, at least so far as the south of the country was concerned. Haverfield's interpretation of Romanisation has been fundamental to the development of theory in Romano-British archaeology in the twentieth century.

Romanisation theory: initial definitions

'Romanisation' is not a concept that was used by Roman authors to describe the effect of their control and influence; rather, it was invented in modern times and has been used in various ways by a wide range of authors.[1] Archaeologists during the twentieth century have used various forms of the term – Romanisation, Romanization, romanisation and romanization.[2] The use of the 's' and 'z' are spelling differences while the use of the initial capital or lower case reflects differing attitudes to the value of the concept. The use of the lower case 'r' perhaps sometimes focuses upon a more critical evaluation of the significance of the term than the use of the upper case letter. The variant *Romanisation* will be used in this work to refer to the use of the concept in past works; where quoting from works which use an alternative spelling, the given variant will be used.

There have been recent calls for the abandonment of the use of the term 'Romanisation' due to the intellectual baggage that accompanies it.[3] Jane Webster, however, has suggested that from the perspective of colonial discourse theory, the cultural imperialism that the theory is founded upon helps to inform us about the discourses that have shaped Roman studies. The abandonment of the term would leave dominant discourses even less open to reflexive critique[4] in the form of almost a denial of the past. Romanisation, therefore, might be allowed to stand as a term as long as we are aware of the cultural baggage that it incorporates. I accept this view, although I have doubts about the value of the term in the context of an understanding of social change in the Roman Empire.[5]

I therefore intend to restrict my usage of the term Romanisation to the context of the type of reflexive consideration of dominant discourses that Jane Webster supports. I wish to subject Haverfield's account to critique in order to expose its cultural baggage. I shall argue below that the fundamental influence of Haverfield's account during the twentieth century requires such a critique as part of the attempt to build a more coherent approach to social change in the Roman Empire. In creating this historical critique of the development of the concept, my intention is to enable progress beyond the limitations inherent in these past accounts of Romanisation. The aim should be to develop accounts that provide alternative perspectives of social change in the Roman Empire and move beyond the limitations of the perspectives that have been characterised by past approaches. I feel that, in the context of the development of these alternative perspectives, the concept of 'Romanisation', or even that of 'romanisation', should have no place. Romanisation will therefore be used to refer to the approaches that have been adopted by past generations of archaeologists to social changes while care should perhaps be taken in future when using the term to interpret social change in the Roman Empire.

The theory outlined by Haverfield's approach to Romanisation was teleological in nature, in that it assumed a simplistic and directional transition from native to Roman that reflected views of social evolution from a state of primitiveness to civilisation. It also contained the same assumed connection between Roman civilisation and modern society – the Romans as 'us' – as featured in much of the work that I have already reviewed in this book. The civilising of the natives by a process of Romanisation enabled a direct connection to be drawn between Romanised natives and 'us' and thus helped to create the domestic link between English national identity and classical Rome.[6] In this way, Haverfield's theory of Romanisation shared an interest in English domestic history with the other late Victorian and Edwardian accounts of Rome and Britain which have been discussed in the chapters on Englishness. A similar interest is also evident in other later works on Romanisation which are considered in the next chapter.

Mommsen and Romanising

Haverfield's European contacts included the German scholar Theodor Mommsen. The fifth volume of Mommsen's important work *Römische Geschichte* was a history of the Roman Empire which was published in 1885 and translated into English in 1886 as *The Provinces of the Roman Empire*.[7] It has been suggested that because of Mommsen's approach, Roman studies grew in a way that tended to place emphasis on the homogeneity of the Roman Empire and the centralisation of power.[8] Any local variation in the nature of classical society in Italy and across the Empire tended to be played down in the stress on homogeneity.

In *The Provinces of the Roman Empire* Mommsen discusses: 'The carrying out of the Latin-Greek civilising process in the form of perfecting the constitution of the urban community, and the gradual bringing of the barbarian or at any rate alien elements into this circle'[9] These were actions that took centuries of steady activity and, in a passage which Haverfield was later to draw upon many times, Mommsen suggested that:

> it constitutes the very grandeur of these centuries that the work once planned and initiated found this very long period of time, and the prevalence of peace . . . to facilitate its progress . . . the Roman Empire . . . fostered the peace and prosperity of the many nations united under its sway longer and more completely than any other leading power has ever succeeded in doing.[10]

This statement is a useful initial definition of the theory of Romanisation, although Mommsen did not use the term. He actually used another term — 'Romanising' — to discuss this concept, by which the conquered provinces of the western Empire became more 'Roman'.[11] For instance, 'Roman Britain sustained a relation to *Romanising* similar to that of northern and central Gaul.'[12] Haverfield reviewed Mommsen's contribution in a new introduction that was written for a republished version of Mommsen's book in 1909. He argued that Mommsen's influence had been 'immense'.[13] Haverfield owed much of the theory of Romanisation that he produced at the end of the nineteenth and the beginning of the twentieth century to the theory of Romanising which Mommsen outlined in *The Provinces of the Roman Empire.*

Mommsen contributed to a general reassessment of the value of the concept of imperialism in a British context during late Victorian and Edwardian times – a trend which has been considered in detail above.[14] In addition, Mommsen's stress on the homogeneity of the Roman Empire had an impact on Haverfield's account.

Haverfield's *The Romanization of Roman Britain*

Significantly, in the context of the Romanisation of the northern Empire, the long peace made possible by Roman foreign policy and military organisation created a lasting heritage. The lands protected by the legions were given Roman civilisation and as a result, in the terms used in Haverfield's 1911 address, the natives were 'assimilated' and 'denationalised'.[15] Haverfield studied this process through the development of the theory of 'Romanization'.

Haverfield's theory of Romanisation was built upon the work of Mommsen[16] and developed in a series of publications.[17] The most important was Haverfield's *The Romanization of Roman Britain*, which was first presented as a lecture and was published in the *Proceedings of the British Academy* for 1905; it was also published separately as a short book. The article was later expanded and published as a slightly larger book of 70 pages in 1912 and republished again (with 91 pages) in 1915 and several times thereafter. Through its various editions the work maintained a coherence of argument and grew to be, perhaps, the most influential book on the archaeology of Roman Britain published in the twentieth century. It has also had considerable influence in other areas of Europe.[18]

Haverfield's *The Romanization of Roman Britain* is an exploration of how the civilising mission within the Roman Empire progressed through the process of Romanisation. I shall consider the text of Haverfield's 1905 article, but I will supplement this discussion by reference to the expanded version of the arguments that he produced in 1912 and 1915. I will also draw attention to other works of Haverfield's where they appear to help to explain some of the points that are made in *The Romanization of Roman Britain*.

Despotism and assimilation

Haverfield's text initially drew attention to a negative consideration – the despotic nature of the Roman political system.[19] Haverfield evidently felt that this despotism did not form a valid parallel, or useful model, for the British political system, and in this he expresses a view that was common at this time. A number of the authors who drew a parallel between the Roman and the British imperial systems were highly critical of the autocratic, or despotic, rule of the Roman Emperors; the British political system was felt to be highly superior in this regard.[20] Despite the nature of their political organisation, however, Haverfield agreed with Mommsen and some of his own Edwardian English contemporaries that the Romans were a good thing for the people whom they conquered or subsumed. He wrote that:

> [W]e have come to understand, as not even Gibbon understood it, through the researches of Mommsen . . . the true achievement of the Empire. The old theory of an age of despotism and decay has been overthrown, and the believer in human nature can now feel confident that, whatever their limitations, the men of the Empire wrought for the betterment and the happiness of the world.[21]

It is possible to study Haverfield's interpretation of the Roman's methods of 'denationalisation' by considering the text of *The Romanization of Roman Britain*, where Haverfield outlined the concept of 'Romanization' to explain the gradual transformation of native Britain into a Roman province. Haverfield's study of this topic coincides with the attitudes expressed by a number of contemporary administrators and politicians which were explored earlier – as an imperial power Rome was felt to have been particularly efficient at incorporating and denationalising natives; rather more efficient than the British. Haverfield, through his work on Romanisation, therefore explored in detail a topic that was considered of importance in the British imperial context by a range of politicians, administrators and popular writers.[22]

Cultural coherence, race and assimilation

The Roman Empire became, according to Haverfield, fully Romanised; it 'gained . . . a unity of sentiment and culture which served some of the purposes of national feeling'.[23] In the west of the Empire, Rome conquered 'races' which were not yet 'civilized' but were apparently 'racially capable' of accepting Roman culture:[24]

> Celt, Iberian, German, Illyrian, were marked off from Italian by no broad distinction of race and colour, such as marked off [ancient] Egyptian from Italian, or that which now divides Englishman from Indian or Frenchman from the Algerian Arab. They were marked off, further, by no ancient culture, such as that which had existed for centuries round the Aegean. It was possible, it was easy, to Romanize these western peoples.[25]

In another article, Haverfield considered this point further and argued that in the east Rome came across a coherent Greek civilisation with a long history. Rome did not change these societies, bringing them a measure of good government, but not 'progress'.[26] Here Rome met 'that most serious of obstacles to assimilation, races whose thoughts and affections and traditions and civilisation had crystallised into definitive form'.[27] He continued his text by describing the ways in which this crystallisation might derive from 'political religion', 'national sentiment', or 'memories of the past', and subsequently commented upon attempts by Britain to assimilate people in India and elsewhere.[28]

To Haverfield, as we have seen in Chapter 4, 'coherence' appears to have represented a far greater bar to assimilation in both modern and ancient imperial situations than colour, but racial factors were also of importance.[29] In defining Romanisation, Haverfield argued that race was not a major issue in the Roman Empire: 'races like the negroes were rare in the Roman Empire; they were, therefore, neither dangerous nor obtrusive, and this motive for a colour-sense was absent'.[30] Therefore, no major physical distinction divided the Romans from the pre-Roman inhabitants of Britain. Ancient Italians and Britons were felt to have been genetically similar. In Haverfield's work the Roman Empire is not always viewed as fully unified by a pro-Roman sentiment because of the attitude of the Greek East. In the context of Roman Britain, however, this unity of sentiment did exist and was a result of Roman influence and the absence of pre-Roman crystallisation of society. In making these comments Haverfield appears to have been in broad agreement with Curzon, Cromer and others whose work has been discussed above.[31]

The progress of Romanisation

How did Roman civilisation spread? Haverfield wrote: 'In material culture the Romanization advanced . . . quickly. One uniform fashion spread from Italy throughout central and western Europe, driving out native art and substituting a conventionalized copy of Graeco-Roman or Italian art.'[32] Romanisation was seen by Haverfield in this work as progressive, swift and uniform in the way it affected the landlords and upper classes,[33] involving language, art, religion, urbanisation and the construction of villas. It is suggested that in the towns and amongst the 'upper classes' Romanisation was 'substantially complete'.

The context for this view of Roman control as creating a uniform Roman culture lies in the observation that Haverfield was working in what Freeman has defined as a limited, unitary concept of the Roman Empire. This was a concept which was conditioned by the climate of his times, the historiographical tradition out of which Roman archaeology had developed, and the limited quality and quantity of data available.[34] As Freeman has stated, part of Haverfield's motivation was to stress the cultural homogeneity of the Empire and the common items that occurred across it – such as towns, villas and art – were emphasised and standardised, while elements of local identity were not noticed or were played down.[35] Haverfield's approach was also imbued with the same assumptions about the division between civilisation and barbarism and the inevitability of progress which have been considered above.

Haverfield was not, however, always totally consistent in the various works that he published on this topic. This may suggest that there was some contradiction in his own mind over the evenness of the spread of Roman culture and practices in Britain and over the Western Empire as a whole. In a contribution to the *Victoria History of Somerset* (1906) he suggested that in Britain Romanisation was perhaps comparatively late in date and imperfect in extent. It was Romanisation 'on a low scale'; this was because the more elaborate and wealthy features of Roman civilisation, whether material, intellectual or administrative, were rare or unknown.[36] In general, however, Romanisation spread to all, or most: 'in the end the Britons generally adopted the Roman speech and civilization, and in our island . . . the difference between "Roman" and "provincial" practically vanished'.[37]

In the 1915 version of *The Romanization of Roman Britain* we learn that 'Romanisations' methods of development and its fruits varied with local conditions, with racial and geographical conditions'[38] and other works by Haverfield demonstrate this point. For instance, Haverfield's analysis of the *civitas* capital at Silchester (*Calleva Atrebatum*, Hampshire) illustrates that he was aware that Romanisation, even in the case of the tribal élite, produced a subtle mix of Roman and native, rather than a full transformation of Britain into a image of a Roman-period Mediterranean society (Figure 9.1).

Figure 9.1 The Romano-British town at Silchester. The form and organisation of the town demonstrated to Haverfield that Romanisation could produce a subtle mix of Roman and native, rather than a full transformation of Britain into a image of a Roman-period Mediterranean society. *Source*: J. Thomson (1924).

Romanisation, as expressed in urban plan was not totally consistent across the Empire or the individual province. The Romano-British town of Silchester is, in Haverfield's analysis, a complex amalgam of Celtic and Roman rather than a purely Roman phenomenon. Haverfield felt that this amalgamated nature of Silchester might contain a message for town planning in his own time. He wrote:

> When his town had been 'haussmannized' and fitted with Roman streets, and equipped with Roman Forum and Basilica, and the rest, he [the native town-dweller] yet continued to live – perhaps more happily than the true townsman – in his irregularly grouped houses and cottages amid an expanse of gardens.[39]

In several places Haverfield considered the position of the less wealthy. For instance: 'The rustic poor of a county seldom affect the trend of its history'.[40] Nevertheless, according to his book, he felt that even the poor appeared to have adopted the trappings of Roman culture. The evidence, while not extensive, was taken to indicate that the 'peasantry' were less thoroughly Romanised, although 'covered by a superimposed layer of Roman civilization'.[41] While native settlements in north Wales and on Cranborne Chase may remain primarily non-Roman in appearance, these people swiftly adopted Roman pottery and other items of personal decoration.[42] Haverfield suggests that the villagers at Woodcuts in Dorset (Figure 9.2): 'may well have counted among the less Romanized of the southern Britons. Yet round them too hung the heavy inevitable atmosphere of the Roman material civilization'.[43] According to Haverfield, therefore the poor were involved in much the same process of Romanisation as the wealthy, presumably limited only by their lack of disposable income.

The spiritual character of Roman material culture

In a particularly significant statement in the 1915 edition of *The Romanization of Roman Britain* Haverfield stated that:

> Some scholars . . . write as if the external environment of daily life, the furniture and decorations and architecture of our houses, the buckles and brooches of our dress, bear no relation to our personal feelings, our political hatreds, our national consciousness. That may be true to-day of

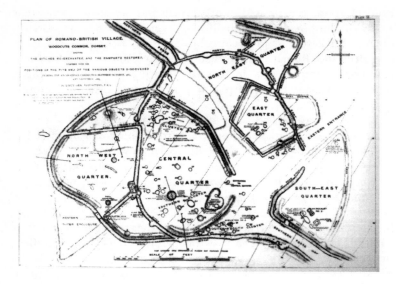

Figure 9.2 The Roman 'village' at Woodcuts (Dorset). Haverfield argued
that Roman pottery and other finds from this settlement indicated the Romanisation of the poorer members of Romano-
British society. *Source*: Pitt Rivers (1887).

Asiatic or African who dons European clothes once or again
for profit or for pleasure. It was not true of the Roman
provincial. When he adopted, *and adopted permanently*, the
use of things Roman, we may say of him, firstly, that he
had become civilized enough to realise their value, and
further, that he had ceased to bear any national hatred
against them . . . We can argue from the spread of Roman
material civilization that provincial sentiment was growing
Roman.[44]

This suggests that, for Haverfield, Roman culture carried with itself
Roman identity. Romanisation had an almost spiritual quality and
by adopting new items and new ideas the whole range of provincials aimed to become Roman and abandon his or her incoherent,
uncrystallised, native identity. He wrote that: 'The definite and
coherent culture of Rome took hold on uncivilized but intelligent
provincials and planted in them the wish to learn its language and
share its benefits'.[45] The coherence of civilisation was to be preferred
by the native to the uncrystallised nature of the inherited native

identity. The poor aspired with the rich to be wealthy and Roman; although they had achieved a lower level of Roman culture, they exhibited the same process in action.

Haverfield, therefore, did recognise some variation across the Empire and suggested that a range of factors possibly lay behind regional patterns; these variations, however, were argued not to relate to any form of national instinct:

> If he felt sometimes the claims of his province and raised a cry that sounds like 'Africa for the Africans,' he acted on a geographical, not on any native or national idea. He was demanding individual life for a Roman section of the Empire. He was anticipating, perhaps, the birth of new nations out of the Romanized populations. He was not attempting to recall the old pre-Roman system.[46]

There is no room for native resistance, after the initial phase of conquest and consolidation, in Haverfield's account of the western Empire. With these comments Haverfield may have been providing a response to a view which he roundly criticised in the 1905 publication of *The Romanization of Roman Britain*. In Britain, as we have seen above, many authors prior to Haverfield had felt that Romans and Britons remained as distinct from each other as modern Englishmen were from Indians. In this context the 'departure of the Romans' in the early fifth century left the Britons almost as native as the Romans had found them. Haverfield argued that this old view had been reinforced in some minds by the 'revival of Welsh national sentiment', and this will be considered further below.

The reification of civilisation and progress

How did Romanisation operate, in Haverfield's view? Evidently, the broad parallel that Haverfield drew between the spread of 'civilisation' in the two empires suggests that Romanisation was thought to be broadly comparable to the spread of ideas and material culture in Britain's empire. While it is not certain that Haverfield was consciously aware of drawing a parallel between Romanisation and the concept of progress in his society, comments that he made in the context of both his 1911 paper and *The Romanization of Roman Britain* suggests that he was.[47]

Haverfield did not consider the parallel in any great detail and drew a contrast between the two distinct historical processes with regard to race. Africans and Asians were unable to adopt civilisation because of cultural and racial factors, while ancient Britons were intelligent and free enough to adopt progress. This suggests that, to Haverfield, the basic spread of ideas and objects in the two contexts were motivated by a shared civilising mission at different times in history, only the context of the civilising process with regard to race varied.[48] The civilising mission linking Rome and Britain appears united in the form of a linear continuity of progress through time.[49]

Haverfield's 'Romanisation' was part of a broader image of progress which was common to many people during his lifetime; an idea which was derived from evolutionary and diffusionist theories. Just as European civilisation was seen to be expanding and carrying new ideas and standards to those 'primitive' and 'uncivilised' cultures incorporated in the empires of Western powers, so Romanisation drove out the pre-Roman material culture in barbarian Europe. Mackenzie has discussed the ways in which Britain's unique imperial mission developed in the late nineteenth century,[50] and Haverfield's work may be seen in this context: it exhibits the logic of its time, with the 'higher' culture replacing the 'lower'. To Haverfield, pre-Roman society in Britain had no coherent 'civilisation' capable of withstanding Rome and all was swept away in a trend towards a standardised (or fairly standardised) Roman civilisation.

In Haverfield's words, Rome had served to spread its classical culture, for which we may read 'civilisation', to the modern world and was, therefore, a major contributor to modern western civilisation.[51] The role of Rome in bringing civilisation to the west and the broad connections between the two processes meant also that Romanisation was evidently 'a good thing', especially since as we have seen – in Haverfield's terms – the men of the Roman Empire achieved a dramatic social improvement in western Europe.[52] This connection between the ancient and the modern world perhaps helped to create the context for the idea of a reified coherent category of civilisation; in this regard, Haverfield followed a common tradition, which has been studied already.

Haverfield's ideas should also be seen as part of a more general development within English academic studies of a rather more 'liberal' attitude to Celtic peoples within Britain at his time, a growing interest in other native peoples within the Empire and also of the development of concepts related to the social duties and burdens of 'white men' towards natives.[53] That Haverfield could even conceive of Roman sites in Britain as the homes of ancient

British natives was in tune with broad changes in social thought occurring during his lifetime. We have seen that many late Victorians had viewed the natives of Roman Britain in the guise of the natives of British India. Haverfield introduced a radical new approach with his study of Romanisation, but this was, itself, evidently based upon broader changes in society. That he may some-times have over-emphasised the degree and uniformity of Romanisation across the south of the province should be seen in the light of these previous accounts which viewed all 'Roman' monu-ments as the work of Roman officers from Italy.

It is even possible that the process of Romanisation, by which the native British became more like the Romans, was conceived by Haverfield as a testament to the fact that the idea of civilisation had real validity in his own world. If Rome had succeeded, why should the British not also? Especially if the English were able to learn lessons from the Roman past. This, in fact, appears to Haverfield to have formed part of the justification for the study of the Roman Empire and to be one of the messages behind Haverfield's comments to his public audience at the Roman Society address in 1911, discussed above. In the 1905 article, however, he seems to be less optimistic about Britain's success in the task of denational-isation, when he suggests that there is a serious racial barrier to 'civilisation' (by which we may read the 'westernisation') of Africans within the Empire.[54] Perhaps the Roman success was seen within a process of definition as highlighting the British failure and the need for Haverfield's contemporaries to strive to succeed and main-tain their own imperial effort[55] – another moral provided by Roman studies for the British to take into account.

The Englishman, the Welshman and the Roman Britain

It is possible that, in discussing Roman Britain, Haverfield felt that he was considering the mental capacity of people who formed part of the genetic make-up of his own society. In this context the comments of Scarth, Ackworth, Henty, Lucas and Weigall during late Victorian and Edwardian times are interesting in that they suggest some genetic connection between ancient Britons and modern English people. It is important in this context that some academic contemporaries of Haverfield's in Oxford were working towards a philosophy which argued that racial mixing led to the strength of the British and the potential future destiny of the British

Empire.[56] Haverfield's work on Romanisation had a role to play in these changing views of English origin in providing an acceptable academic image which helped to support the public image of Englishness. Nevertheless, whatever his attitude about progress in Britain's own Empire, Haverfield was arguing that the pre-Roman inhabitants of Britain had an essential racial compatibility with their conquerors, a very different situation from that between the colonised peoples and the officials of the British Empire.

Haverfield considered the topic of genetic or racial survival from ancient Britain to modern England in his paper *Roman Britain and Saxon England.* This was not published, however, until after his death in 1924, in a collection of his papers. G. Macdonald, who edited them prior to publication, recalled that they were originally the lectures given by Haverfield in 1907, which were amended in 1913 or 1914. In addition, in preparing the papers for publication, Macdonald had taken parts from other works produced by of Haverfield and made his own additions.[57] It is, therefore, not certain that the views in this 1924 article were entirely those of Haverfield.

In this article Haverfield considers the possibility that the Britons were exterminated by the incoming Saxons but argued that some of the British population certainly remained.[58] He felt, however, that: 'from the Romans who once ruled in Britain, we Britons have inherited practically nothing . . . Racially, topographically, culturally, ancient Rome has nothing to do with modern Britain.'[59]

Haverfield continued his arguments by suggesting that Rome had influenced modern Britain as Roman civilisation created much of modern Europe and, in the process, Britain. The idea being expressed at this point is presumably that the Roman civilisation of Britain was lost as a result of Saxon activity, but that it remained on the Continent to be reintroduced to Britain, or was rediscovered and reintroduced during the Renaissance. In arguing this way, Haverfield may also have been drawing attention to the supposed Roman origin of European culture and the place of Britain within Europe.

In addition to his ideas about English origins, Haverfield made observations on the origin of the Welsh. He contested the idea that Celtic social organisation survived the Roman control of Britain in lectures and published works. He noted that an attitude of Welsh superiority had been derived from the medieval writings of Geoffrey of Monmouth and he attacked these views on a number of occasions.[60] In the published version of an article presented in 1909 to the Honourable Society of Cymmrodorion, Haverfield talked about Welsh patriots. He reviewed the attitude of the Welsh in the Middle

Ages which was focused upon the idea that the Roman Empire did not embrace Wales, or even Britain, permanently or continuously. He suggested that this opinion had not totally dissipated in Wales but had grown as the feeling of Welsh nationalism had developed over the past forty or fifty years.[61] In *The Romanization of Roman Britain* he argued in similar terms when he observed: 'the revival of Welsh national sentiment has inspired a hope, which has become a belief, that the Roman conquest was an episode, after which an unaltered Celticisim resumed its uninterrupted supremacy'.[62] In both works Haverfield sought to demonstrate that these nationalistic views of a permanent Celticness were not realistic when viewed with regard to the archaeological evidence for Roman Britain.[63]

The end of Roman Britain and the enigma of the 'Celtic revival'

There are two issues within *The Romanization of Roman Britain* that could be taken to counter the clear emphasis which Haverfield places on a fundamental Roman transformation of Britain. The idea of a 'Celtic revival' appears odd in the context of Romanisation, as do some of his comments about the 'military districts' of the north and west of Britain.

In the eighth chapter of the 1912 edition of the book Haverfield considered the so-called 'Celtic revival' in the later Empire, characterised particularly by the revival of 'Celtic' art. The idea of a Celtic revival after the departure of the Romans in 410 is evident in earlier popular literature, for instance in A.J. Church's novel *The Count of the Saxon Shore*, published in 1887. In Church's novel the revival of Celtic sentiment in Britain at this time is seen in an entirely negative light.[64]

Such a revival in Haverfield's account of Roman Britain might appear to conflict with his suggestion that a fundamental Roman transformation of the province occurred; as we have seen, Haverfield argued that Romanisation removed any concept of native origins among the Britons. A Celtic revival suggests a degree of continuity in social organisation from pre-Roman to Roman and post-Roman Britain that would run directly contrary to Haverfield's account of Romanisation. How did Haverfield explain the occurrence of a Celtic revival in the context of a province in which Romanisation had led to a standardised and relatively uniform Roman pattern?

Haverfield suggests that this Celtic revival was due to a number of causes, including the fact that after AD 407 the province was cut off from Rome and Roman influence.[65] The sporadic survival of

Celtic inspiration in art within the province,[66] which is evidently seen by Haverfield as an exception to the general pattern of Romanisation, is one reason for this Celtic survival.[67] Haverfield suggests that this continuity resulted more directly from the influence of the less-Romanised Celtic areas of Cornwall, Ireland and northern Britain on the occupants of the former province, together with the invasion of Irish Celts.[68] The other strong force for change was the destruction of the Romanised parts of Britain by invading Saxons. The Celtic revival in late Roman and sub-Roman Britain therefore had nothing to do with the survival of Celtic society in the lowland areas of the province.

Celtic subalterns and the 'military district'

Haverfield argued that through the process of Romanisation, the Romans could be seen to have passed civilisation on to the south and east of Britain. However, they did not appear to have provided such a lasting heritage of civilisation for the Welsh, Scots or Irish. As we have seen, some of Haverfield's comments indicate that he felt that Roman civilisation was passed onto ancient Britons in Wales through the process of Romanisation.[69] Some parts of his work could, however, be used to develop an alternative image, which drew again upon the image of the Celts as 'other'.

In *The Romanization of Roman Britain*, Haverfield argued that Roman Britain could be divided into two parts – the 'civil district' and the 'military district' (Figure 9.3).[70] The civil district consisted of much of England, while the military district included Wales, northern England and southern Scotland. According to Haverfield, outside the forts and their associated *vici*, little Romanisation occurred in the military district. In the Lake District, for instance, Haverfield mentioned in his 1913 address that 'wild hill-men' survived 'who defied Roman ways'.[71] In *The Romanization of Roman Britain* Haverfield suggested that 'Celtic qualities' may have lingered on' in the military north and west.[72] Therefore, the Romanisation of the British population was confined to the civil districts – the area of southern Britain.

Figure 9.3 The (a) civil and (b) military districts of Roman Britain. In the south and east civil society developed and towns and villas became common. In the north and west the army remained throughout the Roman occupation and natives did not achieve a high level of Romanisation. *Source*: Haverfield (1912).

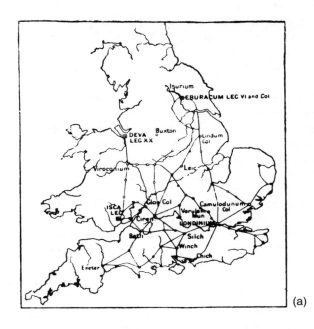

(a)

(b)

Other early twentieth-century works also considered the role of Rome in passing on civilisation to the British.[73] The potential political power of the type of ideas with which Haverfield was working in defining his military and civilian districts can be judged from a work that was published in 1911, in which Fletcher and Kipling wrote:

> It was . . . a misfortune for Britain that Rome never conquered the whole island. The great warrior, Agricola, did . . . penetrate far into Scotland; but he could leave no trace of civilization behind him, and Ireland he never touched at all. So Ireland never went to school, and has been a spoilt child ever since.[74]

In Fletcher and Kipling's account, Rome is seen to have created civilisation in the lowlands but failed to bring this to Scotland and, in particular, to Ireland. In the eighteenth and nineteenth centuries the 'Celts' formed an idea which helped with English self-definition[75] and Haverfield and Feltcher and Kipling drew upon this common tradition. We shall see below that Haverfield's definition of the civilian and the military districts of Roman Britain helped later authors to reconfigure the relationship between the English and the population of the north and west of Britain.[76]

Summary

Romanisation theory came to form part of British imperial discourse due to the fact that it fulfilled a number of roles in Edwardian and later thought. It accounted for how native ancient Britons were brought the benefits of civilisation: as such, it reflected the basic assumption that a joint civilising mission united the Roman Empire with the British. Further, it adopted much of the Edwardian theory of progress, a theory that stressed that the British had a moral right and duty to lead others to the benefits of civilisation.

Romanisation theory also fitted, or was made to fit, with Edwardian and early twentieth-century images of Englishness. This occurred despite the fact that Haverfield appears to have felt that Roman civilisation did not survive the Anglo-Saxon invasion of Britain but was reintroduced from Europe at a later date. A linear conception of English history allowed others in the early twentieth century to develop their own arguments about the inheritance of the imperial burden of the Romans.[77] In addition, as we have seen in earlier chapters, Haverfield argued that the study of Romanisation had a value to British imperialists. Through the consideration of how Rome had assimilated native ancient Britons into imperial culture, modern imperial administrators and politicians could inform their policies and activities among the native peoples of their own empire.

The progressive nature of Haverfield's contribution to imperial discourse was perhaps, as I have already suggested, a product of the time in which he lived. Imperial need in Edwardian times drove English academics to look for ways to shore up the imperial effort. Haverfield's work on Romanisation operated on a number of levels within Edwardian imperial discourse. It also had an important legacy that lasted beyond the dismemberment of the British Empire during the 1950s, 1960s and 1970s. This legacy is evident in the development of the progressive view of Romanisation between 1920 and the 1990s.

10

ROMANISATION
Haverfield's legacy

Introduction

The context for the writing of this book was the suggestion that the imperial legacy has influenced the nature of archaeological research in Britain (see Preface). An earlier chapter contained a brief discussion of the imperial legacy of Roman frontier studies after Haverfield. In that chapter I considered the comments of a number of authors regarding the influences that the Victorian and Edwardian world view had on the study of Roman frontiers. In this chapter I shall study the influence of Haverfield's work on Romanisation in rather more detail, since it interrelates with the topic of English origins that I have already discussed.

Romanisation studies since Haverfield have been characterised by a focus on the role of Rome in the civilising of native peoples. The explicit connection with images of Englishness exhibited by some of the popular and political works discussed in earlier chapters is not clearly evident in this archaeological writing, although we have seen that Robin Collingwood speculated on this topic in 1923 and 1925.[1] Much of the work on Romanisation, however, effectively establishes an unquestioned connection between the Romans and ourselves. The other side of this interpretation is a matching association between the non-Romanised native and the 'other'. Change from Roman to native is conceptualised in a manner which defines what I shall title the 'progressive' theory of Romanisation. This progressive Romanisation establishes a direct connection between the Roman Empire and modern Britain, or modern Europe. In this connection, the aspects of Roman civilisation that are most relevant to research and discussion are those that are seen to have contributed most to modern English or Europe society. In this way the progressive theory

We can study how Collingwood's later interpretation of Roman-isation operated by considering his works of 1932, 1936 and 1939. He argued that the puzzle of the so-called 'Celtic revival' demonstrated a focal problem in the definition of Romanisation – what really happened when people became 'Romanised'?[15] Collingwood's accounts of the province is developed in some detail in his section of the book that he published with J.N.L. Myres in 1936. Roman towns (*colonia* and *civitas* capitals) were the 'vehicle of civilization'.[16] They initially evolved in an impressive way with the support of the native élite and were well developed by the end of the first century AD, at which time they 'had laid down the main lines of their development'.[17]

Interestingly, Collingwood, however, notes the possibility of a degree of native resistance to the process of urban development. The movement for the development of towns in the late first century AD divided the population of Britain into two 'classes' – the educated and cultured town-dwellers and the unromanised country-dwellers in their villages.[18] Collingwood described the decline in Romano-British towns during the mid-third century and suggested that this was the result of factors operating on an empire-wide basis. He also speculated, however, that one factor in this trend could have been due to a 'sense of hostility towards the towns'.[19] The conservatism of the peasants in the villages may have impacted upon the success of the Roman towns, although Collingwood admitted that the evidence did not allow a definite verdict on this topic.

The idea embodied in Collingwood's work is that some natives did not aspire to a Roman image and this forms a clear contrast to Haverfield's idea of unified Romanisation involving all classes of society. It is in the context of their interpretation of the country-side that the contrast between Collingwood and Haverfield becomes particularly stark. For instance, in the expanded 1932 version of *Roman Britain*, Collingwood mentioned that many villages:

> lie close to the zero point in the scale of Romanization, so that even when they are carefully dug they may fail to yield any definitely Roman objects; and moreover, being rather sordid bunches of huts, huddled together inside a rough fence, they offer little to attract excavation, and compara-tively few of them have been dug at all.[20]

He drew a particular distinction between the villa-dwellers and the village-dwellers of southern Britain.[21] The villa, according to Collingwood, was an isolated house, 'romanized in architecture and furniture'.[22] Villages, by contrast, were groups of one-roomed huts, usually circular in shape. Collingwood argued that the origin of the division between villas and villages lay in the pre-Roman period and that, while villas often developed from isolated pre-Roman settlements, the villages continued in use from an Iron Age origin throughout the period.[23]

Collingwood's account of the countryside of Roman Britain contrasts directly with that of Haverfield. In what was presumably a direct counter to Haverfield's comments about the intention of the native who adopted and used Roman material culture, Collingwood argued that the Cranborne Chase 'villages' (Woodcuts and Rotherley) were exceptional in their degree of Romanisation. With regard to Romano-British sites of this sort in Britain generally; 'a native village may obtain its pottery and implements from the civilized world without using them in a particularly civilized way'.[24] He also expanded on the suggestions in another publication, when he argued that:

> Romanization . . . made headway even among the poorest and most backward classes of the population. But the degree of headway which it indicates must not be exaggerated. In scale, it amounts to no more than the Europeanizing of a native village in Africa, where the people have learnt to use cloth and tools and so forth made in Europe, but the houses and language and manners and customs are unchanged.[25]

The characterisation of the spiritual connotations of Roman material which Haverfield produced (above) is entirely absent in these observations. Roman objects could be adopted without any intention to acquire a Roman identity on the part of the village-dweller.

Collingwood was aware of the influence of Rome on these village dwellers, but felt that rural Romanisation was far more evident amongst the villa-dwellers of Britain. The pre-Roman organisation of the rural economy affected the Roman development of the countryside in both the villa- and village-zones. The two types of settlements occurred in distinct zones of the country and, according to Collingwood, were associated with differing types of field system. The nucleated village settlements occurred, for instance, on Cranborne Chase and Salisbury Plain, while the villas occurred on the periphery of the area (Figure 10.1).[26]

For Collingwood, the 'Celtic revival' defined by Haverfield in the final chapter of *The Romanization of Roman Britain* was fundamental

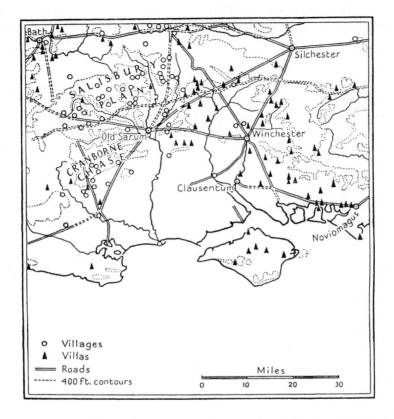

Figure 10.1 Villas and villages in Dorset, Hampshire and Wiltshire. Collingwood argued that the centre of Cranbourne Chase and Salisbury Plain were characterised by native villages, while the outskirts formed a contrasting villa landscape. More recent archaeological work has shown the situation to be rather more complex than this simple model would suggest. *Source*: Collingwood and Myres (1936).

and led to a situation in which by the time of the Anglo-Saxon invasion the civilisation of the lowland zone was not so much Roman as sub-Roman.[27] This is characterised by the fact that:

Its material and spiritual possessions were so deeply and increasingly tinged with Celticism, and what Romanity they had was so typical of the last imperial age, that they would hardly be recognized as Roman at all by persons whose idea of Roman culture is derived from the early empire.[28]

In fact:

> from the late fourth century onwards, Britain became less Roman and more purely Celtic, not because the Roman element was composed of foreigners who left ... but because it was composed of a minority of wealthy Britons of the upper classes, whose wealth and power ... came to an end in the troubles that marked the close of the Roman occupation of Britain.[29]

According to Collingwood, 'revival' means 'survival' and in his terms Romano-British art involved a 'transmutation' of 'naturalistic' Roman style through the influence of 'symbolic' La Tène art[30] – a trend that caused a permanent cultural strain and led to a resistance which resulted in the so-called 'Celtic revival'. Collingwood suggested that any change to a new type of behaviour, such as the Romanisation of 'Celtic' Britons, will leave a desire to go on acting and thinking in the old way.[31] The persistence that caused the 'Celtic revival' was a result of the passing down of tradition through 'folk-memory'.[32] Rather than assisting with the development of Welsh nationalism,[33] Collingwood's conception of a Celtic revival (or survival) perhaps fed an image of the permanence of English identity. This was due to the fact that the passing down of tradition and genetic continuity from the ancient Britons to modern Englishmen was argued to have linked the art and civilisation of Roman Britain with the culture of modern *England*.[34]

Collingwood created a clear Roman-native opposition in his characterisation of the villa (Roman) and village (native) economies and in his analysis of the survival of 'Celtic' imagery in art. Any synthesis of Roman and 'Celtic' in Britain was unstable and did not stand the test of time. Sometimes Collingwood's account appears to suggest that the continued presence of native ('Celtic') imagery and institutions was a result of some form of resistance to Rome. In these ways his account of Romanisation differed dramatically from that of Haverfield and the accounts produced by Rivet and Frere.

A.L.F. Rivet's *Town and Country in Roman Britain*, first published in 1958, still constitutes a useful work. Rivet's book follows Collingwood's example in that it does not contain a detailed discussion of the concept of Romanisation. The concept, however was fundamental to the way in which Rivet interpreted Roman Britain, with chapters on 'Romanisation – towns', and 'Romanisation – countryside'.

Rivet's comments at the beginning of his book pursue some of the ideas explored under the theme of 'Imperialism', above. In considering the nature of the evidence for Roman Britain he discussed literary evidence, epigraphic evidence, archaeological evidence, evidence by analogy and the opinions of modern scholars.[35] With regard to evidence by analogy, he argued that information from other Roman provinces is of use for the analysis of Roman Britain. Analogy is not necessarily, however, restricted to the time at which the Roman Empire flourished. He suggests that:

> Throughout history contacts between *higher* and *lower* civlisations have tended to follow set patterns, and our understanding of the earlier stages of the romanisation of Britain can be deepened by the study of such processes as the westernisation of Africa in the last hundred years.[36]

Differences between the two contexts existed in Rivet's account, for instance in the fact that the Romans never became distracted by the futility of race and colour prejudice; but the similarities, both general and particular, are, according to Rivet, 'sometimes startling'.[37]

With regard to modern analogies, Rivet drew attention in his bibliography to a work on the modern administration of Africa that provides a storehouse of information:

> on the social and administrative problems that arise in the *early stages* of the *assimilation* of *backward societies* to a more *developed* culture and on the various ways – some of them very similar to those adopted by the Romans – in which they have been attacked.[38]

I have already explored general similarities between the approaches of some of the imperial administrators of Rome and those of western imperial powers to 'backward' peoples. I would suggest that these similarities in imperial practice often had a great deal to do with the classical education of the British imperial and administrative élite and the use of classical parallels and lessons in their imperial activities. In this regard these associations were also based on a broadly-conceived assumption of a shared Roman-British civilising mission. Rivet was aware of the incorrect nature of the use of Roman

Britain as an analogy for British India, as we have already seen,[39] but he still appears to have felt general analogies to be useful.[40]

It is of interest that Rivet treated the works of Haverfield and Collingwood in contrasting ways in the section of his book on the opinions of modern scholars. Rivet felt that Haverfield's observations on the relationship of Britons to Romans and the division between a civilian and a military zone were helpful.[41] By contrast, he argued that Collingwood's identification of contrasting village and villa zones in southern Britain had been 'undermined at its base' by the evidence to indicate that villages did not exist in Roman Britain.[42] There appears to be a contrast in the way that Rivet treated the work of these two eminent scholars, which may have resulted from the fact that Rivet's own work reflected in many ways the progressive approach to Romanisation in the work of Haverfield, which I have discussed above.

Rivet considered in general terms the ways that Romanisation operated, although he did not deal with the process in as much detail as Haverfield. A strong division existed between Romans and natives:

> Though the people of Britain at the time of its absorption into the Roman Empire were not naked savages, neither were they *in any way the equals* of their conquerors. . . . The settlement pattern was that of a *primitive society*, depending almost entirely on natural circumstances. . . . Man was the suppliant, not yet the master, of nature.[43]

In Rivet's account, Romanisation is viewed as the spread of civilisation to these primitive communities. The 'Belgae' had acquired 'a veneer of romanisation before the Claudian conquest' and therefore had a 'higher degree of civilization' than the other more 'primitive peoples'.[44] The association between the area covered by the so-called Belgae: 'with that of the civilised part of Roman Britain strongly suggests that it was these people, *rude* and *uncultured* though they were, who laid the foundations on which the prosperity of the Roman province ultimately rested.[45]

Rivet returned to the process of Romanisation at several other points in his book. 'This romanised pattern displays an organic development of its own, and although its point of departure was the natural, native order of things, the key to it is the military, political and technical competence of Rome.'[46] Again, the Roman impact on native society is more fundamental than the native background itself.

It is evident in *Town and Country*, as in the work of Haverfield and Collingwood, that Rome did not totally transform all aspects of native society. For instance: 'the romanisation of the countryside normally took the form of an increased use of Roman goods and the adoption of a Roman style of living by people who continued to farm their land in the old way'.[47] In this regard, Rivet defines a '*normal*' development of the countryside that involved the construction of a villa – a Romanised focus for a landed estate.[48] This villa system, however, was based on a continuity of native agricultural practice by the native élite living within their villas. The villa was a Romanised building but the surplus to build it was drawn from cultivation that continued in a native manner.

Rivet's perspective placed special emphasis on certain aspects of the archaeology of Roman Britain at the expense of others. In doing so he created a problem in defining the idea of 'normal' development. As I have discussed elsewhere, the vast majority of the people of Roman Britain did not live in villas.[49] Even in areas of southern Britain in which villas are common, they do not form more than 15 per cent at the very most of the total number of rural settlements.[50] To suggest that the development of the villa was a 'normal' development within Britain therefore places an emphasis on the archaeological record produced by the élite within the province and negates the information for the less wealthy and powerful. Rivet's 'normal' development was certainly not so in statistical terms: real normality in terms of the vast majority of cases was for no villa house to be built and for the family to continue to live in a village or farm without a substantial Romanised building.[51]

In Rivet's terms the 'abnormal' areas fell naturally into three classes – land alienated for officially sponsored settlers, imperial estates[52] and the native north and west.[53] In the abnormal areas the farms were not Romanised, but Rivet was insistent that Collingwood's division between discrete village-zones and villa-zones was unacceptable.[54] Rivet's brief discussion of the so-called 'native' north and west drew upon Haverfield's definition of the military and civilian districts.[55] Rivet argued that on the highland fringes of the province there were large areas where the 'the impact of civilisation was very slight indeed'.[56] In these areas, rural habitations continued to be 'purely native in character'. As a result, 'civilisation' was largely confined to the lowland zone.[57]

Rivet focused attention on the 'civilising' aspects of Rome – the development of a 'higher degree of civilisation' within Britain under Roman influence.[58] At the same time he was evidently aware that this strictly progressive perspective in which all became equally 'Roman' was a simplification. In a manner similar to that of Haverfield, he was conscious of the native dimension of Romano-British society, but for him this is not fundamental to an understanding of the province. While some native continuity exists in Rivet's account, for instance in agricultural organisation and in the military north and west of the province, this is not fundamental to the understanding of the process of Romanisation. The poorest did not benefit from Roman control at all and even those people who were *slightly above* the 'bottom of the scale . . . benefited little from . . . civilisation'.[59] As a consequence, they were of little relevance to an understanding of the history of Roman Britain. Unlike Haverfield and Collingwood, Rivet does not discuss the ways in which the poor and powerless might have used Roman pottery and other objects, as it is of little relevance to the main part of his narrative which focuses on the Romanisation of settlement and economy. His few comments on the subject do appear to suggest that, like Collingwood, he was more dismissive of the benefits to the poor of Roman civilisation than was the case with Haverfield.

Evidently, Rivet's use of the idea of Romanisation is very different from its use by Haverfield, but the emphasis in the two accounts which are separated by fifty-four years is on the progress from a backward state to an improved condition. Although Rivet perhaps allows for more variation from the Roman norm than is the case with at least some of Haverfield's writings, to him it remains that norm which is of importance for an understanding of the province. As such, Rivet's work built on Haverfield's in helping to define the 'progressive' view of Romanisation. The process was seen to transform all important natives from a state of barbarism to one of civilisation and, as such, made Romano-British domestic history of relevance to the contemporary generations of British people – it helped to draw Roman archaeology into the ambit of English domestic history.

S.S. Frere's influential book *Britannia: A History of Roman Britain* was first published in 1967 and was highly influential well into the 1980s and even into the 1990s. It contains a chapter on 'The Romanisation of Britain' which draws on the work of Haverfield and is critical of the work of Collingwood. Frere argued for the dual character of Romano-British civilisation:

> Outwardly it was Roman, inwardly it remained Celtic; yet it would be wrong to suppose an inner conflict between the two aspects. The result was a synthesis, intended by Rome,

and welcomed by the British people as they came to realise the advantages of peace and wealth conferred by membership of the empire.[60]

Presumably this emphasis on synthesis was, at least in part, a counter to Collingwood's account of contradictions and hostility between natives and Romans.[61] Frere argued for a wide variability within the synthesis, depending on the social class of those involved and the varying conditions of life in Roman Britain: 'At the one end of the spectrum lay considerable approximation to the classical way of life and at the other a substantial survival of native characteristics.'[62] Frere continued, however, with a qualified restatement of Haverfield's views:

> We can measure the Romanisation of Britain only with imprecision, for we have to depend so largely upon the evidence of material things – potsherds, iron tools, bronze brooches, house-plans, towns or statues – rather than upon the much more revealing evidence of contemporary testimony. Not that the evidence of material things is of little account. Haverfield long ago made the point that when the provincial adopted the use of Roman things he could be declared civilised enough to realise their value and, further, could be seen to have abandoned any *national* hostility towards them. Nevertheless, the evidence of the written word is invaluable in such an enquiry, and Romano-British writings are denied us until the fifth century.[63]

Frere's account of Britannia places emphasis on change and on the Roman image of the province, and his account of Romanisation appears to view change as inevitable and positive in character. Terms such as 'advances' and 'progress' are used in this account of the Romanisation of the province. For instance, by the end of the first century towns 'were rapidly *developing*';[64] these towns were the 'vehicle and focus of this *progress*'[65] and the changes in the second century AD led to 'much greater *advances*'.[66] From the perspective adopted in this present study, Frere's account of Roman Britain appears to reflect an over simplistic perception of progress from a lower culture to higher in a way that is familiar from the work of Haverfield and Rivet.

Turning again to the familiar topic of the rural settlements of Rotherley and Woodcuts, which still formed the prime examples of excavated non-villa settlements in the south of Britain in the 1960s, Frere suggested that: 'It is clear that in Roman Britain art was far more pervasive than it had been in the Iron Age, and that all classes according to their means and tastes could enjoy its products.'[67]

The number of bronze objects from the two village sites therefore leaves one *'impressed'* and this demonstrates the extent to which the new 'art' reached even 'the peasant class'.[68] As with Haverfield, all aspired to Roman standards and the only factors operating to limit the extent of Romanisation were the wealth and social position of those below the top of the social hierarchy. Items of material culture and the developing rectangularity of house form demonstrate the spread of this 'civilization' to even the poorest within society. In art, Collingwood's idea that 'Celtic' art was driven underground by the Romans was considered as 'quite unrealistic' by Frere.[69]

With regard to the re-occurring topic of the 'Celtic revival', the revival of 'Celtic' art in the later period may have occurred either through transmission or survival; indeed, 'the Celtic craftsmen who still worked in the west and north during the third to fourth centuries were tinkers rather than artists and practised a peasant craft'.[70] Presumably the pre-Roman and post-Roman art of Britain was also, in some way, inferior to that of Rome. The spread of 'a considerable approximation to the classical way of life' within Roman Britain was only limited by restricted wealth and limited contacts. Frere's observations about Romano-British art should be seen as a reaction to Collingwood's dismissive views, and perhaps Frere was deliberately taking an opposite stance in the discussion. The relevant point, however, is the connection drawn in the works of Rivet and Frere between the idea of Romanisation and that of progress in the modern world.

There has been a good degree of continuity in the theory of Romanisation into the late twentieth century. Martin Millett has analysed the concept in his influential book *The Romanization of Britain* (1990). This book, which draws in its title on Haverfield's important study,[71] also aims to provide views about Romanisation relevant to 'a post-imperial' generation.[72] It can be argued, however, that the interpretation of Romanisation that is developed in the volume draws upon much the same body of thought which is evident in the work of Haverfield, Rivet and Frere. Although the judgmental evaluation of Roman society as *superior* to native is not as evident in this book as in earlier works on this topic, Romanisation is still interpreted as progress. In addition, in Millett's book attention remains focused, as in earlier accounts, on those who were most involved in the process of change, the rich and those who were resident in the south and east of the province.[73]

For the details of Millett's interpretation of Romanisation we have to turn to an article also published in 1990. This defines a fairly simple process of change in which new ideas pass down through the social hierarchy through a process of 'emulation'. The élite of the western provinces adopted Roman material symbols in order to reinforce their social position by identifying themselves with Rome.[74] Romanisation then spread throughout society. 'Progressive emulation of this symbolism further down the social hierarchy was self-generating [,] encouraging others within society to aspire to things Roman, thereby spreading the culture.'[75]

Other Romanists have developed comparable accounts of Romanisation in which similar concepts are utilised. For instance, Whittaker has suggested that Roman culture appealed more to the rich than to the poor. He argued, however, that, since the rich were constantly mobile and were themselves socially entwined with their poorer 'compatriots', there was 'infiltration' from one set of values to another.[76] Elsewhere, the same author describes this process as Romanisation 'by osmosis'.[77]

This type of interpretation of progressive Romanisation is familiar from the work of Haverfield, Rivet and others.[78] Roman ideas and symbols spread through society through a process of emulation and the more wealthy and socially well connected a provincial was, the more Romanisation he or she would exhibit. The relative lack of detailed discussion of the non-élite in a variety of late twentieth-century accounts presumably relates once again to their limited relevance according to this simplistic account of social change.

In selecting the works of Whittaker and Millett for comment it is not my intention to suggest that Roman archaeology has not changed over the past thirty years. I would, however, argue that a basic continuity in thought within Romanisation studies has not taken account of the social context of the development of Haverfield's concept of Romanisation or of changes in the nature of the world over the past eighty years.

Romanisation and progress

Both Rivet and Frere followed Haverfield in drawing upon an interpretation of Romanisation that was built upon twentieth-century ideas of progress, and later twentieth-century scholarship has often followed the same direction. According to Haverfield, Rivet and Frere, Romanisation brought improvement to Roman Britain in leading the natives to civilisation. Collingwood's early work mirrored these ideas, but his later writings of the 1930s were rather different, in that he developed the idea of a certain degree of native resistance to Romanisation. Collingwood's idea of native resistance drew upon earlier images of Celtic identity, but placed them in a new context through the use of the image of Englishness.[79] His general account of Romanisation has been drawn upon in subsequent works that have considered the permanence of native identity, but these will not be discussed in this book.[80]

It is significant that in the dominant works of the twentieth century the concepts of Romanisation and civilisation are reflections of a single common idea, *progress*. I wish to discuss some of the problems with the types of account outlined both in this and the previous chapter. The accounts of Romanisation are based on a very simple model. They view social change in terms that now appear too simple with regard to a contemporary understanding of human society.

Haverfield, Rivet and Frere's approaches to Romanisation appear to derive their character from three fundamental, associated and unquestioned assumptions, each of which draws upon a long history which has been discussed in the first two parts of this book. These assumptions are:

- the coherent nature of the categories of the primitive native Briton/'Celt' and Roman, and the definition of these categories in opposition to each other;
- the definition of the Roman as 'us' and the ancient Briton as 'other'; and
- the progressive interpretation which views social change as a transition from primitive to civilised and which has been used to propose a picture of simple directional change from native to Roman.

The 'progressive'[81] nature of the theory of Romanisation is used to account for how the primitive ancient Britons in the civil district of the province achieved civilisation through contact with Rome. In broader terms, through this process of Romanisation, the ancient Britons ('other') effectively become Romans ('us' or 'more like us').

In the context of adoption of the deep structure of mythic thought by academics in a search for the historical context of national origin, Britain was considered to have progressed through Romanisation

144

towards a state that was more comparable to its present condition of twentieth-century civilisation. Rome, as an image, consequently held a specific and unquestioned historical message for the English involving their national origin, European inheritance of civilisation and place within the twentieth-century world.

Romanisation theory was established by Mommsen and Haverfield at a time when simple models of social evolution were dominant – accounts which stressed directional change from primitive to civilised.[82] Such ideas were derived partly from Greek and Roman classical sources,[83] but 'progress' as an analytical concept had its intellectual origin in the Enlightenment.[84] It developed into a powerful image during the nineteenth century and into the twentieth through the use of the forceful analogy provided by the theory of biological evolution developed by Charles Darwin.[85] In many late nineteenth-century accounts of social evolution, civilisation was felt to be the outcome of progress created through an unquestioned and linear trajectory of history.

The idea of progress operated within a discourse of imperialism that argued for civilising missions in which it was the duty of white men, or westerners, to bring civilisation to 'primitives', or 'natives'. The industrial and political domination which Europeans exerted upon the world in the late nineteenth and early twentieth centuries enabled the development of a theory of progress which held that the West had a moral right and duty to lead other branches of humanity into the light of civilisation. This assumed duty was utilised in this context as partial justification for the creation and maintenance of political control over others who were seen as being lower down the scale of social development. It was also conceived that less evolved forms of humanity would progress some way towards a modern state through the influence of European society.[86] In some cases fairly full progress to a modern state might be possible in time, but for other peoples permanent political guidance was deemed necessary by the imperial power.[87]

This progressive theory of social evolution was used to reconcile the diversity of societies with the unity of the human race through the study of differing people who were seen as less developed but in the image of the West.[88] In interpreting the history and culture of others in this way, western society can be considered to have imposed its own view of history on those whom it colonised[89] and also to have used ideas of progress and civilisation to justify imperial action. The idea of progress formed a fundamental part of social evolutionism and in the western mind it effectively did away with the value of the history and culture of these others, since they were interpreted as an imperfect representation of the early history of western society.[90]

In the context of the British Empire this process of interpretation included the imposition of concepts of progress and evolution on a wide range of peoples which were incorporated within British territory. Imperial discourse was also used, however, to recruit a series of the dead societies which were studied by prehistoric and Roman archaeologists into the same framework, both in Britain and abroad.[91] Within twentieth-century Roman studies, Romanisation was developed as the particular Roman form of a broadly-conceived western civilisation. The power of the image of Rome was derived throughout much of this century from the observation that a general form of civilisation was spread through western Europe (including England) by the expansion of the Roman Empire and that this led directly to the current state of the civilised world. The images of imperial ideology projected the idea of western cultural dominance based upon a lengthy historical tradition which was derived from Greece and Rome.[92]

Ideas of Romanisation and civilisation in the twentieth century have therefore been deeply influenced by the historical context in which they have developed. In the particular context of their twentieth-century usage, ideas of social change in Roman Britain became bound up with the imperial ideology of the ideas associated with progress and the 'white man's burden'.[93] As we have seen in Haverfield's account, this progressive model was transferred to the process of change in Roman Britain. The use of terms such as 'advance', 'progress' and 'higher culture' by Rivet and Frere demonstrates the continuation of this view of progressive Romanisation well into the twentieth century, while a moderated form of progressive Romanisation is evident in certain late twentieth-century works.

In J.M. Scott's popular account of Boadicea, published in 1975, despite the heroic value of Boadicea's example she was perceived as ultimately a bad thing for the British. This was because 'Rome was a civilisation, Britain a collection of barbaric tribes. The influence of Rome must have been progressive.'[94] Boadicea was, therefore, a 'retrogressive influence' in that her activities delayed 'Romanization'.[95] Scott's image of Romanisation in this account of Boadicea's revolt derives its progressive character from some of the academic works discussed in this chapter. Other late twentieth-century children's books and popular accounts of Roman Britain project similar ideas.

This progressive image of social change is why all important individuals, or in Haverfield's account all individuals, in civilian Roman Britain needed to become involved in the same process of Romanisation. Native society had to be transformed into a Roman image because this was a move toward the present in a conception of national origins that drew upon a dominant idea of progress that was felt to be fundamental to western society. The progressive model of social development which was imported without question into the theory of Romanisation did not allow for a branching form of social evolution: to accept that other cultures were equally valid expressions of human nature would imply a relativism of values which most found unacceptable.[96] Different ways of living from the supposedly Roman trajectory were either therefore not considered to exist at all or, if they did exist, were not worthy of study. Roman identity was considered a far more valid expression of humanity than native identity. During the Roman occupation of southern Britain, native society was considered to have swiftly become outmoded and backward and to be of little interest from the perspective of an historical or archaeological account of progress from primitive to civilised. To persist in a native form was a failure of progress, a refusal by uncivilised ancient people to accept the logic of Victorian and twentieth-century ideas of social evolution. Such a refusal was considered conceivable only in the context of poverty or geographical isolation from the civilising power. Poverty-stricken 'village'-dwellers in the province and the natives of the 'military' north and west were acceptable examples of the aberrant uncivilised.

In the military districts of Roman Britain, native or Celtic identity could survive and the image of the Celtic subaltern remained relevant. The use of the image of an historical parallel between British India and Roman Britain, which has been considered above,[97] becomes less apparent once the Indian independence movement gathered force from the 1920s onward.[98] Windle, however, included a chapter in his 1923 book on 'Rome and Britain – Britain and India'. He also proposed that the North-west Frontier in British India is 'reminiscent of "The Wall" and its history'.[99] This comment repeated an idea developed by Haverfield in 1913 – that British India might still form a valid parallel for the military districts of Roman Britain.[100]

Occasionally ideas about parallels between British India and Roman Britain are perpetuated in later works. For instance, Arthur Bryant, in a book published in 1953, considered that during the Roman period: 'The whole northern half of the island [of Britain] remained in a state of permanent unrest, not unlike the north-west frontier of nineteenth-century British India.'[101] The Indian parallel might be thought to be no longer relevant for the 'civilised' areas of southern Roman Britain but was still cited as a relevant parallel for the uncivilised 'military' north and west, where the archaeological evidence suggested that native society did not suddenly change to a supposedly 'Roman' form.

Through the analysis of Romanisation a series of binary oppositions have been set up by a range of authors throughout the twentieth century. These have built upon eighteenth- and nineteenth-century ideas. These oppositions, posited on the distinction between Roman (us) and native (other), include the following categories as shown in Table 10.1.

In many accounts of Romanisation the categories listed in the native column were considered undeveloped or incomplete versions of those in the Roman. In Collingwood's 1930s' accounts, the native categories, after the invasion, were felt to have been continued almost as a form of opposition against Roman control, and there appeared to be a degree of permanence in native identity which Roman control could not change. For Haverfield, Rivet and Frere, however, whatever their character, the native categories did not require serious study because they represented an incomplete version of a simple process of Romanisation which is considered to have included all in the province.[102]

Table 10.1 Differences between 'Roman' and 'Native'

Roman	Native
(us)	('other')
civilised	barbarian
officer	'subaltern'
Englishman	'Celt' (Welsh, Irish, Scot)
south and east	north and west
civilian	native
central	peripheral
élite	peasant
villa	village/farmstead
town	country
Roman town	small town (*oppida*)
Roman art	'Celtic art'
assimilation	resistance
Romanisation	'Celtic survival/revival'
change/progress	stability

A standard idea of Romanisation has been built up using a theory of progress; archaeological work has been dominated by an approach that focused upon the study of those who became Romanised. If people in Roman Britain were seen not to have adopt the standard approach to becoming Roman, this made them of little relevance to Roman studies. This approach to Romanisation, to a degree, created the evidence that was used to support it. The ways that evidence has been collected are based on certain beliefs and assumptions; these approaches have distorted the evidence and made it very difficult to interpret it in different ways.[103] The ways in which assumptions about Romanisation have distorted the archaeological evidence can be explored by considering the nature of the database of excavations undertaken from 1921 to the 1990s.

The creation of archaeological data

The number of Roman period sites excavated in Britain increased during the 1920s and 1930s. In 1921 the amount of archaeological work that was occurring caused the Society for the Promotion of Roman Studies to begin publishing annual accounts of work undertaken; these form a valuable resource in the study of the progress of Roman-period archaeology.[104] The number of sites excavated at this time and up until 1995 is indicated by the figures shown in Table 10.2.[105]

Table 10.2 Numbers of archaeological sites excavated by 5-year period from 1921 to 1995

Date	Numbers of sites excavated
1921–25	135
1926–30	153
1931–35	135
1936–40	148
1941–45	46
1946–50	130
1951–55	168
1956–60	240
1961–65	276
1966–70	483
1971–75	572
1976–80	555
1981–85	483
1986–90	628
1991–95	503

The types of sites that have been studied were, however, largely dictated by the often unconscious research interests of Romano-British archaeologists. As such, the sites excavated comprise a very biased selection focusing mainly on the agenda developed by the approaches to Romanisation outlined above. Table 10.3 shows a quantification of the proportions of various types of sites mentioned in the indexes of excavations from 1921 onward.[106] Several trends are evident in this information.

I wish to draw a distinction between two broad classes of sites – the villas/major towns/military sites, which form the backbone of the dominant accounts of the Romanisation of the province, and the small towns and non-villa settlements.[107] Military sites are relevant to frontier studies and administration, major towns have a relevance to administration and studies of Romanisation, while villas are also of importance for Romanisation. Small towns, particularly unwalled examples, and non-villa settlements are of less obvious relevance for an understanding of administration and Romanisation. The non-villa settlements are assumed to have been the homes of the poor or of those who were not able to adopt a high level of Roman culture. The

Table 10.3 Numbers and proportions of archaeological sites of differing types excavated by 5-year period from 1921 to 1995

Year	Military	Major town	Villa	Small town	Non-villa
1921–25	51 (38%)	16 (12%)	34 (25%)	24 (18%)	10 (7%)
1926–30	69 (44%)	27 (17%)	28 (18%)	28 (18%)	6 (4%)
1931–35	65 (48%)	30 (22%)	18 (13%)	13 (10%)	9 (7%)
1936–40	53 (36%)	31 (21%)	27 (18%)	20 (14%)	15 (10%)
1941–45	15 (33%)	14 (30%)	14 (30%)	1 (2%)	2 (4%)
1946–50	52 (39%)	28 (21%)	31 (23%)	15 (11%)	6 (5%)
1951–55	86 (51%)	33 (19%)	22 (13%)	15 (9%)	12 (7%)
1956–60	103 (43%)	39 (16%)	46 (19%)	36 (15%)	18 (7%)
1961–65	92 (33%)	43 (15%)	70 (25%)	51 (18%)	20 (7%)
1966–70	143 (32%)	52 (12%)	107 (24%)	85 (19%)	62 (14%)
1971–75	148 (26%)	61 (11%)	132 (25%)	95 (18%)	102 (19%)
1976–80	177 (35%)	64 (13%)	91 (18%)	86 (17%)	90 (18%)
1981–85	161 (38%)	80 (18%)	76 (17%)	70 (16%)	57 (13%)
1986–90	179 (34%)	137 (26%)	88 (17%)	61 (12%)	64 (12%)
1991–95	154 (36%)	92 (22%)	42 (10%)	40 (9%)	96 (23%)

Notes: Military = all military sites.
Large town = London, *colonia*, *civitas* capitals, provincial centres.
Villas = villa buildings and associated structures.
Small towns = small town sites with walls and without.
Non-villa = non-villa settlements – various 'villages', 'farmsteads', hillforts with Roman-period domestic occupation, etc.

small towns, according to Rivet,[108] are perhaps an Iron Age problem in relating to native organisation rather more fully than to the Roman control of the country.

Table 10.3 illustrates that the proportions of sites studied between 1921–25 and 1956–60 do not vary in a particularly significantly way. Military sites constituted between 33 per cent and 51 per cent of the sites excavated at this time, while non-villa settlements at no time formed more than 10 per cent. Between 1920 and 1960, the villas, major towns and military sites together accounted for around 75 per cent–95 per cent of the total of the five classes of sites. In the period from 1960 to 1995, the figures change. This is indicated most clearly by the increase in the number of non-villa settlements that have been excavated. The proportion of excavations on military sites and villas declined during this period. The figures given in Table 10.3 suggest that a change in emphasis in the proportions of sites excavated has occurred during the late twentieth century.

If we look at the figures prior to 1965, they demonstrate that the emphasis in the past has been on the supposedly 'Roman' attributes of the province – the elements of the archaeological record that fit easily into the standard accounts of the Roman province. These sites include the forts, walled towns and villas – sites indicative of the administrative and military organisation. These sites are also the ones that usually produce the most substantial quantity of Romanised artefacts, and which also sometimes produce inscriptions.[109] This bias in archaeological research led to a general avoidance of sites that did not fit so easily into the accounts of the Romanisation of the province – the small towns, other rural sites and non-villa settlements. These sites did not so clearly relate to the élite, the literary sources, the administration, or the military – and were therefore of only limited relevance to a perspective that focused on progress. In Haverfield and Frere's view they were assumed to demonstrate the same process of Romanisation as the more Romanised sites, but to a lower level, as a result of the poverty of their inhabitants. They were also only of limited relevance according to the perspective on Romanisation that was developed by Millett.

As we have seen, Collingwood commented that there had been a lack of work on 'village' settlements. In the 1960s a greater interest developed in the rural settlement of the province. Charles Thomas edited a volume in 1966 that attempted to study the broad range of rural settlement in Roman Britain, and since this time there has been an increase in the proportion of excavations on non-villa sites in relation to villas. This change may have resulted, at least in part, from the development of Rescue archaeology from the 1960s onward and also the rise of developer-funded archaeology during the 1980s and 1990s. Romano-British sites have come to be excavated because they were threatened rather than because they fitted into some pre-conceived research framework.[110] The types of site that are now receiving increased attention take on a direct relevance in any attempt to build approaches alternative to those of the Romanisation school of research.

Romanisation and post-imperial archaeology

I have reviewed Haverfield's addresses and his work on frontiers and Romanisation in order to consider how his work operated within the context of British imperial discourse. It is evident that the necessity to found the analysis of Romanisation on the publications of Haverfield and the other authors discussed indicates the continuing importance of this seminal work.[111]

The context of Haverfield's times caused him to take a certain approach to the Roman past of Britain and this approach was of political value to some of his contemporaries. It is relevant, however, that Haverfield appears to have been clearly aware of the value of Roman studies in the context of British imperial philosophy. He also knew that the contemporary political significance of the subject could be used to the advantage of Roman studies. His comments regarding the value of Roman studies in his four addresses between 1910 and 1913 can not be dismissed and demonstrate these points.[112]

I have attempted to show that his work derived much of its direction from a broader idea of the fundamental role of Rome in the foundation of modern Britain and Europe. In this context, Rome had a vital role in the destiny of the British Empire as a provider of the civilisation that created modern England. By a circular process, this political value claimed for Roman studies, to an extent, resulted in their reinvention in the context of modern issues. This involvement in present concerns in turn drew Roman archaeology further into the context of imperial discourse. Haverfield's focus on frontier studies formed part of a long-term tradition of research in Romano-British archaeology, which has been studied above. His work on Romanisation formed part of a developing interest in English (and European) origins that drew upon the lessons that Britain had learnt from Rome.

His account of Romanisation was based upon the polarisation of barbarians and civilised peoples and a simple image of progress from the former to the latter. Some of the influential twentieth-century accounts of Romanisation derived much of their power through the linear connection that was created between the Roman history of England and its modern state. Haverfield and his successors in the 1900s to 1990s based their ideas of social change on the same simple notion of progress. The English have often argued a similarity between themselves and the Romans and this is part of the basis for the progressive theory of Romanisation.

Over the past sixty years a vast body of research has been undertaken which suggests that Victorian and Edwardian notions of progress and social evolution can no longer be considered to be valid. This critique of progress should cast doubt on the image of national stability and that of the inheritance of the imperial spirit. Some Victorians were critical of notions of progress[113] and the critical attention addressed to this idea has increased since 'the fall of the British Empire'. The period since 1960 has been a time during which other academic disciplines have become increasingly critical of such teleological and progressive accounts. Much of this criticism derives from those studying the subjects of recent imperialism, but there is a growing amount arising from the descendants of those actually subjected to imperialism.[114]

Hoogvelt, for instance, has written: 'Eighteenth- and nineteenth-century evolutionism expounded an optimistic idea of human progress which the twentieth century, having witnessed two world wars, the atom bomb, and the ruthless extermination of entire races could no longer accept.'[115] As a result, evolutionary theory in the social sciences gave way to neo-evolutionary theory, development theory and other more critical forms. Increasingly many have suggested that western imperialism has created a state of 'underdevelopment' which assisted in the economic exploitation of the victims of imperialism.[116]

The British Empire has now gone, but it can be argued that many of the images which formed imperial discourse still remain in British society in general and in Roman studies in particular. This book has directed critical analytical attention towards the subject because times have changed and the attitudes of scholars in many fields regarding the concept of progress have altered with them. Through its contribution to British imperial discourse, Roman archaeology in Britain has in the past contributed modestly in maintaining the world-order in which these unequal relations exist. Yet, until the late 1970s, 1980s and 1990s, archaeologists dealing with the Roman period did not attempt critical assessments of the assumptions on which Roman archaeology is based.[117] The vast majority of academic publications remain unwilling to indulge in debate about the origins of Roman archaeology, and their authors often appear to consider that the answers to the Roman past are straightforward and easily knowable.

Roman archaeology in Britain has grown up in the context of imperial discourse and it is time for a critical re-evaluation of the approaches that derived from our imperial past. The inheritance of the simple ideas of social change that lie behind Roman archaeology suggested to me back in the early 1980s that a critical assessment of our interpretations of Romanisation would be profitable; this provided the motivation for the research which has resulted in the writing of this book. Romano-British archaeology now needs to move forward and to build new ideas that are not imbued with the same simplicity of direction and lack of critical, self-reflective, assessment as expressed by past approaches to Romanisation. Those undertaking archaeological analysis and the writing of archaeological texts might indeed seek in future to attempt to challenge the images of linear national history which exist in society by demonstrating that there is actually a wide variety of alternative readings of the past.[118]

In this context, members of a post-imperial generation have now begun to produce interpretations which move beyond the type of explanation involved in paternalistic views such as those explored above; views which express the idea that 'the Britons did what they were told by the Romans because it represented *progress*'.[119] These accounts are beginning to challenge the over-simple interpretations of progress which lie behind past approaches to Romanisation. Some of these approaches have begun to show that many of the people of Roman Britain were denied their own history through the writing of the works of progressive Romanisation.[120] A number of relevant studies over the past few years are beginning to move Roman archaeology into new and fertile territory.[121] The relevant studies are united by an attempt to look beyond the simplistic dual categorisation that has been fundamental to accounts of Romanisation. I shall return to this topic in another study rather than addressing these works here.

At the same time, changes in the nature of British field archaeology in the past thirty years have led to an alteration in the nature of the Roman sites which are being investigated (Table 10.3). In recent years, the number of non-villa settlements that have been excavated has surpassed the number of villas. This demonstrates a change in the practise of archaeology that is resulting in the excavation of a more varied range of sites. This should in time produce the evidence to construct new accounts that take a wider view across the social spectrum of the Romano-British population.

Is the change in the proportion of sites that have been excavated adequate? I have calculated that in areas of the southern British countryside where villas occur, no more than 15 per cent of the settlements are villas and at least 85 per cent are non-villa settlements.[122] A small percentage of the settlement is therefore still receiving far more than its share of the excavations. We still do not have an adequate sample of non-villa settlements on which to base an informed understanding of the Roman province.[123] Further work will be required to address this imbalance if we are to be able to build convincing new ways to understand the archaeology of Roman Britain.

11

CONCLUSIONS

'Island stories'[1]

Introduction

My starting point in this book has been to suggest that the British and Roman Empires were very different in organisation and development and that the use of the Roman Empire to form an analogy for the British has stretched and distorted the archaeological and historical evidence. I have contended that many of the apparent similarities between the two imperial situations are a result of the British borrowing ideas from the Roman imperial context, and do not constitute some form of direct imperial inheritance.

One of the aims of this book is to draw attention to the linear connections which have been drawn between periods so far apart in time; I have also attempted to indicate how these connections have influenced our understanding of the pre-Roman and Roman past. A close relationship was held to have existed between the English and the Romans. This relationship presumably provided the reason for the observation made in the Preface of this book regarding the feeling among some present-day academics that challenging the role of the Roman Empire as a force for good is also an attack on the British imperial mission.

The starting point for much of the discussion of Rome and Britain in this book is the perception that archaeological research has served a range of purposes in the context of the definition of British imperial thought. Through this action, Roman archaeology has become implicated in the creation of imperial discourse. The use of the image of the Roman Empire and that of native resistance in the context of British imperialism and nationalism is far from unique in the European context. The image of Rome as the ancestor of western civilisation is common to a range of European countries whose area had formed part of the Roman Empire. For instance, people in France, Germany and Italy, among others, drew upon the Roman image at various times.[2] Images drawn from the resistance of native heroes to Rome are also common to a wide range of countries. The use to which the valiant Celtic leader Vercingetorix was put by Napoleon III during the nineteenth century and the use of imperial Rome by Mussolini in the creation of Italian imperial discourse have been considered above.[3] I have, however, focused the study of imperial discourse in this book on England, the country of my own origin.

A summary of three themes

To conclude this book, I wish to summarise the three themes that I have drawn upon in my discussion of imperial discourse. The themes are: Imperialism; Englishness; and Romanisation.

Each does not form a clearly defined and distinct area of thought operating at a distinct time. In fact, each theme contains a range of ideas that were sometimes used in combination and sometimes in isolation. They interacted in a variety of ways and were called upon in different contexts throughout English history.

Imperialism

I have shown that the English often identified themselves with the classical Romans. This identification resulted from a number of factors. The classical literary sources formed a core element of the education of gentlemen; Greek and Roman authors talked in the first person to the English gentleman. In addition, it appears to have been of vital significance to a range of writers that the Roman history of England drew the ancient Britons of the south and east into the ambit of Mediterranean civilisation. This enabled the English to push further forward the 'boundaries of civilisation'. During the English expansion into Scotland in the eighteenth century the invaders felt themselves to be fulfilling a role comparable to that of the first- and second-century Roman army – pushing forward the frontier with the barbarians.

The Roman Empire had an ambiguous image in the early to mid-nineteenth century because of its associations with contemporary French despotism. A growing association between the English and the Romans in the late nineteenth century, however, fed the definition of the newly reinvented concept of imperialism. At this time earlier images were redefined and received new emphasis. England, it was argued, was the heir to the Roman imperial mission and also to the civilisation of ancient Rome. The Roman occupation of southern Britain had introduced civilisation – including roads, towns, laws, government, taxes, an organised army and Christianity – to England. The English had exported civilisation to the Scots and also used their inheritance to great effect by making the British Empire the next great world power in succession to Rome. Britain was thus exporting this inherited civilisation to vast new areas of the globe. The Christian inheritance, in some relevant accounts, appears to provide part of the context for inherent teleology. Rome enabled the British to achieve salvation; the British were seen to be exporting salvation to the non-Christian areas of their empire. According to some works, therefore, Britain and Rome had a strong religious purpose in their imperial activities that presumably formed part of the 'divine plan'.

The inheritance of the imperial mission also caused some concern. In a linear conception of history, Britain could be seen to have inherited from and improved upon the Roman example. From a more cyclical perspective, however, Britain might take a warning from the decline and fall of earlier empires. It was difficult for many Victorians to accept the inevitable decline of their own empire, although with the rise of Germany this came to be seen as a possibility. In the early years of the twentieth century, the image of decline and fall became a significant element in the view of Britain as the heir to Rome and was drawn upon extensively by a wide range of writers.

The most dramatic indication of the imperial value that was attributed to the classics during this time was the appointment of a number of imperial administrators and politicians to the presidency of the Classical Association (including Cromer in 1909–10 and Baldwin in 1926). The perceived value of the classics to the education of the imperial élite has been explored in detail above. Archaeology formed a useful sideline to the classics. It provided detailed information on imperial frontiers and the process of the assimilation and incorporation of natives (which, under Mommsen and Haverfield, became the theory of Romanisation). At the same time the imperial role of Roman archaeology caused early twentieth-century military men and administrators to take serious notice of the new academic discipline.

I have suggested that the importance of decline and fall to the study of the history of the development of archaeological theory lies in the contribution made by Haverfield, W.T. Arnold and others

158

to a widespread Edwardian search for imperial lessons. Late nineteenth- and early twentieth-century British imperial concerns focused archaeological attention on certain valuable topics of research.[4] In turn, the knowledge derived from archaeology and ancient history, both in Britain and abroad, was seen to be useful in the context of Britain's own imperial mission.

Englishness (and otherness)

We have seen that during the Hanoverian military operations in Scotland there was a tendency amongst the English to see the occupants of northern Britain as being in the guise of the ancient 'barbarians' with whom Roman imperialists came into contact in northern Europe. The population of the periphery of the British Isles was felt to have inherited the character of the ancient peoples who lived there. This idea drew upon the image of a united and historically-coherent barbarian society, which was used as a way of uniting peoples far apart in time by drawing upon classical images of the Celts. This image of the threatening barbarian at the edge of the civilised world was also used to help to justify the military campaigns that were fought against these people.[5]

The identification of these barbarian 'others' formed part of the way by which the English defined themselves at this time. When the English travelled overseas they carried ideas of the relationship between Romans and natives in the Roman Empire with them and also used classical inspiration to inform their imperial actions. In this process the concept of the barbaric 'other' was often transferred by the British to the native peoples of parts of the world which the Greeks and Romans never reached;[6] Cowper's 'regions which Caesar never knew' from his poem on Boadicea.

In the late nineteenth and the early twentieth centuries Roman Britain came to be viewed as an historical parallel for British India, with the ancient British in the guise of what I have termed the 'Celtic subalterns'. This image derived its strength from the perceived inheritance through classical education of Roman civilisation by the English, and also from the subservient position into which the 'Celtic' population of ancient Britons tended to be placed at this time. The Teutonic image of English origins, to which many adhered at this time, allowed a clear racial distinction to be drawn between the ancient Britons and the contemporary English, descendants of the Anglo-Saxon. The ancient British were considered to be the ancestors of the Welsh and Scots, not of the English.

This idea of Roman Britain as the home of resident but racially distinct Roman settlers living in 'stations' surrounded by a population of savage barbaric Celtic subalterns had a strong influence on nineteenth-century antiquarian studies. The image of the Celtic subaltern, through a circular process of antiquarian and archaeological practice, perhaps assisted in reinforcing the identification felt by the English with the Romans and led to the use of the Roman Empire as a provider of imperial lessons. The excavations undertaken on Roman villas, forts and towns in the nineteenth century uncovered the remains of Roman stations that were interpreted as the homes of the Roman equivalent to the British officers in India. The nature of the Teutonic origin myth meant, however, that for many Victorians any association between the Englishman and the Roman was derived from the classical nature of education, the inheritance of western civilisation and an imperial mission; it was not related to any from of genetic relationship. As we have seen, however, the image of a Roman racial contribution to the character of the English developed in the late nineteenth and early twentieth centuries.

A number of Victorian and Edwardian authors sought to establish this type of direct racial connection between ancient Romans and the contemporary English. While the ancient Britons where represented as a type of ancient subaltern, racially and culturally distinct from the ruling Romans, there was no easily defined area of racial encounter between the civilisation of the classical Romans and the modern English. As the idea of the Celtic subaltern went into decline, many late nineteenth- and early twentieth-century works struggle with the problem of how a modicum of Roman civilisation might have been transferred from the ruling Romans to the subservient British population.

For instance, we have seen that Coote, in two books published in 1864 and 1878, argued for the passing of classical civilisation (and Christianity) on to modern England through racial inheritance. The idea that Britain's imperial greatness arose as a result of the mixing of races which created the island race was developed in a significant way in a range of works which drew upon the inspiration of Coote's account. A political need had developed to replace the Teutonic image of origin – a narrowly English image – with one that could encompass the whole of the United Kingdom. This new image could also be extended to encompass the white peoples of the Empire and developed as a form of opposition to the German menace.[7]

It could be argued that this image of mixed racial origins was rather less exclusive than the Teutonic myth. In time, however, it came to be inward-looking and exhibited strongly nationalistic overtones. The mixed spirit of the English was often connected with the idea of Britain's imperial greatness. The complexity and variety of the English character were considered to have been particularly suited to the duties of imperial rule. The representation could draw upon both the valiant spirit of ancient British resistance and the civilisation and imperial spirit introduced into England by Rome. This is because, in the myth of mixed racial origins, there was room for the gifts provided by the various races that were felt to have contributed to modern England. In these accounts the native Britons provided a brave spirit of resistance to foreign invaders; the Romans a superior civilisation, bath-houses, roads, taxes and so on; the Anglo-Saxons a love of freedom and a healthy attitude to family life; and the Normans order and government, etc. In this progressive image of national origins, it was often only the positive elements of racial character which were considered to have been passed on from former races to the English. The perceived barbarity of Boadicea and the Anglo-Saxons and the despotism of the Roman Empire were not conceived to be relevant to the current political position or character of England and the English.

Haverfield provided a seminal account that allowed Edwardian and later authors to imagine the creation of a Roman civilisation in Britain, which included the native élite of the province in addition to resident peoples from other provinces. The power of his work was that it broke the image of the Celtic subaltern in many minds and caused the gradual abandonment of the concept, at least so far as the south and east of the province was concerned. Haverfield's work on Romanisation was recruited as part of the representation of the racial mixing which created the English race. This transferred Roman civilisation could then be used by other thinkers more effectively to explain the civilisation and the imperial character which the Romanised ancient Britons passed on to England through racial inheritance.

Romanisation

Progressive interpretations of Romanisation helped the English to understand their place in the world; this was achieved through the image of the incorporation of Roman civilisation into the English character. Haverfield's comments on the devastating effect of the

Anglo-Saxon invasion suggest that if he had lived longer he might well not have approved of the way in which his interpretation of Romanisation was appropriated by Baldwin and others during the 1920s. Owing to the European dimension of Roman culture, accounts of Romanisation have not always pursued a directly nationalistic line. This is due to the fact that it is possible to conceive that the classical civilisation of Rome was actually reintroduced to Britain from Europe after the perceived crisis of the 'Dark Ages'.[8] We have also seen, however, that popular and political works, and on occasions academic works, developed the idea of the English inheritance of classical Roman civilisation in a specifically nationalistic manner.

I have discussed the relationship that exists in a number of the works inspired by Haverfield between the theory of Romanisation and contemporary ideas of progress. Theories of progress have developed in Europe since the Enlightenment and, although they have drawn upon classical origins, the classical Romans had no comparable concept. I have argued that, in the context of Edwardian and early twentieth-century Britain, concerns about national identity and imperial destiny drove academics to use terms such as 'advance' and 'improvement' in their accounts of the 'progress' of 'civilisation' that was introduced to Britain by the Romans. In these accounts the Romans were compared to the educated modern man while the unromanised native Briton was seen in the guise of the 'other'. Haverfield's definition of a 'military district' in Roman Britain allowed the image of the Celtic (or the native) subaltern to survive well into the twentieth century for the north and west of Britain.[9] The theory that Roman civilisation was inherited by the English thus appears to have allowed twentieth-century writers to continue a long tradition which represented English identity in contradiction to the Celtic (or native) 'other'. The Roman contribution to the character of the British has often been felt to focus distinctly upon the English and Haverfield's Roman archaeology did not seek to contradict this idea.

Island stories

The argument of *continuity* from the Roman past to the nineteenth and twentieth centuries in the British context is the result of the use of the classical past to provide lessons for modern society. My review of late Victorian, Edwardian and later texts suggests that two factors came to be felt to be fundamental in the inheritance of

162

traditions from the Roman past. The first factor was the geographical connection between the ancient donor and the modern recipient,
while the second factor related to a proposed direct racial connection between the two populations. The supposed racial connection
between Britain and Rome that was created through the Roman
conquest and domination of Britain came to be of particular interest
to a range of authors in the late nineteenth and early twentieth
centuries. This connection led to writers placing a particular
emphasis on the Roman archaeological monuments of the province.

Few of the Roman literary sources that deal with Britain addressed
the native population. Those Roman authors who did write about
the ancient Britons produced accounts that often appeared to be
dismissive and critical.[10] The classical account provided a picture
of peoples who were often felt by Victorians and Edwardians to
resemble the natives of their own Empire. Such accounts, and the
experience of various native peoples in the British Empire, had
helped to create the Victorian notion of the Celtic subaltern. The
image of the ancient Britons changed to a more positive one in the
late nineteenth and early twentieth centuries. At this time, the study
of the Roman monuments of Britain – the forts, roads, cities, towns
and villas – promised a direct contact with the civilised Romans of
Britain. The classical literary sources did not provide clear evidence
for a civilised Roman culture in Britain, but the Roman monuments could be used for this purpose. The increasing relevance of
Roman archaeological monuments to English national history may
partly explain the growing fascination with Roman archaeology
during the 1900s through to the 1930s and beyond. As a consequence, Romanisation studies have been pursued to an extensive
degree in the twentieth century because of the desire to establish
lines of continuity in national history.

Popular accounts of Englishness often focused on the racial spirit
of national life – the idea that the English have inherited their
national spirit from people who have lived in the country in the past.
In a search for national origin, the concerns and images of the present
were projected back into the past. Roman archaeology was recruited
directly as part of this discourse.

Archaeologists have on occasions attempted to dismiss popular
images of Roman Britain that sought to project nationalistic concerns.[11] It is an irony, however, that academic texts also focused
upon national concerns. The idea of Romanisation provided the
context for the reaffirmation of a mythical continuity in national
history over a long period. Romanisation defined a progressive idea

by which civilisation was introduced to the English by the Romans and this idea could be assimilated with ease into the agenda of those searching for the origins of national life as a root of contemporary stability.

Academics and the general public inherit unquestioned assumptions about the stability and permanence of national life. Collingwood contributed directly to the images of the stability of English domestic life,[12] but Romano-British studies also have a rather less obvious legacy. David Braund has argued that Romano-British scholarship has often been no less an island than its subject.[13] By and large, Britain has formed the preserve for a clearly defined group of scholars who conduct work of a specific type which is cut off to an extent from broader classical scholarship. Braund's comments echo those of Rivet's about popular images of Roman Britain as a nation state (p. 107). Popular images conveyed a picture of a province so British that no Roman would dare set foot in it and archaeological theory has perhaps been developed upon a broadly comparable basis. I feel that both the popular images and the archaeological interpretations reflect a common character, a concern with English national origins. Romanisation studies in the first seventy years of the twentieth century can therefore be argued to have contributed to English imperial discourse as part of a broad range of images which have been used to justify and support the superiority of England and the West. The continuity in Romano-British archaeology of this type of explanation into the 1990s is evident from the review of my book *Rural Settlement in Roman Britain* (1989), which was considered in the Preface of this volume.

Progressive views of national history therefore continued to inspire images of Roman Britain during the 1990s. The focus of this book has been upon the use of Roman archaeology as imperial discourse – the ways in which the Roman past has been used in the definition of imperial purpose. The idea that much of the imperial legacy lives on in modern British society has been discussed above,[14] and continuity in the theory of Roman archaeology can be viewed in this light. Nevertheless, I consider that times *have* changed and that Roman archaeology no longer needs to reflect imperial lessons. We need to distance ourselves to a greater degree from the accounts that see the past as a direct forerunner of the present. I do not consider it useful to perceive history as a process in which the past existed merely as an evolutionary stage in the development towards our present society. In this context it is vital to examine the archaeological evidence from Britain in the context of the Roman Empire in general if we are to avoid a nationalistic emphasis in building our future accounts. Romano-British studies require to be reintegrated into classical archaeology,[15] but we also need to beware of linear accounts of the development of European civilisation from an imagined Roman past.

NOTES

PREFACE

1 For instance, Daniel (1950); Piggott (1966, 1976) and Smiles (1994).
2 For exceptions see Potter (1986) and S. Johnson (1989a).
3 For particularly useful accounts of imperial identity see Eldridge (1996), Mackenzie (1984), Judd (1996) articles in Mackenzie (ed.) (1986a) and P. Marshall (ed.) (1996a). For English and British identity see Daniels (1993), Colley (1992), Colls and Dodd (eds) (1986), Robbins (1998) and Samuel (1998). Other relevant accounts are mentioned below.
4 See pp. 6–9 for a definition of imperial discourse and pp. 96–7 for a discussion of 'Englishness'.
5 Brunt has considered how modern conceptions of imperialism have influenced ancient history (1964, 268), while Turner has discussed how a perceived analogy between Britain and Rome has impacted upon modern accounts of the ancient world (1993, 231). For an up-to-date discussion of associated issues see Stray (1998).
6 For instance, Scholte (1970; 1981); Diamond (1974; 1975); Wolf (1972); and Diamond et al. (1975).
7 For earlier attempts to discuss some of these issues see Hingley (1989, 2–3; 1991; 1993; 1995a; and 1996).
8 Stray has produced a thorough survey of the role of the classics in English society from 1830 to 1960 (1998). He has discussed the way in which the decline of the classics was formally completed when the Universities of Oxford and Cambridge abandoned a long-standing insistence on a qualification in Latin for entrance at the end of the 1950s (ibid., 12). This was the end of what Stray has called a kind of 'Indian summer for the classics' (ibid., 293).
9 See P. Marshall (1996c) and Judd (1996) for the dismembering of the British Empire.
10 Millett (1990a, xv).
11 C. Thomas (1990, 184).
12 See Freeman (1997b) for the lack of any direct association between modern and ancient imperialism.
13 For instance, Raychaudhuri (1996, 358).
14 For the value of colonial discourse theory in the context of Roman

archaeology see J. Webster (1995); Hingley (1995a); Webster and Cooper (eds) (1996) and Mattingly (1997). For general works on colonial discourse theory see p. 6.

15 Samuel (1998, 76).

16 For the Theoretical Archaeology Conference see individual contributions to E. Scott (ed.) (1993); Rush (ed.) (1995); Cottam *et al.* (eds) (1995); Meadows *et al.* (eds) (1997), Forcey *et al.* (eds) (1998); Laurence and Berry (ed.) (1998) and Leslie (ed.) (1999).

17 For instance, J. Webster (1995); Hingley (1995a, 1996); Barrett (1997); S. Jones (1997) and Mattingly (1997).

18 See particularly Freeman (1991, 1996 and 1997a).

1 IMPERIAL DISCOURSE

1 Relevant works produced by women would appear to be considerably less common than those by men at this time. It is of interest that a bias towards men is evident in the current employment structure of Roman academic studies; see E. Scott (1993a; 1998) and this appears to reflect the Victorian and Edwardian pattern.

2 Smiles (1994, 1). A range of differing concepts of identity, of which Rome is one, has been drawn upon in the English and British contexts – for instance, Trojans, Celts, ancient Britons, Greeks, Romans, Anglo-Saxons, Vikings and Normans. Some of these images form specific origin myths and some form rather more general historical analogies of varying types. For the Trojans see Kendrick (1950) and MacDougall (1982). For the important Teutonic or Anglo-Saxon image see MacDougall (1982), Stocking (1987, 62–4) and Smiles (1994, 113). For the role of the Celts see Chapman (1992), and Sims-Williams (1998). Chapman (1992, 131–4) considers the relationship. of the Celtic image to the Germans. The image of Greece was also used actively to help to define British identity as a result of a perceived historical continuity in Western history, although Greece never had an active impact on the British islands (see Cross (1968), Turner (1981 and 1989) and Jenkyns (ed.) (1980)). For the comparative lack of work on the image of the Vikings, the Normans and later historical images, see for instance, Black (1997). This present book is concerned primarily with the uses to which the image of classical Rome has been put, although certain aspects of ancient British/'Celtic' and Anglo-Saxon identity will also be considered where these are relevant to the definition of imperial discourse.

3 Smiles (1994, 1).

4 (1998, 14).

5 *Ibid.*

6 The character of the relationship. of the English, Scots, Welsh and Irish to each other through time is a complex one (see, for instance, Colley (1992); Grant and Stringer (ed.) (1995); Matless (1998, 17); Robbins (1998); and Samuel (1998, 3–73)) and not a topic that is discussed in detail in this book. Much of the material considered relates to English origin myths rather than those of the Irish, Scots or the Welsh and images of origin relating to the area that some English writers have

titled the 'Celtic periphery' will only be considered where they relate specifically to topics of relevance to English self-identification.

7 Braund (1996, 179) and Laurence (1998, 6).

8 Stobart (1912, 3); Turner (1999, 173) and Vance (1997, 16).

9 Victorian novels which focus upon Christianity in the Roman Empire have been discussed by Turner (1999). For the introduction of civilisation see below.

10 In the context of Europe, Pagden provides a summary of the use of the image of Rome during the sixteenth to the eighteenth centuries in France, Spain and Britain (1995). Moatti has considered a variety of ways in which the image has been used in a number of countries (1993). Vance has looked at the ways in which the Victorians used Rome (1997), while the volume of articles edited by Edwards (ed.) (1999) examines various perspectives on the use of the image of Rome in a number of eighteenth- to twentieth-century European countries. A range of authors have provided summaries of late Victorian and Edwardian conceptions (see Chapter 2, note 35). Wyke has studied cinematic images of Rome in twentieth-century Italy and America (1997). Other relevant references to the use of the image of Rome in Britain and elsewhere are included below.

11 See for instance, Edwards (1999a), Moatti (1993), Pagden (1995) and Vance (1997).

12 See, for instance, Church (1895), MacGregor (1912), Turner (1999), Unstead (1957) and Wyke (1997).

13 See, for instance, Church (1887), Henderson (1929), Henty (1887) and (1893), Treece (1954), Sutcliff (1954; 1978).

14 Vance (1997, 236).

15 Samuel (1998, 81). See also Koebner and Schmidt (1964, 135–65) and Judd (1996, 9). This is the period of Baumgart's 'Classical Imperialism' (1982, 3).

16 Eldridge (1996, 2); see also Mackenzie (1986b, 3) and Judd (1996, 139).

17 For significant works on colonial discourse see for instance, Said (1978, 1993); articles in Ashcroft et al. (eds) (1989), Williams and Chrisman (eds) (1993); Fabian (1983); Tiffin and Lawson (eds) (1994); N. Thomas (1994); Spurr (1993) and Cohn (1996). For an introduction see Ashcroft et al. (1998, 41–3). For a recent review of colonial discourse theory and the British Empire see Washbrook (1999).

18 Said (1978) and (1993).

19 (1993, 1–2).

20 A similar concept of 'imperial core ideology' is developed by Mackenzie in his important *Propaganda and Empire* (1984), while Vance occasionally uses 'imperial discourse' in his study (1997, 229). Rome has been used in the creation of imperial discourse in a range of other times and places (see, for instance, Stone (1999) on Mussolini and Italy and Losemann (1999) on Hitler and Germany).

21 Koebner and Schmidt have provided a detailed account of the changing meanings of the concept of imperialism between the 1840s and 1964 (1964).

22 Baumgart (1982, 1–2); Said (1993, 8).

23 (1964, xx).
24 J. Webster (1996a, 5); Ashcroft *et al.* (1998, 122).
25 It should be noted that for this reason in this book I will not adopt Said's distinction of the use of 'imperialism' for the ideological force and 'colonialism' for the practice of imperial expansion (1993, 8).
26 Baumgart (1982, 48–55) discusses some relevant subjects that are defined as imperial discourse in this text. See also Said (1993, 18–19).
27 For instance, see Eldridge (1996), Mackenzie (1984), Mackenzie (ed.) (1986a) and Samuel (1998, 74–95).
28 Symonds (1986, 25).
29 See, for instance, Eldridge (1996), Hynes (1968), Mackenzie (1984), Mackenzie (ed.) (1986a), Said (1993) and N. Thomas (1994).
30 Doyle (1986).
31 *Ibid.*
32 See Koebner and Schmidt's comments on propaganda at this time (1964, 280).
33 P. Marshall (1996c, 62).
34 (1993, 128).
35 Baumgart (1982, 10).
36 Samuel (1998, 82).
37 See Mackenzie (1984, 257); P. Marshall (1996d, 92) and Samuel (1998, 83) for the decline of the British Empire and the continuing role of literature during this period.
38 (1998, 123).
39 For some examples of the imperial discourse of classical Rome see, for instance, Alston (1996), J. Webster (1996b), Wells (1972, 3–14), Woolf (1998, 54–76) and Zanker (1988). Vance has considered some of the uses to which Roman imperial discourse was put by in Victorian times (1997). For works about Roman imperialism see Brunt (1964) and (1990), Garnsey and Whittaker (ed.) (1978), Millar (1967) and Wells (1972).
40 See, in particular Bernal (1987; 1994). See also the comments of Patterson (1997) on the role of Greece and Rome in the 'invention of western civilisation'.
41 For the classical input into education from 1500 onward see M. Clarke (1959). For Victorian classical education see education M. Clarke (1959, 74); Martindale (1992, 178), Vance (1997) and Stray (1998).
42 Betts (1971); Cross (1968, 35); Stray (1998) and Turner (1989, 63).
43 M. Clarke (1959, 74); Cross (1968, 35).
44 Cross (1968, 35); Symonds (1986). For the use of classical allusions in politics see Betts (1971, 151).
45 Symonds (1986, 1–2); see also Levine (1986, 137–40) and Stray (1998, 53–4). For an alternative interpretation of the relative importance of the classics to the training of members of the Indian Civil Service see Majeed (1999).
46 Turner (1989, 63).
47 (1998, 11).
48 Stray (1998, 47).
49 *Ibid.*, 10.
50 Bernal (1994, 119). See articles in Lefkowitz and Maclean Rogers (eds) (1996) for a number of responses to the main issues raised by Bernal.

51 For the classical definition of the barbaric other see, for instance E. Hall (1989); Romm (1992); Shaw (1983); J. Webster (1996b; 1999).

52 See Spivak (1988) for the use of the concept of the subaltern in colonial discourse theory. The concept is used widely in 'historical archaeology' (see Bond and Gilliam (1994) and M. Hall (1999). This use of the term draws upon the inspiration of the writings of Antonio Gramsci. For the general background to the dismissive views of the English about the 'Celts' of Ireland, Scotland and Wales at various times see, for instance, McDonald (1986, 335–6); Smiles (1994, 116–18); and Robbins (1998, 27). Sims-Williams (1998, 15) has considered the early eighteenth century contribution of Edward Lhuyd to the development of coherent view of Celtic society. Some English archaeologists and social anthropologists have attacked the value of the term 'Celtic' during the 1980s and 1990s (see particularly Chapman (1992) and archaeological works referred to in Sims-Williams (1998)). In a persuasive article, Sims-Williams has argued, however, that the concept of the 'Celt' has a degree of validity in the context of linguistic and historical study, as long as its limitations are acknowledged (1998). I will use the terms 'Celt' and 'Celtic' in this book when referring to the usage adopted by other authors, although I am not suggesting that the concept necessarily has widespread analytical significance within archaeology. I am grateful to Alex Woolf for the reference to Sims-William's article.

53 The writings of Caesar, Diodorus Siculus, Strabo and others portrayed a barbaric people, far removed from the civilisation of Rome (for a collection of these writings in translation, see Ireland (1986)). Mikalachki (1998, 4) has considered the reception of these classical sources by the English in the period after the Renaissance and has also discussed the wish for a more civilised image of the prehistoric past. For classical concepts of Britain see Braund (1996) and Stewart (1995).

54 Spurr (1993, 1).

55 For travel writing and anthropology see N. Thomas (1994) and Spurr (1993); for history see articles in Schwartz (ed.) (1996); for ancient history and archaeology see Webster and Cooper (ed.) (1996) and a number of the articles in Mattingly (ed.) (1997).

56 For a discussion of the general background to Haverfield's work and the influences that he derived from Theodor Mommsen, Henry Pelham and others, see Freeman (1996).

57 G. Macdonald provided a detailed note of Haverfield's life (1924b) from which this brief discussion is taken. Freeman (1997a) has also considered Haverfield's life and influences.

58 Richmond (1957, 1).

59 Frere (1988, 31). For other comments on the fundamental nature of Haverfield's work see also, for instance, Potter (1986); R. Jones (1987, 87); Freeman (1996; 1997a).

60 Including Freeman, Hingley and Laurence; see Freeman (1991; 1996; 1997a); Hingley (1991; 1995a; 1996) and Laurence (1994a).

61 Stray (1998, 136). See further on pp. 55–6.

62 Freeman (1996, 19).

63 Smiles (1994) and Levine (1986, 4–5).

64 See comments on W.T. Arnold and Francis Haverfield (below). For an additional example in another European country, see Dietler's comments about the ways in which archaeology served to legitimise the efforts of the French state in the nineteenth and twentieth century to draw upon the power of certain Iron Age monuments as 'memory factories' (1998). Also see comments on Mussolini's use of classical Roman archaeology (pp. 106–7).

65 Some of this work sought to break the popular link between the British in India and the Romans in Britain (see below, p. 91).

66 For instance, the writings of J.A. Hobson on imperialism (1902); see Eldridge (1996, 87–8). Also see Vance's comments on Robert Lowe and J.M. Robertson (1997, 228–9, 235).

2 REPUBLICANISM TO IMPERIALISM

1 Betts (1971); Harris (1993) and Stray (1998, 17).
2 Cross (1968), Jenkyns (ed.) (1980), Stray (1998, 17) and Turner (1981, 1989).
3 Betts (1971, 158); Edwards (1999a, 4) and Harris (1993, 247–8).
4 Vance (1997, 16).
5 See Huet (1999) for Napoleon's adoption of Augustan imagery and Koebner and Schmidt (1964, 1–2), Vance (1997, 141) for Napoleon III and British attitudes to the concept of 'imperialism'. See also Eldridge (1996, 14) and Turner (1989, 70).
6 Koebner and Schmidt (1964, 27–49).
7 Levine (1986, 82).
8 Sheppard (1861, 104–5).
9 Kingsley (1864, 17).
10 *Ibid.*, 37.
11 See Miket (1989) and Bidwell (1999) for discussion of Bruce and his work.
12 Bruce (1851, 40–1). See Smiles (1994, 144) for this reference.
13 Bruce (1851, 449–50).
14 Harris (1993, 247–8); Vance (1997, 233–4).
15 During the seventeenth and eighteenth centuries, politicians and others drew upon the political power of the image of the Roman Republic to help to define the British constitution. After the Restoration of the monarchy in (1660) people invoked Roman parallels in the hope of securing a Roman-style peace; see Jenkyns (1992, 5); Vance (1997, 11–12); Black (1997). Rome offered the historical image of a virtuous, flourishing and militarily successful commonwealth so long as she had remained a republic; see Porter (1988, 27–8). The particular value of the historical analogy in this context was an idea which was held dear by British republicans, that the despotic tendencies of central government could be held in check by the independent property holders of the nation (*ibid.,* 27). Associations were also drawn between the respective architectural traditions and in the creation of landscape gardens; see Turner (1989, 65–70); for the Roman contribution to post-medieval architecture see Summerson (1964). During the eighteenth century the Republican image continued to be of focal importance, although

occasional allusions were made to the British Empire as a successor to Rome; see Vance (1997, 12). In contrast to its Republican history, however, the Roman Empire was often felt at this time to provide an image of arid despotism, its patricians corrupted by luxury, its plebeians by 'bread and circuses'; see Porter (1988, 28).

16 See p. 91.
17 Koebner and Schmidt (1964, 1); Baumgart (1982, 2) and Vance (1997, 228).
18 Vance (1997, 228–32).
19 Eldridge (1996); Koebner and Schmidt (1964), Stray (1998, 23) and Vance (1997, 228) have discussed the context of this political development and the range of critical and supportive attitudes to the granting of the imperial title. For the context of the Royal Titles Bill in the broader adoption of the imperial cause by Disraeli see, for instance Morris (1973, 379–82). For Disraeli's (1879) speech in which he appears to have bowdlerised comments of Tacitus' to define Britain's purpose as *imperium et libertas* see Baumgart (1982, 76–7).
20 Baumgart (1982, 48).
21 Koebner and Schmidt (1964, 132).
22 Terrenato (1998, 21). See Freeman (1997a, 30) for the context of Mommsen's work in the light of events of Europe in 1848.
23 Koebner and Schmidt (1964, 185).
24 Baumgart (1982, 2).
25 (1964, xix).
26 *Ibid.*, xxi and 1; Baumgart (1982, 2).
27 (1971, 158).
28 *Ibid.*
29 Including the article by Monypenny, referred to below.
30 Seeley (1883, 237–8). Partly quoted in Betts (1971, 150).
31 *Ibid.*, 239.
32 Monypenny (1905, 5–6). See Turner (1993, 254) for the general context.
33 Seeley (1883, 238).
34 Levine (1986, 160).
35 The range of modern scholars who have considered the use of the image of Rome in late Victorian and Edwardian times include Betts (1971); Brunt (1964); Hingley (1991, 90–101; 1995a, 1996); Hynes (1968, 15–53); Laurence (1994a); Majeed (1999); Vance (1997); and Wells (1972, ix–x). See Stray (1998) for a discussion of relevant aspects of the study of classics.
36 Examples which are discussed in this book include Seeley (1883); Henty (1893); Lee-Warner (1894); Church (1896); Cramb (1900); Hobson (1902); Henderson (1903); Watson (1903); see Watson (1936, 104); Mills (1905); Monypenny (1905); Kipling (1906); Curzon (1907); Balfour (1908); Baden-Powell (1908); Sands (1908); Cromer (1908; 1910a; 1910b); Haverfield (1910a, 1911a, 1912a, 1914); Fletcher and Kipling (1911); Lucas (1912); Stobart (1912); Bryce (1914).
37 For instance, Windle (1923); Baldwin (1924; 1926); Weigall (1926); Blakeney (1927); Hughes (1927).
38 Cromer (1910a; 1910b); Lucas (1912) and Bryce (1914).

39 These lectures were presented in 1910, 1911, 1912 and 1913 (for their published versions see Haverfield (1910a; 1911a; 1912a; and 1914).
40 As was A. Weigall, whose contribution will be considered in a subsequent chapter.
41 Symonds (1986, 2) has discussed the role of Oxford University as the supplier of imperial administrators to the Indian Civil Service and other branches of the imperial administration and government.
42 Vance (1997, 9).
43 Smiles (1994, 1).
44 Betts (1971, 149–50).
45 Vance (1997, 269).
46 Betts (1971); Turner (1989, 75); Vance (1997, 269).
47 See Monypenny (1905, 8). Betts (1971) also quotes relevant works.
48 Church (1896, 222).
49 Bryce (1914); see also works reviewed by Betts (1971, 155).
50 Majeed (1999).

3 DECLINE AND FALL

1 (1999, 89).
2 See Hingley (1991; 1995a; 1996). Note that Phil. Freeman strongly disagrees with this point, as he does not see any political agenda to Haverfield's scholarship; see Freeman (1996, 30); this is discussed further below (p. 53).
3 Porter (1988); McKitterick and Quinault (1997, 1).
4 Porter (1988, 140); Black (1997, 217).
5 Porter (1988, 161).
6 *Ibid.*, 137.
7 See Vance (1997) for Victorian attitudes to the associated idea of decadence.
8 Eldridge (1996, 4) and Judd (1996, 136, 146).
9 Reynolds (1991, 9).
10 Eldridge (1996, 4).
11 *Ibid.*, 5–6. See also Doyle (1986).
12 Eldridge (1996, 5–6); Hynes (1968). The 'German Peril' is documented in newspapers from 1896 onward; see Baumgart (1982, 87). For the 'Cold War' between Britain and Germany, see Reynolds (1991, 66).
13 Reynolds (1991, 66–86); Eldridge (1996, 6–7); P. Marshall (1996c, 60–8).
14 Hynes (1968); see also, Bowler (1989, 196–200); Broks (1990).
15 Bowler (1989, 198); see also Majeed (1999) has also considered some aspect of the insecurity felt by the British over their own identity at this time.
16 Eldridge (1996, 7).
17 Vance (1997, 246).
18 (1900, 271). He also argued that the parallel was not exact (*ibid.*, 272).
19 Burrow *et al.* (1997, 340–1); Vance (1997, 57–8). Quinault has studied the impact of Gibbon on a range of late Victorians and Edwardians (1997, 318), including J. Bryce, whose contribution will be studied further below (pp. 45 and 49).

20 Watson's poem was republished in Watson (1936, 104).
21 Hynes (1968, 24).
22 Mills (1905). See Hynes (1968) for the context of Mill's book.
23 Hynes (1968, 24). For the context of the relationship of Britain to Japan at this time see Judd (1996, 146).
24 Mills (1905, iii–iv).
25 *Ibid.*, 1–3.
26 *Ibid.*, 12–13.
27 Baden-Powell (1908, 163). Quoted in Hynes (1968, 27).
28 Hynes (1968, 27); Eldridge (1996, 93).
29 Baden-Powell (1908, 240). There are further references to the decline and fall of the Roman Empire on pages 18 and 261–2 of this book.
30 Balfour (1908, 8).
31 See Hynes (1968, 30) for a full discussion of the morals which Balfour drew from the historical parallel.
32 Balfour (1908, 40).
33 (1911, 22).
34 See Mackenzie (1986c, 171) and Stray (1998, 8–11) for a discussion of Stobart's life and work.
35 Stobart (1912, 3).
36 *Ibid.*, 5.
37 See, for instance, Cromer (1910a, 14).
38 For Lucas, see Vance (1997, 222).
39 Lucas (1912, 156).
40 Symonds (1986, 44–5).
41 The *Classical Review* had been published since 1887, while the Classical Association was founded in 1903. See Stray (1998, 237 and 247–8) for the context of the Classical Association and *ibid.* (1998, 135) for the context of the *Classical Review*.
42 Cromer (1910b).
43 Cromer (1910a).
44 *Ibid.*, 1–2.
45 Haverfield (1910a, 105).
46 *Classical Review* 10 (1910, 105–7).
47 Published as Haverfield (1910a).
48 Haverfield (1911a). For a recent discussion of the context and significance of this address see Majeed (1999, 88–9).
49 Haverfield (1912a).
50 Haverfield (1914).
51 (1911a, xix).
52 *Ibid.*
53 *Ibid.*
54 (1910a, 105).
55 *Ibid.*, 106.
56 *Ibid.*
57 (1912a, 27–8).
58 See p. 35 for the context of this address.
59 (1911a, xviii).
60 *Ibid.*
61 *Ibid.*

62 *Ibid.*
63 (1905, 185–6).

4 DRAWING LESSONS FROM ROME

1 Wells has discussed the military origin of some of those who studied
  the military frontiers of Britain and Germany in the sixteenth to the
  nineteenth centuries (1996, 436) and further references are provided
  in his article. S. Johnson (1989a) and (1989b) has also considered the
  early history of Roman military archaeology in Britain. One particular
  case in which an ancient frontier systems was used to provide inspiration for military purposes is an Elizabethan text, written between
  1577 and 1594, which proposed the fortification of the English border
  against the Scots (Bain 1894, 300–2; quoted in Birley 1961, 23–4).
  The anonymous writer of this account wrote a letter to the Queen
  proposing that the border should be defended by an 'Inskonce' 80
  miles long. This was to be an earthwork, provided with encampments
  of soldiers at regular intervals. As an historical parallel, the writer
  quoted the examples of a Roman frontier work which was built against
  the Helvetii, a Greek frontier work constructed to keep out the Turks,
  and the '"Pightes Wall" in Northomberlande' – Hadrian's Wall. The
  Elizabethan author's description of the proposed frontier work has been
  taken by Birley as an indication that he did not have a detailed knowledge of Hadrian's Wall and had not read Camden's account. It does,
  however, demonstrate a general knowledge of Roman frontier systems
  in Britain and abroad (Birley 1961, 24). It also represents an example
  of an ancient monument serving as the inspiration for proposed
  military activity.
2 Vance (1997, 240).
3 Seymour (1980, 4 and 62–3).
4 *Ibid.*, 63.
5 See also Maxwell (1989, 8–10) and Tabraham and Grove (1995,
  11–12).
6 Earl of Ilchester (ed.), letters to Henry Fox (p. 9, 13–4), quoted by
  Black (1997, 217).
7 Forbes (1815, 298). Piggott has written about the parallels drawn
  between Rome and Britain in these eighteenth-century accounts (1965,
  229 and 278).
8 S. Johnson (1775, 51).
9 Similar suggestions continue well into the twentieth century. Piggot,
  discussing Forbes' comments argued that the early Iron Age in Atlantic
  Scotland continued until almost modern times (1965, 229). For the
  archaeological context of Piggott's suggestions see Parman (1990) and
  Hingley (1995b, 185).
10 See Grafton (1992) for the ways in which classical images of barbarians
  were used in encounters with native peoples during the expansion of
  Europeans into the New World. See p. 10 for classical views of civilisation and barbarians.
11 Chapman (1992, 125); Smiles (1994, 117).
12 Porter (1988, 30).

13 For the concept of a continuing Celtic identity see Stocking (1987, 62–3) and McDonald (1986, 336).

14 Vance (1997, 240).

15 It should be noted, however, that although Roy felt his archaeological surveying work to have some value in military terms, he also was at pains to point out that it formed 'the lucubrations of his leisure hours' (1793, ii). It would appear that the Roman element in this mapping was not directly state-sponsored.

16 See Bidwell's comments on medieval use of Vegetius' late Roman treatise *Military Institutions of the Romans* (1997, 110).

17 Sheppard (1861, 12).

18 S. Johnson (1989b, 120).

19 S. Johnson (1989a, 17–19; 1989b, 120) and Wells (1996, 436). J.C. Bruce's *The Roman Wall*, first published in 1851, was a milestone in the study of this major frontier.

20 See Kirk (1979) for the general context of British frontier policy in India.

21 Pelham (1911, 201–2); Haverfield (1911b). See also Strachey (1888). Haverfield's information on the monument was provided by Sir Alfred Lyall of the India Office.

22 Strachey (1888, 92).

23 *Ibid.*; Haverfield (1911b, 323).

24 Strachey (1888), 92.

25 Grant Duff (1876, 71).

26 Pelham (1911, 201); Haverfield (1911b, 323).

27 Roger Miket informs me that the frontier known as the Victoria Lines on Malta, which was built during the 1870s, may also be closely based on Hadrian's Wall (Roger Miket, pers. comm; for the Victoria Lines see Zammit, 1996). It is possible that a wide range of frontier systems of the British Empire derived inspiration from the traces of Roman frontier systems, but this topic requires further research. Other ways in which classical sources were used by the British in India included architecture inspired by the solid classical tradition. The Calcutta Government House, for instance, had a state dining room that was modelled on a Roman atrium and contained marble busts of the twelve Caesars (Metcalfe 1996, 239–40). Other buildings in India drew upon an association with Roman imperial power to stress that western society had ancient roots and had stood the test of time (*ibid.*; Majeed (1999, 109*)*. Later in the nineteenth century the British began to draw upon architectural forms more appropriate to the East in an attempt to project themselves as legitimate rulers.

28 (1997, 198).

29 S. Johnson (1989b, 120); Bidwell (1997, 23–4).

30 The Glasgow Archaeological Society's work at sites on the Antonine Wall is discussed by Maxwell (1989, 13). The Society of Antiquaries' work commenced with work at Birrens and Ardoch and spread to a number of Antonine Wall forts, see Maxwell (1989, 13–15); Bidwell (1997, 22).

31 Whittaker (1994, 2).

32 Bratton (1986, 80).

33 *Ibid.*, 40–1.

34 The focus on the period in which Magnus Maximus ruled Britain (383–5) is significant. This emperor, who was probably born in what is today Spain, overthrew the emperor of the west and for five years ruled Britain, Gaul and Germany from a base in Trier. He was remembered as the last of the Roman rulers of Britain and also the first independent ruler, from whom various Welsh dynasties claimed descent (Robbins 1998, 24–5). The focus that Kipling and other British writers place on the rule of Magnus Maximus presumably related to an interest in a perceived former period of perceived British nationhood. Another example is provided by Charles Lucas who wrote about the relevance of the period from 287–296, when Britain became a kind of separate Roman monarchy (1915, 6). See also Casey's (1994, 186–8) discussion of various eighteenth-century representation of the late third-century usurper Carasius as the leader of a British Navy.

35 Rivet mentions that the villa in this novel is likely to have been based on the example excavated at Brading in 1879–81 (Rivet, 1976, 7). Brading is also likely to have provided the inspiration for the villa in A.J. Church's novel *The Count of the Saxon Shore* (1887); see p. 67 for Church's novel).

36 Rivet (1976, 13). See Kipling (1906, 149) for these terms.

37 (1906, 154). Partly quoted by Carrington (1955, 381).

38 Rivet (1976, 5.) For the so-called Jameson Raid of (1895) see Judd (1996, 159–63).

39 Majeed (1999). See further p. 50.

40 See Wells (1972, ix–x).

41 See, in particular, W.T. Arnold (1906). See Symonds (1986, 32–3 and 90) for a discussion of the work of W.T. Arnold.

42 Fiddes (1906, 5–6).

43 Montague (1906, lxxix).

44 Letter from Sir Ian Hamilton to Mrs Ward, dated 18th May 1906, quoted in M. Ward (1906, cviii). See Symonds (1986, 32–3 and 90).

45 M. Ward (1906, cviii).

46 Curzon (1907). See Davies (1932) for the context of this work.

47 Curzon (1907, 54).

48 (1908, 17).

49 (1912, 61). He suggested, however, that the parallel might have some relevance for some British territories in India, South East Africa and New Zealand, but not for most of the Empire, where 'British trade and colonization have known no limits' (1912, 61–2).

50 (1914, 18–19).

51 These comments may well also have drawn upon the perceived parallel between the Roman control of Britain and the British in India, which will be considered further in the second part of this book.

52 Potter (1986, 75). Haverfield also visited the Roman frontier system in Germany and published notes.

53 For Pelham's contribution to Roman frontier studies see Pelham (1906).

54 (1911a, xix).

55 This was subsequently published as Haverfield (1914). I am grateful to Steve Dickinson for drawing my attention to this work.

56 Haverfield (1914, 433).
57 *Ibid.*, 434.
58 *Ibid.*, 435.
59 (1910b, 13).
60 As time progressed Haverfield's attitude to frontiers and war appears
   to have changed. In a public address to the Somersetshire Archaeological and Natural History Society towards the end of the Great War
   in 1918, the year before his death, he drew attention to the barbarity
   of Attila the Hun. He speculated that if Atilla had won his great battle
   with the Gauls in AD 451, the civilisation and heritage of Rome would
   have been destroyed (Haverfield 1918, xxxvi–xxxvii). Perhaps, in
   Haverfield's opinion, this would in turn have broken the historical link
   that united Rome with western civilisation. The barbarity of the Great
   War in which Haverfield lost most of his protégés (Collingwood 1939,
   120) was surely in Haverfield's mind when he made these comments.
61 That Bryce was one of the original members of the Roman Society (see
   p. 56) presumably suggests that he may have heard Haverfield's presidential address in 1911 and that he was aware of Haverfield's other
   comments on the Roman Empire and the British.
62 (1912b, 10).
63 Smiles (1994, 141–3).
64 Betts has considered Edwardian works which argued that the Romans
   excelled at what might today be called 'race relations' (1971, 156–7).
   See also Majeed's (1999) for a useful consideration of the nature of
   Edwardian accounts of Roman assimilation in the context of British
   imperial policy in India.
65 Bryce (1914); Cromer (1910a, 73–4); Lucas (1912) and Monypenny
   (1905). Cromer in his work also considers the activities of other
   European imperial nations.
66 Monypenny (1905, 6).
67 *Ibid.*, 6–7.
68 Koebner and Schmidt (1964, 219).
69 For instance, Henty (1893, 383). This parallel is discussed further on
   p. 90.
70 See Majeed (1999).
71 Thornton (1978, 50).
72 (1971, 156–7).
73 (1914, contents list and 58).
74 (1912, 100).
75 (1910a, 89–91).
76 Hogarth (1910, 113–14).
77 (1910a, 106).
78 *Ibid.*, 107.
79 *Ibid.*
80 Haverfield (1905, 186). See also (1912b, 12).
81 (1910a, 107).
82 (1905, 186).
83 (1914, 69–70).
84 For instance:

The nations and tribes that were overcome and incorporated by Rome were either, like the Greeks, the possessors of a civilisation as old and as advanced as was her own, or else, like the Gauls and the Germans, belonged to stocks full of intellectual force, capable of receiving her lessons, and of rapidly rising to her level of culture.

(Bryce 1914, 69)

These comments are very similar to observations made by Haverfield in his 1905 paper (see p. 186). Unfortunately, Bryce does not give a list of relevant publications and the inspiration for these comments may not have come directly from Haverfield's work.

85 Majeed (1999, 106). See L. Thompson (1989) and Goldberg (1993) for the absence of a modern concept of race in the ancient world. Goldberg also considers the rise of 'racist culture' from the sixteenth century onward.

86 A full account of relevant administrative analogies which were drawn by the British from the Roman Empire will not be presented in this book. Nevertheless, it can be said that a general interest in the relevance of the administration of the Roman Empire to the British present led several Edwardians to develop a focus on the role of Augustus in providing an administrative framework for the Roman Empire (Turner 1993, 257–8). The publication of three book-length biographies of Augustus between 1902 and 1914 is to be seen in this light (ibid., 258). The value of the view of the academic to the administrator is also indicated by regular reference to W.T. Arnold's book *Roman Provincial Administration*, and in Lucas' book *Greater Britain and Greater Rome* (for instance, Lucas (1912, 179)).

87 Lee-Warner (1894, 8).

88 (1908, 157).

89 Sands (1908, 157–60).

90 *Ibid.*, 158.

91 Fletcher and Kipling (1911, 244).

92 P. 28.

93 See Majeed's comments, quoted above, p. 28.

94 Hingley (1991; 1995a; 1996).

95 Freeman (1996, 30–1).

96 Haverfield quoted by M. Taylor (1960, 129). See also Freeman (1996, 30). Betts (1971, 151) and Stray (1998, 137) have discussed the founding of the Roman Society and its relationship to the Classical Association and the *Journal of Hellenic Studies*.

97 Haverfield (1912a, 28). Freeman does not discuss this paper.

98 Freeman (1996, 33).

99 It also appears to be relevant that the significant observations made about 'Englishness' by R.G. Collingwood during the 1920s (see pp. 97–8) were made in a book aimed at a popular audience (Collingwood 1923, 5) and in a popular pamphlet on the signal station at Scarborough (Collingwood 1925). Popular audiences would appear to have provided both Haverfield and Collingwood with a context in which they could express their feelings about the value of Roman archaeology to

contemporary society. These feelings are not expressed to the same degree by either author in their academic writings.

100 (1910a, 106). Referred to by Freeman (1996, 29).
101 *Ibid.*
102 (1912a, 27–8).
103 See p. 9.
104 (1910a, 105). For comparable comments see Haverfield (1911a, xviii).
105 Freeman (1996; 1997a).
106 Freeman (1996). See also G. Macdonald (1924b).
107 Symonds (1986, 1). See also Stray (1998, 247, note 33) for the founding of various academic societies in a range of fields between 1892 and 1907.
108 The *Classical Review* Volume 24 (1910, 103). See also the volume *English Literature and the Classics* (edited by Gordon in 1912) which is a collection of nine lectures presented during the winter of 1911–12 at the invitation of the Board of English studies at Oxford University and Stray's comments on the context of the classics in the early twentieth century (1998, 258–61).
109 (1911a, xx).
110 Vance (1997, 240).
111 Carrington (1955, 381). Partly quoted by Rivet (1976, 10–11).
112 Rivet (1976, 10–11).
113 (1923, 15).
114 (1976, 10–11).
115 See particularly his comments on Rosemary Sutcliff's work in the context; *ibid.*, 4.
116 Rivet (1976).
117 Wells (1972, x).
118 Whittaker (1994, 2–3). See also Wells (1996, 438).
119 *Ibid.*

PART II ENGLISHNESS

1 Majeed (1999, 108) has explored the problems of too close an identification between Roman Britain and the native population of colonised India at this time.
2 Cunningham (1986).
3 This view itself drew upon earlier concepts of English origins (see Colley 1992, 15).
4 See p. 30 for the 'German menace'.

5 TEUTONS, ROMANS AND CELTS

1 Bowler (1989, 51); Colls (1986); Levine (1986, 4); MacDougall (1982); Robbins (1998, 29); Samuel (1998, 23 and 68); Smiles (1994, 113–28) and Stocking (1987, 62–3).
2 Smiles deals particularly effectively with this topic and the context of these nineteenth-century developments with regard to early evolutionary views of Celtic society (1994, 116–20). See also Samuel (1998, 59).

3 Bowler (1989, 51); Stocking (1987, 62). See Edwards (1999b) for the idea of the inheritance of the political freedom of the barbarian Germanic tribes.

4 Samuel (1998, 68).

5 T. Arnold (1841, 32).

6 *Ibid.*, 35–6.

7 Sheppard (1861, 131).

8 (1864, 46).

9 *Ibid.*

10 Levine (1986, 80).

11 Stapleton has discussed the conflict between the Teutonic myth and the idea of the inheritance of a Latin tradition in the early twentieth century (1994, 75–6, 91).

12 (1905, 59).

13 Fletcher and Kipling (1911, 31).

14 O'Neil (1912, 14).

15 The popular historian Arthur Bryant perpetuated Victorian views by suggesting, in a book published in 1953 that the Anglo-Saxon form of government in England: 'was far simpler and freer than that of Rome ... It was a rough masculine creed, without much subtlety or refinement ... Yet it bred a sense of duty and responsibility without which no nation can be great and endure' (Bryant 1953, 42).

16 See Cohn (1996, 30, 67–70) and Edwards (1999b, 85–6) for the parallels which were drawn between the Roman Empire and the British Empire in India in the eighteenth century.

17 Haverfield (1912b, 19).

18 See p. 10 for the definition of the Celtic subaltern.

19 Haverfield (1912b, 19).

20 Thackeray (1843, 213).

21 *Ibid.*

22 *Ibid.*, 212–13.

23 (1887, 3).

24 See, for instance, Fletcher and Kipling (1911, 21–2), Henty (1893, 384) and Rait and Parrott (1909, 11).

25 (1883, 239). Green, amongst others, also drew a parallel between British India and Roman Britain (1900, 5).

26 Church edited and translated Tacitus and produced a range of novels and books. For other works produced by Church see Vance (1997, 205).

27 Church (1887, 286).

28 *Ibid.*

29 *Ibid.*, 304.

30 *Ibid.*, 304–5.

31 Haverfield and Macdonald (1924a, 84–7); Henig (1995, 186); Levine (1986, 98); Smiles (1994, 125).

32 Despite their apparently limited relevance to English history at this time, Roman remains often appear to have received a greater degree of public attention in Britain than in various countries on the Continent. Perhaps this was a result of the classical education of those who studied them (Haverfield and MacDonald 1924a, 84; Levine 1986, 79–84). During the nineteenth century, in the southern part of the

area which constituted the Roman province of *Britannia*, mosaic pavements were found and recorded (Haverfield and MacDonald 1924a, 84; Henig 1995, 177; Vance 1997, 23). A particularly important contribution was made by Samuel Lyson, with the publication of his *Reliquiae Britannico-Romanae* in three volumes between 1813 and 1817. Public attention sometimes followed when major discoveries were made. For instance, when a new mosaic was found in Queen Victoria Street in London in 1869, people came to see it in their thousands; it was later lifted for the new Guildhall Museum (S. Johnson 1989a, 25; Henig 1995, 187). The excitement which sometimes occurred in Britain at the discovery of mosaics and other objects was an expression of an international climate of interest in Roman remains (Henig 1995, 181). This resulted in part from the discoveries that were made during the excavation of the exceptionally well-preserved sites of Herculaneum and Pompeii in Italy (Levine 1986, 97–8; Henig 1995, 187). Goalen (1995) has discussed the discovery of Pompeii in 1763, the nineteenth-century investigation of the city and the effect of the investigation, and also due to the export market in valuable antiquities. No clear picture of the civilian area of Roman Britain emerged, however, from the discoveries that were made (Haverfield and MacDonald 1924a, 84–7). Roman military archaeology at this time has been discussed above (p. 42).

33 Windle (1897, 11). For comparable views about Roman Britain, see also Green (1900, 4–5) and Rait and Parrott (1909, 11).

34 Fletcher's views were so extreme that the Oxford University Press had misgivings when he approached them with a view to publication, but the involvement of Kipling made the volume irresistible. The book was an immediate success, being republished until 1954 and selling around 134,000 copies (Symonds 1986, 57–8). It was also an extreme book, of which the *Manchester Guardian* protested that 'as a work designed to influence the minds of children, it is the most pernicious we have seen' (quoted in Symonds 1986, 58).

35 Fletcher and Kipling (1911, 19).

36 *Ibid.*, 20.

37 A instructive example of imperial prophesy is provided by one scene in Young's book, *The Island* (1944), which concerns 'The Episode of the Garrulous Centurion'. This scene is set in AD 78 and concerns Caius Petronius, retired centurion of the Second Cohort Augusta, who has moved into the province and lives in retirement in a small villa in 'Middle England'. He utters prophetic words:

And I have often wondered why this empire
of ours should have more permanence that those
which rose and fell before us: Athens, Macedon,
Carthage and Egypt . . . Rome will not last for ever;
And if she withers like a stricken oak,
Maybe – who knows? – that what was best in her
May live in the lands where the acorns were scattered
In her green prime – perhaps even in this Britain
Which she despises. Sometimes I think I see

This Island as the ultimate sanctuary
Of ordered life – in which a new Deucalion
Shall ground his Ark upon a new Parnassus
To populate a world that has been drowned
Beneath barbaric floods with the old stock
Of homely, civil virtues.

(Young 1944, 50–1)

38 Coote (1878, v–vi).
39 *Ibid.*, vi.
40 *Ibid.*, vii–viii.
41 *Ibid.*, ix.
42 *Ibid.*, xi. Even Coote did not, however, wish to totally abolish the Teutonic myth as he adduced from his reading of the evidence that at the time of the Roman conquest the ancient Britons were actually Teutonic rather than Celtic. His writings, however, indicate that he held dismissive views about the ancient Teutons of Britain that contrasted with his positive views about the Roman inheritance (for instance, Coote 1878, 21).
43 *Ibid.*, 4–5.
44 For an account of the lack of continuity between late Roman and Anglo-Saxon urbanism see Ottaway (1992, 117–19).
45 See p. 91.
46 Koebner and Schmidt (1964, 326).

6 ANCIENT HEROES OF THE RESISTANCE

1 Vance (1997, 198). See also Smiles (1994, 148).
2 Bratton (1986, 79). See discussion of Henty, Fletcher and Kipling, below.
3 Locke (1878, 9); see also Bratton (1986, 80). Locke, a Scotsman, was educated in Edinburgh and wished to write a series of stories. It is strange from a modern point of view that this Scotsman wrote a book with a sub-title that refers to England as 'the land that we live in'.
4 Vance (1997, 198–201).
5 (1987, 40).
6 S. Macdonald (1987); Warner (1985, 49) and G. Webster (1978).
7 S. Macdonald (1987, 41). See also Warner (1985, 51), who makes much the same point.
8 Mikalachki (1998, 4).
9 See references to Coote's work above and also the discussion of the work of a number of additional authors in the next chapter.
10 Mikalachki (1998).
11 See Braund (1996, 132–46) for the attitudes of classical writers to Boadicea.
12 'Soft' and 'hard primitivism'; see Smiles (1994, 130).
13 Smiles (1994, 17 and 156–64).
14 Smiles (1994, 137).
15 Cowper (1782).
16 S. Macdonald (1987, 51).

17 Cowper (1782).
18 (1987, 51).
19 (1998, 117).
20 Mikalachki, however, has also noted a number of other more positive interpretations of Boadicea's patriotism during the seventeenth and eighteenth centuries (1998).
21 Smiles (1994, 44–5), 148; Vance (1997, 206–7).
22 S. Macdonald (1987); Mikalachki (1998).
23 S. Macdonald (1987, 52–3).
24 David (1995, 174).
25 David (1995, 52–3). See Mikalachki for rather similar observations about Queen Boadicea and Elizabeth I (1998, 129).
26 Smiles (1994, 45).
27 Boudica and Caratacus were two of a range of British national heroes, including medieval kings and knights and modern soldiers and imperial explorers, who received attention at this time (Bratton 1986).
28 Pp. 67 and 82.
29 For instance, C. Merivale and C. Puller's *School History of Rome*, published in 1877 and A.J. Church's *Stories from English History: from Julius Caesar to the Black Prince*, first published in 1895, H.E. Marshall's *Our Island Story*, published in 1905, C.M. Doughty's monumental and mythic poem *The Dawn in Britain* (1906), and E. O'Neil's *A Nursery History of England*, published in 1912.
30 Church (1887, 109–10).
31 Ackworth (1897–8, Scene VI). For the context of Elgar's work see Crump (1986) and Vance (1997, 212).
32 Kennedy (1977).
33 Dudley and Webster (1962, 126).
34 Thornycroft (1932, 62).
35 *Ibid.,* 69.
36 Treveylan (1900, xiii).
37 'Regions Caesar never knew/Thy posterity shall sway'.
38 Treveylan (1900, xi).
39 *Ibid.*, x.
40 *Ibid.*, xi.
41 For the context of this 'revival' see Judd's comments on the crisis in January 1900 and the response of the British (1996, 154). Despite Trevelyan's optimism, the Boer War continued until 1902 and was associated with a massive crisis of British self-confidence.
42 Trevelyan (1900, xi).
43 *Ibid.,* xii. My emphasis.
44 *Ibid.*
45 *Ibid.*, xiii.
46 *Ibid.*, 319.
47 *Ibid.*, 381.
48 *Ibid.*, 295.
49 *Ibid.*, xi.
50 In addition to the references below, see for instance *ibid.*, 272.
51 *Ibid.*, xii.
52 Collins (1900, xxxiii).

53 *Ibid.*, lxiv.
54 G. Webster (1978, 2). The same comments are attributed to V. Kiernan by Warner (1985).
55 S. Macdonald (1987, 53).
56 Thornycroft (1932, 69).
57 Thornycroft (1932, 69). See also Dudley and Webster (1962, 128).
58 See in particular Dietler's (1998) comments on Napoleon III and the construction of a 'memory factory' for Vercingetorix at Alésia in France. Silberman (1999) has discussed two additional sites which were the scenes of bitter defeats but have served, like Alésia in the process of national building (Masada and Little Bighorn).
59 Warner (1985, 49).
60 For the context of the 'Indian Mutiny' see, for instance, Judd (1996, 67).
61 Henderson (1903, 210). This work is referred to in Dudley and Webster (1962, 129).
62 Henderson (1903, 210).
63 *Ibid.*, 216.
64 Eldridge (1996, 68–71) and Mackenzie (1984, 210). See Vance (1997, 201) for an account of the novel *Beric the Briton*.
65 In addition to *Beric*, Henty also wrote other classical adventure stories, including *A Young Carthaginian or a Struggle for Empire: A Story of the Time of Hannibal* (1887), which contains comments on the beneficial value of Roman civilisation.
66 Henty (1893), especially pp. 382–3 for these final points.
67 See various sections of *Beric the Briton*. According to Mason (1982, 16), being conscious of one's status, consistency, integrity and obligation were the characteristics of a Victorian gentleman.
68 Henty (1893, 380). My emphasis.
69 (1911, 17).
70 Vance (1997, 201).

7 THE RISE OF A THEORY OF MIXED RACIAL ORIGINS

1 Vance (1997, 198).
2 Bowler (1989, 19); see also Levine (1986, 74). See also p. 151 for some exceptions.
3 Bowler (1989, 200–1).
4 *Ibid.*, 9. See Bowler's suggestion that the tension between progressionist and cyclical ideas of history enlivened the whole range of historical studies in the Victorian period. See also the comments of Stanley Baldwin quoted on pp. 101–2 for a later example of the same logic.
5 See Bowler for a discussion of Cramb (Bowler 1989, 57–8).
6 Cramb (1900, 262). My emphasis. Partly quoted in Bowler (1989, 57).
7 Stobart (1912, 5). For Stobart's life and work see p. 33.
8 *Ibid.*
9 (1915, 11). My emphasis. These comments drew upon earlier observations made by Mommsen which will be discussed below (p. 113) and also, perhaps, show the influence of the first year of the Great War.

10 Although Stobart and Haverfield considered that Britain was merely a part of a broader European civilisation some other authors at this time were less open-minded about the value of European civilisations outside the shores of Britain.

11 See p. 40.

12 (1911, 18–19).

13 See Smiles (1994, 140–4), where works of art of Victorian date which deal with the civilising of the British by the Romans are discussed.

14 Forsey (1997). See also p. 113 for the work of Mommsen.

15 P. 112.

16 Rhys (1882, 100).

17 *Ibid.*

18 Collingwood and Myres described this book as the work of a scholar (1936, 465).

19 Scarth (1883, 220).

20 *Ibid.*, 181.

21 *Ibid.*, ix.

22 Henty (1893, 380).

23 (1900, xiii).

24 P. 68.

25 See further on p. 107.

26 See pp. 127–8.

27 Scarth (1883, ix and 181).

28 (1883, ix).

29 For instance, see Conybeare (1903), Locke (1878) and Scarth (1883). The volumes by Scarth and Conybeare represent early accounts of the history of Roman Britain which shown a particular concern with the early history of Christianity, as befits book published by the Society for Promoting Christian Knowledge. See Vance (1997, 206–7) for the general context.

30 Seebohm (1883, x). He specifically mentions Kemble and Freeman.

31 *Ibid.*

32 *Ibid.*, 418.

33 Seebohm also suggested that English history did not begin with primitive Germanic freedom but was constituted by a 1200-year history of a growing freedom based on original serfdom; *ibid.*, 423–38.

34 Henty (1893, v–vi).

35 *Ibid.*

36 Green (1900, 234).

37 P. 78.

38 Vinogradoff (1905, 112–20).

39 (1907, 372).

40 *Ibid.*, 456.

41 (1915, 6). For the career of Lucas, see p. 34.

42 *Ibid.*

43 For Egerton's contribution see Symonds (1986, 51–3).

44 Smiles (1994, 127). See p. 30 for the stress caused by the expansion of Germany. In addition, a growing knowledge of the anthropology of

'primitive' society at this time created a more coherent understanding of the potential role of social evolution in Europe's past that that provided by extreme versions of the Teutonic myth (Smiles 1994, 127).

8 RACIAL MIXING AND THE ROLE OF ROME

1 Howkins (1986); Stray (1998, 173–9).
2 Giles and Middleton (1995, 8); Breese (1998).
3 Recent studies of Englishness include Breese (1998), Daniels (1993), Doyle (1986), Giles and Middleton (1995), Howkins (1986), Matless (1998), Samuel (1998) and Stapleton (1994).
4 Giles and Middleton (1995, 6).
5 (1998, 82).
6 For instance, Breese (1998), Daniels (1993), Doyle (1986) and Samuel (1998).
7 Daniels (1993, 32.)
8 *Ibid.*, 6.
9 Howkins (1986); Matless (1998).
10 A range of the relevant books focus on the southern English countryside and ignore the north and west (Breese 1998).
11 Giles and Middleton (1995, 7–8); Breese (1998).
12 Collingwood (1923, 100). See p. 93 for Rice-Holmes.
13 *Ibid.*, 101.
14 Collingwood (1925, 2). See Boucher (1989, 20) for a discussion of these comments.
15 *Ibid.*
16 (1939, 143). For Collingwood's analysis of this concept, see p. 136.
17 Collingwood's views were, however, clearly not shared by everyone at this time. The archaeologist Sir Ian Richmond published *Huddersfield in Roman Times* in 1925. In this work he argued that Rome had performed a major role in civilising Europe but that the civilisation had been lost in the Huddersfield area and only reintroduced by the Medieval monasteries (Richmond 1925, 10, 107).
18 Collingwood and Myres (1936, 465).
19 (1923, 225).
20 Baldwin (1867–1947) had been educated at Harrow and Trinity College, Cambridge, and was a cousin of Rudyard Kipling. He was Prime Minister of Britain several times between 1923 and 1936. Baldwin's *On England and the West* was a fundamental work in the development of the representation of Englishness (Breese 1998, 156).
21 See Baldwin (1924) and (1926, 1–9).
22 Baldwin (1924, 7).
23 See Chapter 4 for the Edwardian use of the image of decline and fall.
24 According to the Notes and News of the Classical Association, the thanks of the Association were voiced by Lord Finlay in 'enthusiastic language', although apparently Lord Sumner's touch of cynicism in seconding 'struck the wrong note' (Notes and News 1926, 1). Baldwin's address was published later in the same year under the title *The Classics and the Plain Man*.

25 Other relevant statements about the political value of the classics are not uncommon in the proceedings of *the Classical Review* and in other publications in the early part of the twentieth century. Baldwin was succeeded as President in 1926 by Lord Hewart of Bury, the Lord Chief Justice. Lord Hewart presented an address on 26 November on the topic of 'What do we owe the Classics?' (Notes and News 1926, 145). The writer of the Classical Association's Notes and News in 1926 concluded that:

> The real justification for the Classics lies in the list of those who have held the office of President ... and have confessed their faith in the Classics, culminating in the present year in the Prime Minister and the Lord Chief Justice.
>
> (*ibid.*)

Other papers delivered between 1909 and 1927 deal with associated topics, for instance, Nicklin (1909) and Blakeney (1927). Not all references to the classics were positive, as some felt that classical education did not form a good basis for an imperial career. A range of contrasting views are included, for instance, in the book *Classics and the Average Boy: a question for the nation* (1912). See Stray (1998, 259) for the context of this work. Positive references to the classics in their imperial role survive the 1930s (for the work of Grose-Hodge see p. 106). See also *Journal of Roman Studies* (1937) for the teaching of Roman archaeology and history in British schools and universities.

26 Baldwin (1926, 4).

27 *Ibid.* For the context of Baldwin's claim to be a 'common man' see D. Smith (1986, 263).

28 Baldwin (1926, 9).

29 *Ibid.*, 5.

30 *Ibid.*

31 *Ibid.*, 6.

32 *Ibid.*, 5–6.

33 Symonds (1986, 239–40).

34 Weigall (1926, 16).

35 *Ibid.*, 20. He did allow for a certain Anglo-Saxon and Norman admixing of blood but evidently wished to stress the connection of modern British populations with civilised Roman Britons.

36 Weigall (1926, 20).

37 *Ibid.*, 28.

38 *Ibid.*, 331.

39 *Ibid.*, 330.

40 Quoted in Matless (1998, 79).

41 Weigall (1926, 325).

42 *Ibid.*, 80.

43 *Ibid.*, 325.

44 Hughes (1927, 13). Hughes also suggested that the Germans and the Celts have no such ability (*ibid.*).

45 *Ibid.*, 13.

46 P. 72.

47 Hughes (1927, 14).

48 *Ibid.*, 13–14.
49 See Stray for the role of compulsory Latin from the 1920s to the late 1950s and its continued character as a 'paradigmatic exemplar of disciplinary virtue' (1998, 276–7). It is possible, however, to see the supportive comments on the value of the classics voiced in some contexts during the 1900s to 1940s in the form of a reaction to the steady growth of the study of English. The development of English at this time perhaps occurred at the expense of the classics. See Doyle (1986, 93) and Stray (1998, 237 and 258–61).
50 (1944, 10).
51 *Ibid.*, 68. See also references to republicanism and local government (p. 90), and comments on 'nationalism, religion and colour' (p. 105).
52 *Ibid.*, 10.
53 Mussolini's fascist Italy used the imperial Roman past during the 1920s to early 1940s; see Manacorda and Tamassia (1985); Stone (1999). Fascist symbolism drew very heavily on the idea of *romanità* in a variety of ways. Mussolini directed archaeological attention to the Roman-period monuments of Rome and Ostia, carrying out large-scale excavation of a range of important sites and also the reconstruction of monuments to Roman imperialism which could be used as a direct projection of his imperial ambitions. He ordered the rebuilding of Augustan Rome. In particular, the building of the *Via del Mare*, the Road to the Sea formed a symbol of the extension of Roman power toward the Mediterranean (Moatti 1993, 130–42).

   The idea of Italian racial purity was developed at this time; this stressed the superiority of the Italians over 'inferior cultures, notably those of English-speaking origin' (Quatermaine 1995, 211). Mussolini drew directly on the Roman imperial image during a speech in 1934 in which he argued that the Mediterranean should be 'converted from an Anglo-Saxon lake into a Latin sea' (quoted in Quatermaine 1995, 204).

   One particular action of Mussolini's was to arrange for four great marble maps to be set into the wall of the basilica of Constantine (Clark 1939, 199). These portrayed the growth of the Roman Empire from the city state of the eighth century BC to its maximum extent under the Emperor Trajan (AD 98–117), when Britain formed a part of the Empire. The maps were unveiled during the Abyssinian War in 1935 and a fifth was added in due course, displaying the empire of Fascist Italy in the fourteenth year of the fascist era (*ibid.*). Clark's work referred to *The Illustrated London News* as a source for many of Mussolini's actions and this demonstrates that the use of ancient Rome in Italian political action would have been well known to the British at this time. Clark's disapproval of these activities is clearly evident from his comments. In this context references to comparisons between the British and the Roman imperial missions become less popular in England during the 1930s and 1940s.
54 In terms of the response of ancient historians to the fascist menace, Wells and Turner have suggested that Syme's book *The Roman Revolution*, published in 1939 was deeply influenced by Mussolini's actions, for instance in its deliberate criticism of the actions of Augustus (Wells 1972, vii–viii; Turner 1993, 260).

55 Trigger has also written about the use of nationalistic and imperial archaeology in a number of societies throughout the world (1984). In particular, he has suggested that in England in the late nineteenth century there was a trend toward the idea that the pre-eminence of the country was a result of successive waves of invaders. He argues that this development was the result of the growing insecurity of the middle classes (*ibid.,* 364–5). Such a suggestion fits the interpretation offered in this book. The Teutonic myth of origin is an example of one of Trigger's nationalistic interpretations in that it attributed national greatness to ethnic and cultural purity. In this context the development of mythical history in late nineteenth and early twentieth century England moves the dominant image from a nationalistic to an imperialistic form.

56 Rice-Holmes' work is considered on p. 93. For an influential archaeological example of the theory of mixed racial origins, see for instance, the article published by Jacquetta and Christopher Hawkes in 1947 in the book *The Character of England* (edited by E. Barker). They argued that a Roman-British 'stock' were derived from the earlier settlers of Britain. This people became mixed with the: 'more purely Germanic Anglo-Saxons and Scandinavians, [which] under a final hammering from the Normans was to fuse into the much-mixed and abundantly creative people, the English' (Hawkes and Hawkes 1947, 19–20).

57 Rivet (1958, 29).

58 (1976).

9 FRANCIS HAVERFIELD AND ROMANISATION

1 The literature on Romanisation has become very extensive over the past ten years. For a variety of recent perspectives, see, for instance: Alcock (1997); Barrett (1997); Freeman (1993); Hanson (1997); Hingley (1995a; 1997); S. Jones (1997); Millett (1990a; 1990b); J. Webster (1996a) and Woolf (1998, 1–23). For additional studies see articles in Wood and Queiroga (eds) (1991), Metzler *et al.* (eds) (1995) and Hoff and Rotroff (eds) (1997).

2 Alcock (1997, 1).

3 See for instance, Hingley (1996); Alcock (1997, 3).

4 J. Webster (1996a, 15).

5 See Hingley (1995a; 1996; 1999).

6 It is accepted that the drawing of this telelogical link between Roman civilisation and the modern English may not have been a direct intention of Haverfield's but that his work was used in this way by others.

7 Mommsen (1886). See Freeman (1997a) for a discussion of the general context of this work

8 Freeman (1993; 1997a).

9 Mommsen (1886, 4).

10 *Ibid.,* 4–5.

11 Forsey (1997).

12 Mommsen (1886, 193). My emphasis.

13 Haverfield (1909, xiii.)

14 P. 22.

NOTES

15 P. 37.
16 See Freeman (1997a, 39–43). Freeman (1996) also considers Haver-field's debt to Mommsen.
17 Particularly Haverfield (1900; 1905; 1906; 1912b; 1915).
18 See chapter 9, note 1.
19 (1905, 185; 1912b, 9).
20 See p. 27.
21 Haverfield (1912b, 9–10). In his introduction to a reprinted version of Mommsen's *Provinces of the Roman Empire*, Haverfield uses very similar language to this quote, talking of 'progress' and 'happiness' rather than 'betterment' and 'happiness' (1909, xii).
22 Including Curzon, Cromer, Bryce and Baden-Powell. See chapters 3 and 4.
23 (1915, 11). Majeed has quoted directly comparable remarks which were made by Bryce; see Majeed (1999, 101) quoting Bryce (1914, 123–4), and this, presumably is another example of the complementary nature of the work of the academic and politician (see p. 50).
24 (1905, 186; 1912b, 12).
25 (1905, 186.)
26 (1910a, 106).
27 *Ibid.*
28 *Ibid.*, 107.
29 See p. 50.
30 (1910a, 107).
31 See pp. 48–51.
32 (1905, 188; 1912b, 15).
33 (1905, 210–11; 1912b, 58–9).
34 Freeman (1993, 443).
35 See Haverfield (1905, 188).
36 (1906, 211).
37 *Ibid.*, 210.
38 (1915, 12).
39 Haverfield (1913, 132). See Laurence's comments on this issue (1994a, 13).
40 (1912b, 16).
41 (1905, 210–11; 1912b, 58–9).
42 (1905, 203; 1912b, 45–60).
43 (1905, 203; 1912b, 46).
44 (1915, 20). For a similar earlier statement see Haverfield (1905, 203). My emphasis.
45 (1915, 14). See Haverfield (1905, 188) for similar sentiments.
46 (1905, 188).
47 In addition to Haverfield's introduction of the Edwardian concept of progress into the Roman world, see Laurence (1994a, 15) for the way in which Haverfield introduced twentieth-century concepts of town planning into his consideration of Roman towns and cities.
48 See also the comments of Majeed (1999), quoted above on p. 50.
49 Hingley (1995a). See Patterson (1997) for a discussion of the reification of 'civilisation' in the invention of Western civilisation.
50 (1986b, 2).

51 Haverfield (1911a, xix; 1912b, 11).
52 (1912b, 10).
53 See Mackenzie (1984, 63; 1986b, 5) for the general context.
54 (1905, 186); Haverfield does not express his views on Indians in this context.
55 This is certainly one possible reading of Bryce's and Lucas' arguments, although neither author appears to expect success; see Lucas (1912); Bryce (1914). Majeed has emphasised a rather different but complementary reading of the comments of Lucas and Bryce. He has argued that the stress that these authors place on the barrier to assimilation of Indians into British culture should be seen to reflect the insecurity of the British about their own racial identity (1999).
56 For the work of Egerton and Lucas and others see p. 94.
57 G. Macdonald (1924a, 7).
58 Haverfield and Macdonald (1924b, 284).
59 *Ibid.*, 286.
60 Haverfield (1910b, 2; 1912b, 19).
61 Haverfield (1910b, 2–3).
62 (1905, 190) and (1912b, 19).
63 Haverfield's observations on the motives of natives in north Wales who adopted Roman pottery (see p. 119) are relevant in this context.
64 P. 67.
65 (1912b, 60).
66 *Ibid.*, 39.
67 Henig (1995, 9) has suggested that Haverfield viewed Roman contact as having driven out the inspiration and originality of native art and also that Haverfield was influenced by the views of Morris and Burne-Jones on art in late Victorian society.
68 (1912b, 61).
69 P. 119.
70 Haverfield (1905, Fig. 1).
71 Haverfield (1914, 233). See quote on p. 46.
72 (1905, 210–11; 1912b, 58–9).
73 See for instance the comments of Lucas on p. 93.
74 (1911, 21). It should, however, be noted that this work shows little sign that its authors were directly influenced by Haverfield.
75 Pp. 40–1.
76 Pp. 147–8.
77 See comments on the writings of Baldwin, Weigall and others (pp. 100–6).

10 ROMANISATION: HAVERFIELD'S LEGACY

1 Pp. 97–8.
2 For a general discussion of Collingwood's archaeological work, see Potter (1986, 76). For an introduction to his work on political philosophy see Boucher (1989). Freeman has assessed Collingwood's contribution to Roman studies (1997a). Collingwood's interest in Roman archaeology was stimulated by his father, William. Robin Collingwood was a student of Haverfield's and became involved in his excavation

programme at Corbridge and Ambleside during the late 1900s and 1910s. Collingwood inherited Haverfield's 'School of Romano-British studies' as the only student of Haverfield's resident in Oxford after the First World War; most of his fellow students having been killed during the 1914–18 War. (Collingwood 1939, 120).

3 Potter (1986, 76).

4 (1923, 5).

5 (1939, 121). I shall focus on the significant sections of Collingwood's book *Roman Britain*, first published in 1923 and republished in 1932 (the text of the book was first presented as a series of lectures in Oxford in 1921). This was a popular book written for an audience that was not familiar with the subject matter (Collingwood 1923, 5). I shall also consider Collingwood's section of the book that he co-wrote with J.N.L. Myres, *Roman Britain and the English Settlement*, first published in 1936, and also Collingwood's autobiography, published in 1939.

6 Collingwood's address 'The Prussian Philosophy' was presented to the Belgian Student Conference at Fladbury in 1919. Part of this presentation is reproduced in Collingwood (1989, 201–6). For the reference comparing Roman and European imperialism see p. 201. See also Boucher (1989, 20)

7 Collingwood (1923, 14).

8 *Ibid.*, 15.

9 Collingwood (1932, 12).

10 Collingwood (1939, 137).

11 Henig (1995, 9). See also Boucher (1989, 20).

12 For Mussolini see pp. 106–7. For the nature of the German menace in the mid-1930s see Reynolds (1991, 118–20).

13 Bowler (1989, 200–1).

14 Boucher (1989, 20–1), quoting Collingwood's (1919) presentation (see Chapter 8, note 14).

15 (1939, 140).

16 Collingwood and Myres (1936, xvii).

17 *Ibid.*, 191.

18 *Ibid.*, 194.

19 *Ibid.*, 205.

20 (1932, 86–7). It is of interest that archaeologists have been making similar observations about the lack of excavation on non-villa settlements in recent years (M. Jones and Miles (1979); Hingley (1989, 23; 1991); Evans (1995, 34); see also p. 151). It has, however, taken a long time for these issues to be taken on board through archaeological excavation of many of these sites.

21 Collingwood and Myres (1936, 208–9). See also Collingwood (1932, 86).

22 Collingwood and Myres (1936, 209).

23 *Ibid.*, 212–13. Collingwood's use of the archaeological evidence for rural settlement was contested by later authors. Rivet attacked Collingwood's use of the idea of village on the basis that his villages were actually isolated farms (1958, 30; 1969a, 176), while Bowen argued that nucleated settlements and villas occurred interspersed in the countryside and that distinct villa and village economies did not

exist (1969, 32). However, Collingwood's villa-village model has been reapplied recently (Hingley 1989, 122).

24 Collingwood and Myres (1936, 222).

25 Collingwood (1932, 88).

26 According to Collingwood, two economic systems existed side by side. The village economy was rigid and unprogressive, because the minute subdivision of land and the smallness of 'capital' (surplus wealth) commanded by any individual made reform of the economic system all but impossible. The capital to build a villa was therefore not available; see Collingwood and Myres (1936, 211–12).

The isolated family groups on the periphery of Cranborne Chase, by contrast, were able to exploit the new conditions offered by Rome and to expand their agricultural operations, thus creating agricultural surplus for exchange. These groups were then able to accumulate surplus wealth and to build villas (*ibid.*, 212–13). Therefore, the organisation of the pre-Roman society and of the landscape had a major impact on development that occurred in the Roman period. As we have seen, it is even conceivable – according to Collingwood – that this rural conservatism inherent in the village-system added to the decline of the towns of Roman Britain.

27 Although he dismisses the idea of a Celtic revival as a survival of the 'old view' of a distinct division between Roman and Celt in his early book (1923, 99).

28 Collingwood and Myres (1936, 316).

29 Collingwood (1932, 93).

30 (1939, 259–60).

31 (1939, 141).

32 For the details of this process see Collingwood (1939, 143).

33 For this image see the comments made by Haverfield quoted on p. 125.

34 Collingwood (1923, 101; 1925, 2). See further on pp. 97–8.

35 Rivet (1958, 16–32).

36 *Ibid.*, 27. My emphasis.

37 *Ibid.*

38 *Ibid.*, 28. My emphasis. For more recent approaches to the same issue see Oliver (1979), Birmingham (1979) and B. Hodder (1979).

39 P. 107.

40 See a particular analogy which he drew between the development of houses in Roman Britain and in modern East Africa (Rivet 1958, 108–10).

41 (1958, 29).

42 *Ibid.*, 30. Rivet's observations were based on Christopher Hawkes' reassessment of the Cranborne Chase sites excavated by Pitt-Rivers. Hawkes used the results of Bersu's excavations at Little Woodbury to argue that Pitt-River's 'villages' were actually farms. Since Rivet's time, however, the idea that village-type settlements occurred within Roman Britain has been revived (Hingley 1989, 23).

43 *Ibid.*, 33. My emphasis. It is of interest that with regard to this final point, Rivet believed that Iron Age people were only able to cultivate the lighter less fertile soils of Britain because of their technology. The 'Belgae' are argued to have been able to cultivate heavier soils because

they possessed a heavier plough (Rivet 1958, 43). Actually, Rivet's suggestion is based on the fact that the archaeological evidence that he had access to was biased to the lighter soils as a result of the fact that air photographs, which had produced evidence for many of the sites, only regularly produce cropmark evidence on light soils. It is now known that later prehistoric sites occur over all soil types, which suggests a rather greater 'mastery' over nature on the part of Iron Age people.

44 Rivet (1958, 45).
45 *Ibid.*, 53. My emphasis.
46 *Ibid.*, 72.
47 *Ibid.*, 101.
48 *Ibid.*, 103–5.
49 Elsewhere in *Town and Country* Rivet recognised that villas were actually in the minority in Roman Britain (1958, 116).
50 Hingley (1989, 4, 121; 1991, 95).
51 See Hingley (1989).
52 Rivet (1958, 101).
53 *Ibid.*, 116.
54 *Ibid.*, 120.
55 For this distinction see p. 134.
56 (1958), 116.
57 *Ibid.*, 116–17.
58 *Ibid.*, 45.
59 *Ibid.* 118–19.
60 (1967, 303).
61 To which Frere refers in his discussion about Collingwood's consideration of the survival of Celtic inspiration in Roman art; see Frere (1967, 315).
62 *Ibid.*, 304.
63 *Ibid.* My emphasis.
64 *Ibid.*, 305. My emphasis.
65 *Ibid.* My emphasis.
66 *Ibid.*, 306. My emphasis.
67 *Ibid.*, 321.
68 *Ibid.* My emphasis.
69 *Ibid.*, 315.
70 *Ibid.*, 316.
71 Millett (1990a, 1).
72 *Ibid.,* xv.
73 Freeman (1993); Hingley (1995a, 18).
74 Millett (1990b, 38).
75 *Ibid.*
76 (1997, 149).
77 *Ibid.*, 155.
78 Freeman (1993); Hingley (1995a; 1996).
79 See pp. 97–9.
80 For instance, Stevens (1947; 1966); J.T. Smith (1978; 1982; 1985; 1997), Hingley (1989). See Forcey (1997) for a brief review of these 'nativist' works and their relationship to the dominant Romanist

perspective in Roman studies. Collingwood's account drew upon the image of the permanence of national life in a way that was compatible to the use of the image of the Roman ancestor in the representation of Englishness, but I will not pursue this topic further in this context.

81 Bowler (1989) describes the concept of a 'progressionalist' tradition in British and western society; the idea of the 'progressive' approach to Romanisation is derived from his work.

82 See Bowler (1989); Gardner and Lewis (1996) and Rist (1997, 40) for considerations of such views of progress.

83 Rist (1997).

84 *Ibid.*, 35–6.

85 Bowler (1989, 5); Rist (1997, 42).

86 Bowler (1989, 19).

87 *Ibid.*, 33; N. Thomas (1994, 109). See Sand's comments on the 'Protected Princes of India', quoted on p. 51.

88 Rist (1997, 42–3).

89 Bowler (1989, 43–4).

90 *Ibid.*, 43.

91 For examples of British imperial archaeology abroad see, for instance: Cook (1998); Wheeler (1954; 1976).

92 Patterson (1997); see Bernal (1994) for the ideological context of ideas of 'civilisation'.

93 For associated points see Patterson (1997).

94 J. Scott (1975, 133).

95 *Ibid.*, 133–4.

96 Bowler (1989, 19).

97 P. 65.

98 See Judd (1996) for the Indian independence movement.

99 (1923, 228).

100 Discussed on p. 126.

101 (1953, 27).

102 See pp. 119, 140 and 142.

103 Hingley (1989, 3–5; 1999, 141); S. Jones (1997, 106–8).

104 M. Taylor and Collingwood (1923, 200); Frere (1988). The lists are to be found in the annual volumes of the *Journal of Roman Studies* and then from 1971 in *Britannia*. I have compiled the figures in Tables 10.2 and 10.3 from a swift survey of these lists and the information provides a rough summary of the amount of work conducted rather than a fully accurate figure.

105 The serious study of Hadrian's Wall continued after the World War One; see S. Johnson (1989a, 34; 1989b, 121–2). Works also occurred on other military sites in Scotland, England and Wales; see S. Johnson (1989a) and Potter (1986) for reviews of Roman archaeology during the twentieth century. Gradually during the twentieth century a wider range of sites came to be excavated using higher standards. In particular, the development of aerial photography in the 1930s to 1960s resulted in the discovery of important evidence for dense Iron Age and Roman settlement in various areas of Britain during the 1930s; see Potter (1986, 77); S. Johnson (1989a, 42). Urban archaeo-

logy also developed after the Second World War and the increasing threat from development to the archaeology of Roman Britain during the 1960s led to the creation of Rescue archaeology. Major summaries of various classes of site have been published over the past thirty years, including Roman forts, towns, small towns, villas and temples, which have increased the general understanding of the archaeology of the province; see Bidwell (1997), Burnham and Wacher (1990), Hingley (1989); J.T. Smith (1997), Wacher (1995) and Woodward (1992).

106 This is an updated version of the information provided on the pie diagrams in Hingley (1991).

107 Non-villa settlements are the farms and villages in Roman Britain that did not have dwelling houses which can be defined as villas (see, for instance, Hingley (1989, 23–5). The class of non-villa settlements includes the 'villages' and 'farms' discussed by Haverfield, Collingwood, Rivet and Frere. For the comparative lack of work on non-villa settlements prior to the 1960s; see Hingley (1989, 4). For the scarcity of work on unwalled small towns prior to the same decade see Burnham (1993, 99–100).

108 (1958, 75).

109 Collingwood and Myres (1936, 86–7).

110 Frere (1988, 34). Frere characterises this as a loss of the conception of what is important in Roman archaeology. I do not disagree with him about the need for a research framework in Roman archaeology to enable the definition of what is significant in the subject, but I do feel a need for a rather more flexible and open definition of what is 'important'.

111 As we have seen, Haverfield's writings on frontier issues and administration were perhaps less fundamental but still had an important influence on his contemporaries (pp. 58–9).

112 See pp. 53–4.

113 Betts (1971). See above p. 15.

114 For instance, see Diamond (1974); Scholte (1981); Hoogvelt (1974); Fabian (1983); Kuper (1988); Ashcroft et al. (1989); Said (1993); N. Thomas (1994); Patterson (1997); Rist (1997).

115 (1974, 12). See also concerns over environmental degradation expressed in Gardner and Lewis (1996).

116 See, for instance Amin (1976); J. Taylor (1976) and Rist (1997).

117 For some early exceptions see M. Jones and Miles (1979) and Cunliffe (1984).

118 Mattingly (1997).

119 See Millett (1990a, xv) for this concept.

120 For instance, see Hingley (1989; 1997); Mattingly (1997a) and J. Webster (1996a).

121 For instance, see various articles in Webster and Cooper (eds) (1996); Mattingly (ed.) (1997b) and in the TRAC volumes listed in Preface, note 16.

122 Hingley (1989).

123 *Ibid.*

11 CONCLUSION

1 The title 'Island stories' is taken from H.E. Marshall's *Our Island Story* (1905) and Samuel's *Island Stories: Unravelling Britain* (1998).
2 See, for instance, Edwards (1999a). See Mattingly (1996) for a study of North Africa.
3 Pp. 81 and 106–7. See also Diaz-Andreu's discussion of the way in which the Roman imperial past was studied in Spain under Franco because it was the first time that the country had been united (1995, 46).
4 The imperial value of the classics and of Roman archaeology remained relevant into the 1920s and beyond (see p. 106).
5 J. Webster (1995; 1999).
6 J. Webster (1995, 2).
7 Cunningham (1986).
8 See p. 124.
9 Pp. 147–8.
10 See p. 10.
11 We have seen that Haverfield attacked the view of the Roman invasion that was held by 'Welsh patriots' as a short period of discontinuity in a continuation of unaltered Celticism (see p. 125). In addition, Rivet wrote of a myth of Roman Britain as a province so thoroughly British that no Roman would dare to set foot in it (p. 107).
12 See Collingwood's comments on art and civilisation, pp. 97–8.
13 (1996, 179). See also comments by Ray Laurence (1998, 6). Laurence suggests that Roman Britain has always been seen as very different from the rest of the Roman Empire and has considered some of the reasons for this state of affairs.
14 P. xiv.
15 Laurence (1998, 1–2).

BIBLIOGRAPHY

Ackworth, H.A. (1897–8) *Libretto to E. Elgar's opera Caractacus,* London: EMI Records, 1977.

Alcock, S. (1997) 'The problem of Romanisation, the power of Athens', in M.C. Hoff and S.I. Rotroff (eds) *The Romanization of Athens,* Oxford: Oxbow.

Alston, R. (1996) 'Conquest by text: Juvenal and Plutarch on Egypt', in J. Webster and N. Cooper (eds) *Roman Imperialism: post-colonial perspectives,* Leicester: Leicester Archaeological Monographs No. 3.

Amin, S. (1976) *Unequal Development: an essay on the social formations of peripheral capitalism,* London: Harvester.

Arnold, T. (1841) *An Inaugural Lecture on the Study of Modern History Delivered in the Theatre, Oxford, Dec. 2, 1841,* Oxford: John Henry.

Arnold, W.T. (1906) *Studies of Roman Imperialism,* edited by Edward Fiddes, Manchester: Manchester University Press.

Ashcroft, B., Griffiths, G. and Tiffin, H. (1989) *The Empire Writes Back: theory and practice in post-colonial literatures,* London: Routledge.

Ashcroft, B., Griffiths, G. and Tiffin, H. (1998) *Key Concepts in Post-Colonial Studies,* London: Routledge.

Baden-Powell, R.S.S. (1908) *Scouting for Boys: a handbook of instructions in good citizenship,* London: C. Arthur Peterson.

Bain, J. (ed.) (1894) *The Border Papers: calendar of letters and papers relating to the affairs of the Borders of England and Scotland preserved in Her Majesty's Public Record Office, London,* Edinburgh: Her Majesty's General Register House.

Baldwin, S. (1924) 'On England and the West: address at the annual dinner of the Royal Society of St George at the Hotel Cecil, 6th May 1924', reprinted in S. Baldwin (1926) *On England and Other Addresses,* London: Philip Allan & Co.

Baldwin, S. (1926) *The Classics and the Plain Man. Presidential Address delivered to the Classical Association in the Middle Temple Hall, 8th January, 1926,* London: John Murray.

Balfour, A. (1908) *Decadence,* the Henry Sidgwick Memorial Lecture, Cambridge: Cambridge University Press.

Barrett, J. (1997) 'Romanization: a critical comment', in D. Mattingly (ed.) *Dialogues in Roman imperialism: power, discourse, and discrepant experiences in the Roman Empire*, Portsmouth, Rhode Island: Journal of Roman Archaeology, Supplementary Series, No 23.

Baumgart, W. (1982) *Imperialism: the idea and the reality of British and French colonial expansion, 1880–1914*, Oxford: Oxford University Press.

Bénabou, M. (1976) *La résistance africaine à la romanisation*, Paris: François Maspero.

Bernal, M. (1987) *Black Athena: the Afroasiatic roots of classical civilization – Volume 1, the fabrication of ancient Greece 1785–1985,* London: Free Association Press.

Bernal, M. (1994) 'The image of Ancient Greece as a tool for colonialism and European hegemony', in G.C. Bond and A. Gilliam (eds) *Social Construction of the Past: representations as power*, London: Routledge.

Betts, R.F. (1971) 'The allusion to Rome in British imperial thought of the late nineteenth and early twentieth centuries', *Victorian Studies*, 15: 149–59.

Bidwell, P. (1997) *Roman Forts in Britain*, London: Batsford.

Bidwell, P. (1999) 'The pilgrimages of Hadrian's Wall', in P. Bidwell (ed.) *Hadrian's Wall 1989–1999: a summary of recent excavation and research prepared for the Twelfth Pilgrimage of Hadrian's Wall, 14–21 August 1999*, 1–6, Kendal: Cumberland and Westmorland Antiquarian and Archaeological Society and Society of Antiquaries of Newcastle upon Tyne.

Birley, E. (1961) *Researches on Hadrian's Wall*, Kendal: Titus Wilson & Son.

Birmingham, D. (1979) 'Portugal and the African Iron Age', in B. Burnham and H. Johnson (eds) *Invasion and Response: the case of Roman Britain*, Oxford: British Archaeological Reports, British No. 73.

Black, J. (1997) 'Gibbon and international relations', in R. McKitterick and R. Quinault (eds) *Edward Gibbon and Empire*, Cambridge: Cambridge University Press.

Blakeney, E.H. (1927) 'Some thoughts on the Classics', *Classical Review*, 41, 105–10.

Bond, G.C. and Gilliam, A. (1994) 'Introduction', in G.C. Bond and A. Gilliam (eds) *Social Construction of the Past: representations as power*, London: Routledge.

Boucher, D. (1989) 'Introduction', in R.G. Collingwood *Essays in Political Philosophy: edited with an introduction by David Boucher*, Oxford: Clarendon Press.

Bowen, H.C. (1969) 'The Celtic background', in A.L.F. Rivet (ed.) *The Roman Villa in Britain*, London: Routledge & Kegan Paul.

Bowler, P.J. (1989) *The Invention of Progress: the Victorians and the past*, Oxford: Blackwell.

Bratton, J.S. (1981) *The Impact of Victorian Children's Fiction*, London: Croom Helm.

Bratton, J.S. (1986) 'Of England, home and duty: the image of England in Victorian and Edwardian juvenile fiction', in J.M. Mackenzie (ed.) *Imperialism and Popular Culture*, Manchester: Manchester University Press.

Braund, D. (1996) *Ruling Roman Britain: kings, queens, governors and emperors from Julius Caesar to Agricola*, London: Routledge.

Breese, S. (1998) 'In search of Englishness; in search of votes', in J. Arnold, K. Davies and S. Ditchfield (eds) *History and Heritage: consuming the past in contemporary culture*, Shaftesbury, Dorset: Donhead.

Broks, P. (1990) 'Science, the press and empire: "Pearson's" publications 1890–1914', in J.M. Mackenzie (ed.) *Imperialism and the Natural World*, Manchester: Manchester University Press

Brown, I.G. (1980) *The Hobby-Horsical Antiquary: a Scottish character 1640–1830*, Edinburgh: National Library of Scotland.

Bruce, J.C. (1851) *The Roman Wall: a historical, topographical and descriptive account of the barrier of the lower isthmus, extending from the Tyne to the Solway*, London: John Russell Smith.

Brun, P., Leeuw, S. van der and Whittaker, C. (eds) (1993) *Frontières d'Empire: nature et signification des frontières romaines*, Actes de la Table Ronde Internationale de Nemours 21–22–23 mai 1992, Nemours: Musée de Préhistoire d'Ile-de-France.

Brunt, P.A. (1964) 'Reflections on British and Roman imperialism', *Comparative Studies in Society and History*, 7: 267–88.

Brunt, P.A. (1990) *Roman Imperial Themes*, Oxford: Clarendon Press.

Bryant, A. (1953) *Makers of the Realm*, London: Collins.

Bryant, A. (1982) *Spirit of England*, London: Collins.

Bryce, J. (1914) *The Ancient Roman Empire and the British Empire in India: the diffusion of Roman and English law throughout the world*, Oxford: Oxford University Press.

Burnham, B. (1993) 'The "small towns" of Roman Britain – the last fifty years', in S.J. Greep (ed.) *Roman Towns: the Wheeler inheritance – a review of 50 years' research*, London: CBA.

Burnham, B. and Wacher, J. (1990) *The 'Small Towns' of Roman Britain*, London: Batsford.

Burrow, J.W. McKitterick, R. and Quinault, R. (1997) 'Epilogue', in R. McKitterick and R. Quinault (eds) *Edward Gibbon and Empire*, Cambridge: Cambridge University Press.

Carrington, C. (1955) *Rudyard Kipling: his life and work*, London: Macmillan & Co.

Casey, P.J. (1994) *Carausius and Allectus: the British usurpers*, London: Batsford.

Chapman, M. (1992) *The Celts: the construction of a myth*, London: St Martin's Press.

Church, A.J. (1887) *The Count of the Saxon Shore or the Villa in Vectis – a tale of the departure of the Romans from Britain*, London: Seeley & Co.

Church, A.J. (1895) *Stories from English History: from Julius Caesar to the Black Prince*, London: Seeley.

Church, A.J. (1896) *Stories from English History: from the Lord Protector to Victoria*, London: Seeley.

Clark, G. (1939) *Archaeology and Society*, London: Methuen & Co.

Clarke, M.L. (1959) *Classical Education in Britain 1500–1900*, Cambridge: Cambridge University Press.

Classics and the Average Boy: a question for the nation (1912), articles and correspondence reprinted from the columns of *The Times*, with contributions from the Headmasters of Seven Public Schools and other representative opinions, London: The Times Office.

Cohn, B.S. (1996) *Colonialism and its Forms of Knowledge: the British in India*, Princeton, NJ: Princeton University Press.

Colley, L. (1992) *Britons: forging the nation 1707–1837*, reprinted 1996, London: Vintage.

Collingwood, R.G. (1923) *Roman Britain*, London: Oxford University Press.

Collingwood, R.G. (1925) *The Roman Signal Station on Castle Hill, Scarborough,* Scarborough: Corporation of Scarborough.

Collingwood, R.G. (1932) *Roman Britain*, new edition, Oxford: Clarendon Press.

Collingwood, R.G. (1939) *An Autobiography*, Oxford: Oxford University Press.

Collingwood, R.G. (1946) *The Idea of History*, Oxford: Clarendon Press.

Collingwood, R.G. (1989) *Essays in Political Philosophy*, edited with an introduction by David Boucher, Oxford: Clarendon Press.

Collingwood, R.G. and Myres, J.N.L. (1936) *Roman Britain and the English Settlement*, Oxford: Clarendon Press.

Collins, E. (1900) 'The prediction fulfilled', in M. Trevelyan *Britain's Greatness Foretold: the story of Boadicea, the British Warrior-Queen*, London: John Hogg.

Colls, R. (1986) 'Englishness and the Political Culture', in R. Colls and P. Dodd (eds) *Englishness: Politics and Culture 1880–1920*, London: Croom Helm.

Colls, R. and Dodd, P. (eds) (1986) *Englishness: Politics and Culture 1880–1920,* London: Croom Helm.

Conybeare, E. (1903) *Early Britain: Roman Britain,* London: Society for Promoting Christian Knowledge.

Cook, B.F. (1998) 'British archaeologists in the Aegean', in V. Brand (ed.) *The Study of the Past in the Victorian Age*, Oxford: Oxbow.

Coote, H.C. (1864) *A Neglected Fact in English History*, London: Bell & Daldy.

Coote, H.C. (1878) *The Romans of Britain*, London: Fredrick Norgate.

Cottam, S., Dungworth, D., Scott, S. and Taylor, J. (eds) (1995) *TRAC94: proceedings of the fourth annual Roman Theoretical Archaeology Conference, Durham 1994*, Oxford: Oxbow.

Cowper, W. (1782) 'Boadicea: an ode', in H.S. Milford (ed.) 1967 *Cowper: poetical works*, fourth edition, London: Oxford University Press.

Cramb, J.A. (1900) *Reflections on the Origins and Destiny of Imperial Britain*, London: Macmillan.

Earl of Cromer (Baring, E.) (1908) 'The government of subject races' (Edinburgh Review, January 1908), reprinted in Earl of Cromer (1912), *Speeches and Miscellaneous writings 1882–1911, Volume 2*, privately published for private circulation.

Earl of Cromer (Baring, E.) (1910a) *Ancient and Modern Imperialism*, London: John Murray.

Earl of Cromer (Baring, E.) (1910b) 'Ancient and modern imperialism: address to the Classics Association at Oxford, May 9, 1910', reprinted in Earl of Cromer (1912), *Speeches and Miscellaneous Writings 1882–1911, Volume 2*, privately published for private circulation.

Cross, C. (1968) *The Fall of the British Empire, 1918–1968*, London: Hodder & Stoughton.

Crump, J. (1986) 'The identity of English music: the reception of Elgar 1898–1935', in R. Colls and P. Dodd (eds) *Englishness: Politics and Culture 1880–1920*, London: Croom Helm.

Cunliffe, B.W. (1984) 'Images of Britannia', *Antiquity* 58: 175–8.

Cunningham, H. (1986) 'The Conservative Party and patriotism', in R. Colls and P. Dodd (eds) *Englishness: Politics and Culture 1880–1920*, London: Croom Helm.

Curzon, G.N. (Lord Curzon of Kedleston) (1907) *Frontiers, The Romanes Lecture 1907, delivered in the Sheldonian Theatre, Oxford, November 2, 1907*, Oxford: Clarendon Press.

Daniel, G.E. (1950) *A Hundred Years of Archaeology*, London: Duckworth.

Daniels, S. (1993) *Fields of Vision: landscape, imagery and national identity in England and the United States*, Cambridge: Cambridge University Press.

David, D. (1995) *Rule Britannia: women, empire, and Victorian writing*, London: Cornell University Press.

Davies, C.C. (1932) *The Problem of the North-west Frontier 1890–1908, with a Survey of Policy since 1849*, Cambridge: Cambridge University Press.

Diamond, S. (1974) *In Search of the Primitive: a critique of civilization*, reprinted 1981, New Brunswick: Transactions Books.

Diamond, S. (1975) 'The Marxist tradition as a dialectical anthropology', *Dialectical Anthropology*, 1: 1–5.

Diamond, S., Scholte, B. and Wolf, E.R. (1975) 'On defining the Marxist tradition in anthropology: a response to the "American Anthropologist"', *Critique of Anthropology*, 4–5: 110–26.

Diaz-Andreu, M. (1995) 'Archaeology and nationalism in Spain', in P.L. Kohl and C. Fawcett (eds) *Nationalism, Politics, and the Practice of Archaeology*, Cambridge: Cambridge University Press.

Dietler, M. (1998) 'A tale of three sites: the monumentalization of Celtic oppida and the politics of collective memory and identity', *World Archaeology* 30: 72–89.

Dodd, P. (1986) 'Englishness and the national culture', in R. Colls and P. Dodd (eds) *Englishness: Politics and Culture 1880–1920*, London: Croom Helm.

Doughty, C.M. (1906) *The Dawn in Britain* (6 volumes), London: Duckworth.

Doyle, B. (1986) 'The invention of English', in R. Colls and P. Dodd (eds) *Englishness: Politics and Culture 1880–1920,* London: Croom Helm.

Dudley, D.R. and Webster, G. (1962) *The Rebellion of Boudicca*, London: Routledge & Kegan Paul.

Edwards, C. (1999a) 'Introduction: shadows and fragments', in C. Edwards (ed.) *Roman Presences: receptions of Rome in European culture, 1789–1945*, Cambridge: Cambridge University Press.

Edwards, C. (1999b) 'Translating Empire? Macaulay's Rome', in C. Edwards (ed.) *Roman Presences: receptions of Rome in European culture, 1789–1945*, Cambridge: Cambridge University Press.

Edwards, C. (ed.) (1999c) *Roman Presences: receptions of Rome in European culture, 1789–1945*, Cambridge: Cambridge University Press.

Eldridge, C.C. (1996) *The Imperial Experience from Carlyle to Forster*, London: Macmillan.

Evans, J. (1995) 'Roman finds, assemblages, towards an integrated approach', in P. Rush (ed.) *Theoretical Roman Archaeology: second conference proceedings*, Aldershot: Avebury.

Fabian, J. (1983) *Time and the Other: how anthropology makes its objects*, London: Cambridge University Press.

Fiddes, E. (1906) 'Introduction', in W.T. Arnold *Studies of Roman Imperialism*, edited by Edward Fiddes, Manchester: Manchester University Press.

Fletcher, C.R.L. and Kipling, R. (1911) *A School History of England (Pictures by Henry Ford)*, Oxford: Clarendon Press.

Forbes, D. (1815) *Culloden Papers*, London: T. Cadell & W. Davies.

Forcey, C. (1997) 'Beyond "Romanization": technologies of power in Roman Britain', in K. Meadows, C. Lemke and J. Heron (eds) *TRAC96: Proceedings of the Sixth Annual Theoretical Roman Archaeology Conference, Sheffield 1996*, Oxford: Oxbow.

Forcey, C., Hawthorne, J. and Witcher, R. (eds) (1998) *TRAC97: Proceedings of the Seventh Annual Theoretical Roman Archaeology Conference, Nottingham 1997*, Oxford: Oxbow.

Freeman, P.W.M. (1991) 'The study of the Roman period in Britain: a comment on Hingley', *Scottish Archaeological Review*, 8: 102–4.

Freeman, P.W.M. (1993) '"Romanization" and Roman material culture', *Journal of Roman Archaeology*, 6: 438–45.

Freeman, P.W.M. (1996) 'British imperialism and the Roman Empire', in J. Webster and N. Cooper (eds) *Roman Imperialism: post-colonial perspectives*, Leicester: Leicester Archaeological Monographs No. 3.

Freeman, P.W.M. (1997a) 'Mommsen through to Haverfield: the origins of Romanization studies in late 19th-c. Britain', in D. Mattingly (ed.) *Dialogues in Roman imperialism: power, discourse, and discrepant experiences in the Roman Empire*, Portsmouth, Rhode Island: *Journal of Roman Archaeology*, Supplementary Series, No 23.

Freeman, P.W.M. (1997b) ' "Romanization" – "Imperialism" – What are we talking about?', in K. Meadows, C. Lemke and J. Heron (eds) *TRAC96: Proceedings of the Sixth Annual Theoretical Roman Archaeology Conference, Sheffield 1996*, Oxford: Oxbow.

Frere, S.S. (1967) *Britannia: a history of Roman Britain*, London: Routledge & Kegan Paul.

Frere, S.S. (1988) 'Roman Britain since Haverfield and Richmond: a lecture delivered in All Souls College on 23 October 1987', *Alan Sutton: History and Archaeology Review*, 3, Oxford: Sutton.

Gardiner, S.R. (1887) *Outline of English History B.C. 55–A.D. 1886*, second edition, London: Longmans, Green & Co.

Gardner, K. and Lewis, M. (1996) *Anthropology, Development and the Postmodern Challenge,* London: Pluto.

Garnsey, P.D.A. and Whittaker, C.R. (eds) (1978) *Imperialism in the Ancient World*, Cambridge: Cambridge University Press.

Giles, J. and Middleton, T. (1995) 'Introduction', in J. Giles and T. Middleton (eds) *Writing Englishness 1900–1950: an introductory sourcebook on national identification*, London: Routledge.

Goalen, M. (1995) 'The idea of the city and the excavations at Pompeii', in T.J. Cornell and K. Lomas (eds) *Urban Society in Roman Italy*, London: University College.

Goldberg, D.T. (1993) *Racist Culture: philosophy and the politics of meaning,* Oxford: Blackwell.

Golden, M. and Toohey, P. (1997) 'Introduction', in M. Golden and P. Toohey (eds) *Inventing Ancient Culture: historicism, periodization and the ancient world*, London: Routledge.

Gordon, G.S. (ed.) (1912) *English Literature and the Classics*, Oxford: Clarendon Press.

Gosden, C. (1994) *Social Being and Time*, Oxford: Blackwell.

Grafton, A.T. (1992) (with Shelford, A. and Siraisi, N.) *New Worlds, Ancient Texts: the power of tradition and the shock of discovery*, London: Harvard University Press.

Grant, A. and Stringer, A.K. (eds) (1995) *Uniting the Kingdom? The making of British history*, London: Routledge.

Grant Duff, M.E. (1876) *Notes of an Indian Journey*, London.

Graves-Brown, P., Jones, S. and Gamble, C. (eds) (1996) *Cultural Identity and Archaeology: The Construction of European Communities*, London: Routledge.

Green, G.E. (1900) *A Short History of the British Empire for the Use of Junior Forms*, London: Dent & Co.

Grose-Hodge, H. (1944) *Roman Panorama: a background for to-day*, Cambridge: Cambridge University Press.

Hall, E. (1989) *Inventing the Barbarian: Greek self-identification*, Oxford: Clarendon Press.

Hall, M. (1999) 'Subaltern voices? Finding the spaces between things and words', in P. Funari, M. Hall and S. Jones (eds) *Historical Archaeology: back from the edge*, London: Routledge.

Hanson, W.S. (1997) 'Forces of change and methods of control', in D. Mattingly (ed.) *Dialogues in Roman Imperialism: power, discourse, and discrepant experiences in the Roman Empire*, Portsmouth, Rhode Island: Journal of Roman Archaeology, Supplementary Series, No. 23.

Harris, J. (1993) *Private Lives, Public Spirits: Britain 1870–1914*, Oxford: Oxford University Press.

Haverfield, F. (1900) 'Romano-British Hampshire', in *The Victoria History of the Counties of England: Hampshire and the Isle of Wight*, London: Archibald Constable & Co.

Haverfield, F. (1905) 'The Romanization of Roman Britain', *Proceedings of the British Academy*, 2: 185–217.

Haverfield, F. (1906) 'Romano-British Somerset', in *The Victoria History of the Counties of England: Somerset*, London: Archibald Constable & Co.

Haverfield, F. (1909) 'Prefactory Notes', in T. Mommsen *The Provinces of the Roman Empire, from Caesar to Diocleatian, Parts 1 and 2*, trans. W.P. Dickson, revised edition, London: Macmillan & Co.

Haverfield, F. (1910a) 'Introduction: Roman Empire', *Classical Review* 24: 105–7.

Haverfield, F. (1910b) 'Military aspects of Roman Wales', paper read before the Honourable Society of Cymmrodorium at 20 Hanover Square, on Thursday 18 March 1909, Oxford: Ashmolean Library.

Haverfield, F. (1911a) 'An inaugural address delivered before the First Annual General Meeting of the Society, 11th May 1911', *Journal of Roman Studies*, 1: xi–xx.

Haverfield, F. (1911b) 'Appendix: The Indian Customs' Hedge', in H.F. Pelham *Essays by Henry Francis Pelham*, edited by F. Haverfield, Oxford: Clarendon Press.

Haverfield, F. (1912a) *The Study of Ancient History in Oxford: a lecture delivered to undergraduates reading for the literae humaniores school, May 1912*, London: Oxford University Press.

Haverfield, F. (1912b) *The Romanization of Roman Britain,* second edition, Oxford: Clarendon Press.

Haverfield, F. (1913) *Ancient Town-Planning*, Oxford: Clarendon Press.

Haverfield, F. (1914) 'By Professor Haverfield', in F. Haverfield, R.G. Collingwood and L.B. Freeston 'Report on the excavation of the Roman fort of Ambleside, 1913', *Transactions of the Cumberland and Westmorland Antiquarian and Archaeological Society* 14: 433–35.

Haverfield, F. (1915) *The Romanisation of Roman Britain*, third edition, Clarendon Press: Oxford.

Haverfield, F. (1916) 'Some Roman conceptions of Empire', *Occasional Publications of the Classical Association* 4, Cambridge.

Haverfield, F. (1918) 'The character of the Roman Empire as seen in West Somerset – The Presidential Address', *Proceedings of the Somersetshire Archaeological and Natural History Society*, 64: xxiii–xxxvii.

Haverfield, F. and Macdonald, G. (1924a) 'The study of Roman Britain: a retrospect', in F. Haverfield and G. Macdonald *The Roman Occupation of Britain: being six Ford Lectures delivered by F. Haverfield*, Oxford: Clarendon Press.

Haverfield, F. and Macdonald, G. (1924b) 'Roman Britain and Saxon England', in F. Haverfield and G. Macdonald *The Roman Occupation of Britain: being six Ford Lectures delivered by F. Haverfield*, Oxford: Clarendon Press.

Hawkes, J. and Hawkes, C. (1947) 'Land and people', in E. Barker (ed.) *The Character of England*, Oxford: Clarendon Press.

Henderson, B.W. (1903) *The Life and Principate of the Emperor Nero*, London: Methuen & Co.

Henderson, B.W. (1929) *Michael the Roman and Other Tales for Boys*, Oxford: Blackwell.

Henig, M. (1995) *The Art of Roman Britain*, London: Batsford.

Henty, G.A. (1887) *The Young Carthaginian, or a Struggle for Empire: a story of the time of Hannibal*, London: Blackie.

Henty, G.A. (1893) *Beric the Briton: a story of the Roman invasion*, Glasgow: Blackie.

Hingley, R. (1989) *Rural Settlement in Roman Britain*, London: Seaby.

Hingley, R. (1991) 'Past, present and future: the study of the Roman period in Britain', *Scottish Archaeological Review*, 8: 90–101.

Hingley, R. (1993) 'Attitudes to Roman imperialism', in E. Scott (ed.) *Theoretical Roman Archaeology: first conference proceedings*, Aldershot: Avebury.

Hingley, R. (1995a) '*Britannia*, origin myths and the British Empire', in S. Cottam, D. Dungworth, S. Scott, and J. Taylor (eds) *TRAC94: proceedings of the fourth annual Roman Theoretical Archaeology Conference, Durham 1994*, Oxford: Oxbow.

Hingley, R. (1995b) 'The Iron Age in Atlantic Scotland: searching for the meaning of the substantial house', in J.D. Hill, and C.G. Cumberpatch (eds) *Different Iron Ages: studies on the Iron Age in Temperate Europe*, Oxford: British Archaeological Reports, International, No. 602.

Hingley, R. (1996) 'The "legacy" of Rome: the rise, decline and fall of the theory of Romanization', in J. Webster and N. Cooper (eds) *Roman Imperialism: post-colonial perspectives*, Leicester: Leicester Archaeological Monographs No. 3.

Hingley, R. (1997) 'Resistance and domination: social change in Roman Britain', in D. Mattingly (ed.) *Dialogues in Roman Imperialism: power, discourse, and discrepant experiences in the Roman Empire*, Portsmouth, Rhode Island: *Journal of Roman Archaeology*, Supplementary Series, No 23.

Hingley, R. (1999) 'The imperial context of Romano-British studies and proposals for a new understanding of social change', in P. Funari, M. Hall and S. Jones (eds) *Historical Archaeology: back from the edge*, London: Routledge.

Hobsbawm, E. and Ranger, T. (eds) (1983) *The Invention of Tradition*, Cambridge: Cambridge University Press.

Hobson, J.A. (1902) *Imperialism: a study*, London: James Nisbet.

Hodder, B. (1979) 'The European impact on indigenous nucleated settlements in West Africa', in B. Burnham and H. Johnson (eds) *Invasion
and Response: the case of Roman Britain*, Oxford: British Archaeological
Reports, British No. 73.

Hoff, M.C. and Rotroff, S.I. (eds) (1997) *The Romanization of Athens*, Oxford:
Oxbow.

Hogarth, D.G. (1910) 'Assimilation', *Classical Review*, 24: 112–14.

Hoogvelt, A.M.M. (1974) *The Sociology of Developing Societies*, London:
Macmillan.

Howkins, A. (1986) 'The discovery of rural England', in R. Colls and
P. Dodd (eds) *Englishness: Politics and Culture 1880–1920*, London:
Croom Helm.

Huet, V. (1999) 'Napoleon I: a new Augustus?', in C. Edwards (ed.) *Roman
Presences: perceptions of Rome in European culture, 1789–1945*, Cambridge:
Cambridge University Press.

Hughes, M.V. (1927) *About England*, London: J.M. Dent & Sons.

Hynes, S. (1968) *The Edwardian Turn of Mind*, reprinted 1991, London:
Pimlico.

Ireland, S. (1986) *Roman Britain: a sourcebook*, New York: Croom Helm.

Jenkyns, R. (ed.) (1980) *The Victorians and Ancient Greece*, Oxford: Blackwell.

Jenkyns, R. (1992) 'The legacy of Rome', in R. Jenkyns (ed.) *The Legacy
of Rome: a new appraisal*, Oxford: Oxford University Press.

Johnson, S. (1775) 'A Journey to the western islands of Scotland', reprinted
in S. Johnson and J.A. Boswell *Journey to the Western Islands on Scotland
and the Journal of a Tour to the Hebrides*, reprinted 1984, London: Penguin.

Johnson, S. (1989a) *Rome and its Empire*, London: Routledge.

Johnson, S. (1989b) *Hadrian's Wall*, London: Batsford.

Jones, M. and Miles, D. (1979) 'Celts and Romans in the Thames Valley:
approaches to cultural change', in B. Burnham and H. Johnson (eds)
Invasion and Response: the case of Roman Britain, Oxford: British Archaeological Reports, British No. 73.

Jones, R. (1987) 'The archaeologists of Roman Britain', *Bulletin of the
Institute of Archaeologists of London*, 24: 85–97.

Jones S. (1997) *The Archaeology of Ethnicity: constructing identities in the past
and present*, London: Routledge.

Journal of Roman Studies (1937) 'Report on the discussion of "Roman Britain
as a subject of teaching"' held on January 12th, 1930', *Journal of Roman
Studies*, 27: 250–4.

Judd, D. (1996) *Empire: the British imperial experience, from 1765 to the present*,
London: HarperCollins.

Kendrick, T.D. (1950) *British Antiquity*, London: Methuen.

Kennedy, M. (1977) 'Introduction', to Elgar, E. (1897–8) *Caractacus*,
London: EMI Records.

Kiernan, V.G. (1995) *Imperialism and its Contradictions*, London: Routledge.

Kingsley, C. (1864) *The Roman and the Teuton: a series of lectures delivered
before the University of Cambridge*, London: Macmillan & Co.

Kipling, R. (1906) *Puck of Pook's Hill*, reprinted 1989, London: Macmillan.

Kirk, W. (1979) 'The making and impact of the British imperial North-West Frontier in India', in B. Burnham and H. Johnson (eds) *Invasion and Response: the case of Roman Britain*, Oxford: British Archaeological Reports, British No. 73.

Koebner, R. and Schmidt, H. Dan (1964) *Imperialism: the story and significance of a political word, 1840–1960*, Cambridge: Cambridge University Press.

Kuper, A. (1988) *The Invention of Primitive Society: transformations of an illusion*, reprinted in 1991, London: Routledge.

Laurence, R. (1994a) 'Modern ideology and the creation of ancient town planning' *European Review of History*, 1: 9–18.

Laurence, R. (1994b) *Roman Pompeii: space and society*, London: Routledge.

Laurence, R. (1998) 'Introduction', in R. Laurence and J. Berry (eds) *Cultural Identity in the Roman Empire*, London: Routledge.

Laurence, R. and Berry, J. (eds) (1998) *Cultural Identity in the Roman Empire*, London: Routledge.

Lee-Warner, W. (1894) *The Protected Princes of India*, London: Macmillan & Co.

Lefkowitz, M.R. and MacLean Rogers, G. (eds) (1996) *Black Athena Revisited*, London: University of Carolina Press.

Leslie, A. (ed.) (1999) *Theoretical Roman Archaeology and Architecture: the third conference proceedings*, Glasgow: Cruithne.

Levine, P. (1986) *The Amateur and the Professional: antiquarians, historians and archaeologists in Victorian England, 1838–1883*, Cambridge: Cambridge University Press.

Locke, W. (1878) *Stories of the Land We Live in: or England's history in simple language*, London: James Nisbet.

Losemann, V. (1999) 'The Nazi concept of Rome', in C. Edwards (ed.) *Roman Presences: perceptions of Rome in European culture, 1789–1945*, Cambridge: Cambridge University Press.

Lucas, C.P. (1912) *Greater Rome and Greater Britain*, Oxford: Clarendon Press.

Lucas, C.P. (1915) *The British Empire: six lectures*, London: Macmillan.

Macdonald, G. (1924a) 'Preface', in F. Haverfield and G. Macdonald *The Roman Occupation of Britain: being six Ford Lectures delivered by F. Haverfield*, Oxford: Clarendon Press.

Macdonald, G. (1924b) 'Bibliographical notice', in F. Haverfield and G. Macdonald *The Roman Occupation of Britain: being six Ford Lectures delivered by F. Haverfield*, Oxford: Clarendon Press.

Macdonald, S. (1987) 'Boadicea: warrior, mother and myth', in S. Macdonald, P. Holden and S. Ardener (eds) *Images of Women in Peace and War*, London: Macmillan.

McDonald, M. (1986) 'Celtic ethnic kinship and the problem of being English', in *Current Anthropology* 27: 333–47.

MacDougall, H.A. (1982) *Racial Myths in English History: Trojans, Teutons and Anglo-Saxons*, London: Montreal Harvest House.

MacGregor, M. (1912) *The Story of Ancient Rome: from the earliest times to the death of Augustus. Told for boys and girls*, London: Nelson.

Mackenzie, J.M. (1984) *Propaganda and Empire: the manipulation of British public opinion 1880–1960*, Manchester: Manchester University Press.

Mackenzie, J.M. (ed.) (1986a) *Imperialism and Popular Culture*, Manchester: Manchester University Press.

Mackenzie, J.M. (1986b) 'Introduction', in J.M. Mackenzie (ed.) *Imperialism and Popular Culture*, Manchester: Manchester University Press.

Mackenzie, J.M. (1986c) '"In touch with the infinite": the BBC and the Empire', in J.M. Mackenzie (ed.) *Imperialism and Popular Culture*, Manchester: Manchester University Press.

McKitterick, R. and Quinault, R. (1997) 'Introduction', in R. McKitterick and R. Quinault (eds) *Edward Gibbon and Empire*, Cambridge: Cambridge University Press.

Majeed, J. (1999) 'Comparativism and references to Rome in British imperial attitudes to India', in C. Edwards (ed.) *Roman Presences: receptions of Rome in European Culture, 1789–1945*, Cambridge: Cambridge University Press.

Manacorda, D. and Tamassia, R. (1985) *Il Piccone del Regime*, Rome: Biblioteca di Archeologia, Armando Curcio.

Marshall, H.E. (1905) *Our Island Story: A history of Britain for boys and girls*, London: Thoman Nelson & Sons.

Marshall, H.E. (1906) *Scotland's Story: A history of Britain for boys and girls*, London: T.C. & E.C. Jack Ltd.

Marshall, P.J. (ed.) (1996a) *The British Empire*, Cambridge: Cambridge University Press.

Marshall, P.J. (1996b) 'Introduction: the world shaped by empire', in P.J. Marshall (ed.) *The British Empire*, Cambridge: Cambridge University Press.

Marshall, P.J. (1996c) '1870–1918: The Empire under threat', in P.J. Marshall (ed.) *The British Empire*, Cambridge: Cambridge University Press.

Marshall, P.J. (1996d) '1918 to the 1960s: keeping afloat', in P.J. Marshall (ed.) *The British Empire*, Cambridge: Cambridge University Press.

Martindale, C. (1992) 'Horace, Ovid and others', in R. Jenkyns (ed.) *The Legacy of Rome: a new appraisal*, Oxford: Oxford University Press.

Mason, P. (1982) *The English Gentleman: the rise and fall of an ideal, reprinted in 1993*, London: Pimlico.

Matless, D. (1998) *Landscape and Englishness*, London: Reaktion.

Mattingly, D. (1996) 'From one colonialism to another: imperialism and the Maghreb', in J. Webster and N. Cooper (eds) *Roman Imperialism: post-colonial perspectives*, Leicester: Leicester Archaeological Monographs No. 3.

Mattingly, D. (1997a) 'Dialogues of power and experience in the Roman Empire', in D. Mattingly (ed.) *Dialogues in Roman Imperialism: power, discourse, and discrepant experiences in the Roman Empire,* Portsmouth, Rhode Island: Journal of Roman Archaeology, Supplementary Series No. 23.

Mattingly, D. (ed.) (1997b) *Dialogues in Roman Imperialism: power, discourse, and discrepant experiences in the Roman Empire.* Portsmouth, Rhode Island: Journal of Roman Archaeology, Supplementary Series, No 23.

Maxwell, G.S. (1989) *The Romans in Scotland,* Edinburgh: James Thin.

Meadows, K., Lemke, C. and Heron, J. (eds) (1997) *TRAC96, Proceedings of the Sixth Annual Theoretical Roman Archaeology Conference, Sheffield 1996,* Oxford: Oxbow.

Merivale, C. and Puller, C. (1877) *School History of Rome: from the foundation of the city to the extinction of the Empire of the west,* abridged from Dean Merivale's *General History of Rome,* London: Longmans, Green & Co.

Metcalfe, T.R. (1996) 'Imperial towns and cities', in P.J. Marshall (ed.) *The British Empire,* Cambridge: Cambridge University Press.

Metzler, J., Millett, M., Roymans, N and Slofstra, J. (eds) (1995) *Integration in the Early Roman West: the role of culture and ideology,* Luxembourg: Dossiers d'Archéologie du Musée National d'Histoire et d'Art 1.

Mikalachki, J. (1998) *The Legacy of Boadicea: gender and nation in early modern England,* London: Routledge.

Miket, R. (1989) 'John Collingwood Bruce and the Roman Wall controversy: the formative years, 1848–1958', in R. Miket and C. Burgess (eds) *Between and Beyond the Walls: essays on the prehistory and history of northern Britain in honour of George Jobey,* Edinburgh: John Donald.

Millar, F. (1967) *The Roman Empire and its Neighbours,* London: Weidenfeld & Nicholson.

Millett, M. (1990a) *The Romanization of Britain: an essay in archaeological interpretation,* Cambridge: Cambridge University Press.

Millett, M. (1990b) 'Romanization: historical issues and archaeological interpretation', in T. Blagg and M. Millett (eds) *The Early Roman Empire in the West,* Oxford: Oxbow.

Mills, E.E. (1905) [Anon] *The Decline and Fall of the British Empire: a brief account of those causes which resulted in the destruction of our late ally, together with a comparison between the British and Roman Empires. Appointed for use in the National Schools of Japan. Tokio, 2005,* Oxford: Alden & Co.

Moatti, C. (1993) *The Search for Ancient Rome,* London: Thames & Hudson.

Mommsen, T. (1886) *The History of Rome, The Provinces from Caesar to Diocletian, Parts 1 and 2,* trans. W.P. Dickson, London: Richard Bentley & Son.

Mommsen, T. (1909) *The Provinces of the Roman Empire, from Caesar to Diocleatian, Parts 1 and 2,* trans. W.P. Dickson, revised edition, London: Macmillan & Co.

Montague, C.E. (1906) 'Memoir: middle life', in W.T. Arnold, 1906 *Studies of Roman Imperialism,* edited by Edward Fiddes, Manchester: Manchester University Press.

Monypenny, W.F. (1905) 'The imperial ideal', in *The Empire and the Century: a series of essays on imperial problems and possibilities by various writers,* London: John Murray.

Morris, J. (1973) *Heaven's Command: an imperial progress,* reprinted 1981, London: Faber & Faber.

Nicklin, T. (1909) 'The aims of classical study with particular reference to public schools', *Classical Review,* 33: 33–5.

Notes and News (1926) *Classical Review,* 40: 1–3 and 145–6.

Oliver, R.A. (1979) 'Colonization and decolonization in tropical Africa' in B. Burnham and H. Johnson (eds) *Invasion and Response: the case of Roman Britain,* Oxford: British Archaeological Reports, British No. 73.

O'Neill, E. (1912) *A Nursery History of England,* London: Nelson.

Ottaway, P. (1992) *Archaeology in British Towns: from the Emperor Claudius to the Black Death,* London: Routledge.

Pagden, A. (1995) *Lords of All the World: ideologies of Empire in Spain, Britain and France c.1500–c.1800,* London: Yale University Press.

Parman, S. (1990) *Scottish Crofters: a historical ethnography of a Celtic Village,* London: Rinehart & Winston.

Patterson, T.C. (1997) *Inventing Western Civilization,* New York: Monthly Review Press.

Pelham, H.F. (1906) 'A chapter in Roman frontier history', *Transactions of the Royal Historical Society,* 20: 14–47.

Pelham, H.F. (1911) *Essays by Henry Francis Pelham,* edited by F. Haverfield, Oxford: Clarendon Press.

Piggott, S. (1965) *Ancient Europe: from the beginnings of agriculture to Classical Antiquity,* Edinburgh: Edinburgh University Press.

Piggott, S. (1966) *Celts, Saxons and the Early Antiquarians,* the O'Donnell Lecture 1966, Edinburgh: Edinburgh University Press.

Piggott, S. (1976) *Ruins in a Landscape: essays in Antiquarianism,* Edinburgh: Edinburgh University Press.

Pitt Rivers, Lieutenant-General (Lane-Fox, A.) (1887) *Excavations in Cranborne Chase near Rushmore on the Borders of Dorset and Wilts: Volume 1, excavations in the Romano-British village on Woodcuts Common, and Romano-British antiquities in Rushmore Park,* London: Harrison & Son.

Porter, R. (1988) *Gibbon: making history,* reprinted 1995, London: Phoenix.

Potter, T. (1986) 'A Roman province: Britain AD 43–410', in I. Longworth and J. Cherry (eds) *Archaeology in Britain since 1945,* London: British Museum.

Quartermaine, L. (1995) ' "Slouching towards Rome": Mussolini's imperial vision', in T.J. Cornell and K. Lomas (eds) *Urban Society in Roman Italy,* London: University College.

Quennell, M. and Quennell, C.H.B. (1924) *Everyday Life in Roman Britain,* London: Batsford.

Quinault, R. (1997) 'Winston Churchill and Gibbon' in R. McKitterick and R. Quinault (eds) *Edward Gibbon and Empire,* Cambridge: Cambridge University Press.

Rait, R.S. and Parrott, J.E. (1909) *Finger-Posts to British History: a summary with notes, of the historical events from the earliest time to the year 1908,* London: Thomas Nelson & Sons.

Raychaudhuri, T. (1996) 'British rule in India: an assessment', in P.J. Marshall (ed.) *The British Empire*, Cambridge: Cambridge University Press.

Reynolds, D. (1991) *Britannia Overruled: British policy and world power in the 20th century,* Harlow: Longman.

Rhys, J. (1882) *Early Britain – Celtic Britain,* London: Society for the Promotion of Christian Knowledge.

Rice-Holmes, T. (1907) *Ancient Britain and the Invasion of Julius Caesar,* reprinted in 1936, Oxford: Oxford University Press.

Richmond, I.A. (1925) *Huddersfield in Roman Times,* Huddersfield: Tolson Museum Publications.

Richmond, I.A. (1955) *Roman Britain,* London: Penguin.

Richmond, I.A. (1957) *The Archaeology of the Roman Empire: a scheme of study, an inaugural lecture delivered before the University of Oxford on 14th May 1957,* Oxford: Clarendon Press.

Rist, G. (1997) *The History of Development: from western origins to global faith,* London: Zed Books.

Rivet, A.L.F. (1958) *Town and Country in Roman Britain,* London: Hutchison University Library.

Rivet, A.L.F. (1969a) 'Social and economic aspects', in A.L.F. Rivet (ed.) *The Roman Villa in Britain,* London: Routledge & Kegan Paul.

Rivet, A.L.F. (ed.) (1969b) *The Roman Villa in Britain,* London: Routledge & Kegan Paul.

Rivet, A.L.F. (1976) *Rudyard Kipling's Roman Britain: fact or fiction, an inaugural lecture by Professor A.L.F. Rivet given at the University of Keele on Thursday 6th November 1976,* Keele: Keele University Library.

Robbins, K. (1998) *Great Britain: identities, institutions and the idea of Britishness,* London: Longmans.

Romm, J.S. (1992) *The Edges of the Earth in Ancient Thought: geography, exploration, and fiction,* Princeton, NJ: Princeton University Press.

Roy, W. (1793) *The Military Antiquities of the Romans in Britain,* London: Society of Antiquaries of London.

Rush, P. (ed.) (1995) *Theoretical Roman Archaeology: second conference proceedings,* Aldershot: Avebury.

Said, E.W. (1978) *Orientalism: Western conceptions of the Orient,* reprinted 1991, London: Penguin.

Said, E.W. (1993) *Culture and Imperialism,* London: Chatto & Windus.

Samuel, R. (1994) *Theatres of Memory, Volume I: past and present in contemporary culture,* London: Verso.

Samuel, R. (1998) *Island Stories: Unravelling Britain – Theatres of Memory, Volume II,* London: Verso.

Sands, P.C. (1908) *The Client Princes of the Roman Empire under the Republic,* Cambridge: Cambridge University Press.

Scarth, H.M. (1883) *Early Britain: Roman Britain,* London: Society for the Promotion of Christian Knowledge.

Scholte, B. (1970) 'Towards a self-reflexive anthropology', *Critical Anthropology,* 1/2: 3–33.

Scholte, B. (1981) 'Critical anthropology since its reinvention', in J.S. Kahn and R. Llobera (eds) *The Anthropology of Pre-Capitalist Societies,* London: Macmillan.

Schwartz, B. (ed.) (1996) *The Expansion of England: race, ethnicity and cultural history*, London: Routledge.

Scott, E. (1990) 'In search of Roman Britain: talking about their generation', *Antiquity* 64: 953–6.

Scott, E. (1993a) 'Writing the Roman Empire', in E. Scott (ed.) *Theoretical Roman Archaeology: first conference proceedings*, Aldershot: Avebury.

Scott, E. (ed.) (1993b) *Theoretical Roman Archaeology: first conference proceedings*, Aldershot: Avebury.

Scott, E. (1998) 'Tales from a Romanist: a personal view of archaeology and "equal opportunities"', in C. Forcey, J. Hawthorne and R. Witcher (eds) *TRAC97: Proceedings of the Seventh Annual Theoretical Roman Archaeology Conference, Nottingham 1997*, Oxford: Oxbow.

Scott, J.C. (1990) *Domination and the Arts of Resistance: hidden transcripts*, London: Yale University Press.

Scott, J.M. (1975) *Boadicea*, London: Constable.

Seebohm, F. (1883) *The English Village Community Examined in its Relation to the Manorial and Tribal Systems and to the Common of Open Field System of Husbandry: an essay in economic history*, London: Longmans, Green & Co.

Seeley, J.R. (1883) *The Expansion of England: two courses of lectures*, London: Macmillan & Co.

Sellar, W.C. and Yeatman, R.J. (1930) *1066 and All That: a memorable history of England, comprising all the parts you can remember, including 103 good things, 5 bad kings and 2 genuine dates*, reprinted 1998, London: Arrow Books.

Seymour, W.A. (1980) *A History of the Ordnance Survey*, London: Dawson.

Shaw, B.D. (1983) '"Eaters of flesh, drinkers of milk": the ancient Mediterranean ideology of the pastoral nomad', *Ancient Society* 13/14: 5–31.

Sheppard, J.G. (1861) *The Fall of Rome and the Rise of the New Nationalities: a series of lectures on the connections between ancient and modern history*, London: Routledge, Warne & Routledge.

Silberman, N.A. (1999) 'From Masada to the Little Bighorn: the role of archaeological sites in the shaping of national myths', *Conservation and Management of Archaeological Sites*, 3: 9–15.

Sims-Williams, P. (1998) 'Celts and Celtoscepticism', *Cambrian Medieval Celtic Studies* 36: 1–35.

Smiles, S. (1994) *The Image of Antiquity: Ancient Britain and the romantic imagination*, London: Yale University Press.

Smith, D. (1986) 'Englishness and the liberal inheritance after 1886', in R. Colls and P. Dodd (eds) *Englishness: Politics and Culture 1880–1920*, London: Croom Helm.

Smith, J.T. (1978) 'Villas as a key to social structure', in M. Todd (ed.) *Studies in the Romano-British Villa*, Leicester: Leicester University Press.

Smith, J.T. (1982) 'Villa plans and social structure in Britain and Gaul', *Caesarodunum* 17: 321–51.

Smith, J.T. (1985) 'Barnsley Park Villa: its interpretation and implications', *Oxford Journal of Archaeology* 4: 341–51.

Smith, J.T. (1997) *Roman Villas: a study in social structure*, London: Routledge.

Spivak, G.C. (1988) 'Can the subaltern speak?', in P. Williams and L. Chrisman 1993 (eds) *Colonial Discourse and Post-colonial Theory: a reader*, London: Harvester.

Spurr, D. (1993) *The Rhetoric of Empire: colonial discourse in journalism, travel writing and imperial administration*, reprinted 1994, London: Duke University Press.

Stapleton, J. (1994) *Englishness and the Study of Politics: the social and political thought of Ernest Barker*, Cambridge: Cambridge University Press.

Stevens, C.E. (1947) 'A possible conflict of laws in Roman Britain', *Journal of Roman Studies*, 37: 132–4.

Stevens, C.E. (1966) 'The social and economic aspects of rural settlement', in C. Thomas (ed.) *Rural Settlement in Roman Britain*, London: CBA.

Stewart, P.C.N. (1995) 'Inventing Britain: the Roman creation and adaptation of an image', *Britannia* 26: 1–10.

Stobart, J.C. (1912) *The Grandeur that was Rome: a survey of Roman culture and civilization*, London: Sidgwick & Jackson.

Stocking, G.W. (1987) *Victorian Anthropology*, Oxford: Macmillan.

Stone, M. (1999) 'A flexible Rome: Fascism and the cult of romanità', in C. Edwards (ed.) *Roman Presences: receptions of Rome in European Culture, 1789–1945*, Cambridge: Cambridge University Press.

Strachey, J. (1888) *India*, London: Kegan Paul, Trench & Co.

Stray, C. (1998) *Classics Transformed: Schools, Universities, and Society in England, 1830–1960*, Oxford: Clarendon Press.

Summerson, J. (1964) *The Classical Language of Architecture*, republished in 1980, London: Methuen.

Sutcliff, R. (1954) *The Eagle of the Ninth*, Oxford: Oxford University Press.

Sutcliff, R. (1978) *Song for a Dark Queen*, London: Pelham.

Symonds, R. (1986) *Oxford and Empire: the last lost cause?*, London: Macmillan.

Tabraham, C. and Grove, D. (1995) *Fortress Scotland and the Jacobites*, London: Batsford.

Taylor, J.G. (1976) *From Modernization to Modes of Production: a critique of the sociologies of development and underdevelopment*, reprinted 1981, London: Macmillan.

Taylor, M.V. (1960) 'The Society for the Promotion of Roman Studies, 1910–60', *Journal of Roman Studies* 50: 129–34.

Taylor, M.V. and Collingwood, R.G. (1923) 'Roman Britain in 1921 and 1922', *Journal of Roman Studies* 11: 200–44.

Taylor, W. (1976) *The Military Roads in Scotland*, reprinted 1996, Exeter: SRP.

Tennyson, A. (1864) 'Boadicea', in C. Ricks (ed.) (1969) *The Poems of Tennyson*, London: Longmans.

Terrenato, N. (1998) 'The Romanization of Italy: global acculturation or cultural *bricolage?*', in C. Forcey, J. Hawthorne and R. Witcher (eds) *TRAC97: Proceedings of the Seventh Annual Theoretical Roman Archaeology Conference, Nottingham 1997*, Oxford: Oxbow.

Thackeray, F. (1843) *Researches into the Ecclesiastical and Political State of Ancient Britain under the Roman Emperors: with observations upon the principal events and characters connected with the Christian religion during the first five centuries*, Volume 1, London: Thomas Cadell.

The Empire and the Century (1905) *The Empire and the Century: a series of essays on imperial problems and possibilities by various writers*, London: John Murray.

Thomas, C. (ed.) (1966) *Rural Settlement in Roman Britain*, London: CBA.

Thomas, C. (1990) 'Review of R Hingley's *Rural Settlement in Roman Britain*', *Antiquity* 64: 183–4.

Thomas, N. (1994) *Colonialism's Culture: anthropology, travel and government*, Cambridge: Polity Press.

Thompson, L.A. (1989) *Romans and Blacks*, London: University of Oklahoma Press.

Thompson, M.W. (1977) *General Pitt-Rivers: evolution and archaeology in the nineteenth century*, Bradford-on-Avon: Moonraker.

Thomson, J. (1924) *A Great Free City: the book of Silchester*, volume 1, London: H.O. Lloyd & Co.

Thornton, A.P. (1978) *Imperialism in the Twentieth Century*, London; Macmillan.

Thornycroft, E. (1932) *Bronze and Steel: the life of Thomas Thornycroft, sculptor and engineer*, Long Compton: Kings Stone Press.

Tiffin, C. and Lawson, A. (eds) (1994) *De-scribing Empire: post-colonialism and textuality,* London: Routledge.

Treece, H. (1954) *Legions of the Eagle*, London: Bodley Head.

Trevelyan, M. (1900) *Britain's Greatness Foretold: the story of Boadicea, the British Warrior-Queen*, London: John Hogg.

Trigger, B.G. (1984) 'Alternative archaeologies: nationalist, colonialist, imperialist', *Man* 19: 355–70.

Turner, F.M. (1981) *The Greek Heritage in Victorian Britain*, London: Yale University Press.

Turner, F.M. (1989) 'Why the Greeks and not the Romans in Victorian Britain?', in G.W. Clarke (ed.) *Rediscovering Hellenism: the Hellenistic inheritance and the English imagination*, Cambridge: Cambridge University Press.

Turner, F.M. (1993) *Contesting Cultural Authority: Essays in Victorian intellectual life,* Cambridge: Cambridge University Press.

Turner, F.M. (1999) 'Christians and pagans in Victorian novels', in C. Edwards (ed.) *Roman Presences: receptions of Rome in European Culture, 1789–1945*, Cambridge: Cambridge University Press.

Unstead, R.J. (1957) *People in History: from Caractacus to Alexander Fleming*, London: Adam & Charles Black.

Vance, N. (1997) *The Victorians and Ancient Rome*, Oxford: Blackwell.

Vance, N. (1999) 'Decadence and the subversion of Empire', in C. Edwards (ed.) *Roman Presences: perceptions of Rome in European culture, 1789–1945*, Cambridge: Cambridge University Press.

Vercingetorix et Alésia (1994) *Vercingetorix et Alésia*, Paris: Saint-Germain-en-Laye Musée des Antiquités nationales, Editions de la Réunion des musée nationaux.

Vinogradoff, P. (1905) *The Growth of the Manor*, New York: Swan Sonnenschein and Co.

Wacher, J. (1995) *The Towns of Roman Britain*, second edition, London: Batsford.

Ward, M.A. (1906) 'Memoir: last years', in W.T. Arnold 1906 *Studies of Roman Imperialism*, edited by Edward Fiddes, Manchester: Manchester University Press.

Ward, T. (1911) *The Roman Era in Britain*, London: Methuen.

Warner, M. (1985) *Monuments and Maidens: the allegory of the female form*, reprinted 1996, London: Vintage.

Washbrook, D.A. (1999) 'Orients and Occidents: colonial discourse theory and the historiography of the British Empire', in R.W. Winks (ed.) *The Oxford History of the British Empire: Volume 5, Historiography*, Oxford: Oxford University Press.

Watson, W. (Sir) (1936) *The Poems of Sir William Watson, 1878–1935*, London: George Harrup.

Webster, G. (1969) 'The future of villa studies', in A.L.F. Rivet (ed.) *The Roman Villa in Britain*, London: Routledge & Kegan Paul.

Webster, G. (1978) *Boudica: the British revolt against Rome AD 60*, London: Batsford.

Webster, G. (1981) *Rome against Caractacus: the Roman campaigns in Britain AD 48–58*, London: Batsford.

Webster, J. (1995) 'The just war: Graeco-Roman texts as colonial discourse' in S. Cottam, D. Dungworth, S. Scott and J. Taylor (eds) *TRAC94: proceedings of the fourth annual Roman Theoretical Archaeology Conference, Durham 1994*, Oxford: Oxbow.

Webster, J. (1996a) 'Roman imperialism in the post-imperial age', in J. Webster and N. Cooper (eds) *Roman Imperialism: post-colonial perspectives*, Leicester: Leicester Archaeological Monographs No. 3.

Webster, J. (1996b) 'Ethnographic barbarity: colonial discourse and "Celtic Warrior Societies"', in J. Webster and N. Cooper (eds) *Roman Imperialism: post-colonial perspectives*, Leicester: Leicester Archaeological Monographs No. 3.

Webster, J. (1997) 'A negotiated syncretism: readings on the development of Romano-Celtic religion', in D. Mattingly (ed.) *Dialogues in Roman Imperialism: power, discourse, and discrepant experiences in the Roman Empire*,

Portsmouth, Rhode Island: Journal of Roman Archaeology, Supplementary Series, No 23.

Webster, J. (1999) 'Here be Dragons! The continuing influence of Roman attitudes to northern Britain', in B. Bevan (ed.) 1999, *Northern Exposure: interpretative devolution and the Iron Ages in Britain*, Leicester: Leicester Archaeological Monographs No. 4.

Webster, J. and Cooper, N. (eds) (1996) *Roman Imperialism: post-colonial perspectives*, Leicester: Leicester Archaeological Monographs No. 3.

Weigall, A. (1926) *Wanderings in Roman Britain*, London: Thornton Butterworth.

Welch, G.P. (1972) *Britannia: the Roman conquest and occupation of Britain*, London: Robert Hale.

Wells, C. (1972) *The German Policy of Augustus: an examination of the archaeological evidence*, Oxford: Clarendon Press.

Wells, C. (1996) '*Profuit invitis te dominante capi:* social and economic considerations on the Roman frontiers', *Journal of Roman Archaeology* 9: 436–46.

Wheeler, M. (1954) *Rome Beyond the Imperial Frontier*, London: G. Bell & Sons.

Wheeler, M. (1976) *My Archaeological Mission to India and Pakistan*, London: Thames & Hudson.

Whittaker, C.R. (1994) *Frontier of the Roman Empire: a social and economic study*, London: Johns Hopkins University Press.

Whittaker, C.R. (1997) 'Imperialism and culture: the Roman initiative', in D. Mattingly (ed.) *Dialogues in Roman imperialism: power, discourse, and discrepant experiences in the Roman Empire*. Portsmouth, Rhode Island: Journal of Roman Archaeology, Supplementary Series, No 23.

Whittington, G. and Gibson, A.J.S. (1986) *The Military Survey of Scotland 1747–1755: a critique*, Historical Geography Research Series, No. 18, Lancaster: University of Lancaster.

Williams, P. and Chrisman, L. (eds) (1993) *Colonial Discourse and Post-colonial Theory: a reader*, London: Harvester.

Windle, B.C.A. (1897) *Life in Early Britain: being an account of the early inhabitants of the island and the memorials which they have left behind them*, London: David Nutt.

Windle, B.C.A. (1923) *The Romans in Britain*, London: Methuen & Co.

Wiseman, T.P. (1994) *Historiography and Imagination: eight essays on Roman culture*, Exeter: University of Exeter Press.

Wiseman, T.P. (no date) *A Short History of the British School at Rome*, London: British School at Rome.

Wolf, E.R. (1972) 'American anthropologist and American society', in D.H. Hymes (ed.) *Reinventing Anthropology*, New York: Vintage Books, 251–63.

Wood, M. and Queiroga, F. (eds) (1991) *Current Research on the Romanization of the Western Provinces*, Oxford: British Archaeological Reports, International Series No. 575.

Woodward, A. (1992) *Shrines and Sacrifices*, London: Batsford.

Woolf, G. (1992) 'The unity and diversity of Romanisation', *Journal of Roman Archaeology*, 5: 349–52.

Woolf, G. (1998) *Becoming Roman: the origins of provincial civilization in Roman Gaul*, Cambridge: Cambridge University Press.

Wyke, M. (1997) *Projecting the Past: ancient Rome, cinema and history*, London: Routledge.

Yeo, S. (1986) 'Socialism, the state, and some oppositional Englishness', in R. Colls and P. Dodd (eds) *Englishness: Politics and Culture 1880–1920*, London: Croom Helm.

Young, F.B. (1944) *The Island*, London: William Heinemann.

Zammit, R.C. (1996) *The Victoria Lines: souvenir guide*, Malta: Valletta.

Zanker, P. (1988) *The Power of Images in the Age of Augustus*, trans. A. Shapiro, Ann Arbor, MI: University of Michigan.

INDEX

Ackworth, H. A. 76–7, 123
administration 37, 51–2
Africa 37, 121, 131, 134, 137
Africans 50, 64, 120, 121–3
Agricola 43, 93, 128
Alésia 81
Alfred, Anglo-Saxon king 76
Ambleside, Roman fort 35, 46–7
Ambiorix 67
America xii, 59 *see also* USA
American War of Independence 74
ancient historians xi, 42, 54
ancient history 9–10, 11, 14, 35–6, 98, 159
Anglo-Saxons 3, 61, 63–5, 67, 69, 82, 89, 91–2 94–5, 97–8, 103–5, 107, 128, 135, 159, 161 *see also* Teutons and Saxons
anthropolgists xii, 55
anthropology xii, 11
Antiquity xiii
Antonine Wall 42
Arab 116
architecture 96
Arianrod 79–80
Arnold, Thomas 64, 70
Arnold, W.T. 25, 44, 47, 53–4, 158
art 98–9, 142, 148 *see also* Roman art
Arthur, King 76
Ashcroft, B. 9
Asia 50, 120, 131
Asian 122
assimilation, the concept of 37, 48–51
Atilla the Hun 47

Augustus 44
Australia 7, 31

Baden-Powell, R. 25, 32–3
Baldwin, Stanley 56, 100–3, 106, 158, 162
Balfour, A. 25, 33, 45
barbarians, the concept of 10, 40, 59, 148, 159
Baring, Evelyn *see* Cromer, Lord
Bath 12
Bedford School 106
Belgae 138
Bengal, Gulf of 42
Beric 76, 82–4, 91
Bernal, Martin 10
Betts, R. F. 23, 49
Bevan, E. R. 35
Bismarck, Otto von 30
Boadicea 15, 62, 67, 73–84, 86, 90, 92, 146, 159, 161 *see also* Boudica
Boer War 30, 78, 80, 87
Borrans Field *see* Ambleside
Boudica 73 *see also* Boadicea
Bowler, Peter 86
Boy Scout movement 32
Braund, David 164
Brigantes 73, 82
Britannia 141
British Broadcasting Company 33
Bruce, John Collingwood, 21
Bryant, Arthur 147
Bryce, Lord J. 25–6, 28, 45, 47, 49, 50, 53, 56
Buckingham Palace 20

Caesar, Julius 40, 75, 80, 85, 92–3
Caistor-by-Norwich 90
Caius Muro 83
Calgacus 73
Cambridge 23, 33; Trinity College 33
Camulodunum 83 *see also* Colchester
Canada 7, 31, 100
Caratacus 73–7, 79, 84
Carna 67, 76
Carrington, C. 56–7
Cartimandua 73
Cassius Dio 73–4
Celtic: art 125, 142, 148; revival 125–7, 132–6, 142; subaltern 2, 4, 10, 41, 61, 63, 65–8, 71, 88–9, 91, 111, 126, 147, 159, 160, 162–3
Chinese Empire 20
Chitral 45–7
Christianity 4–5, 22, 63–6, 70, 83, 90–1, 158, 160
Church, A. 25, 27, 67–8, 125
cities *see* Roman cities
'civil district' 126–8, 139, 144
civilising mission 5, 11, 48, 107, 114, 122, 128, 137, 145
classics 9–10, 56, 101–2, 106, 158
Classical Association, The 35–6, 49, 53, 56, 100–1, 158
Classical Review, The 35
Claudius 73
Client princes 51
Clyde, Lord 20
Colchester, 70, 82–3, 90 *see also* *Camulodunum*
Collingwood, R. G. 57, 97–100, 130, 131–6, 138–42, 144, 148, 151, 164
Collins, Edwin 79–80
Colosseum 83
colonial discourse theory xiv, 6, 9, 10, 11, 52, 112
Colonial Office 34
colonies xiv, 22
Conservatives 6, 33 *see also* Tories
Coote, H. C. 69–70, 89, 91, 95, 160
Cornwall 63, 65, 126

Count of the Saxon Shore 67–8, 76
Cowper, William 62, 67, 74–5, 77, 79–80, 86, 159
Cramb, J. A. 30, 87
Cranborne Chase 119, 134–5
Cromer, Lord 25, 28, 34–5, 47, 49, 53–4, 56, 101, 116, 158
Cromwell, Oliver 40
Cumberland and Westmorland Antiquarian and Archaeological Society 35, 45–6, 54
Cunobelin 73
Curzon, Lord G. N. 25, 44–5, 47, 116
'Customs Hedge' 41–2

Daily Mail 103–4
Danes 3, 63, 89, 93–4, 97, 105
Daniel, G. E. 96
'Dark Ages' 162
Darwin, Charles 145
David, D. 76
decline and fall 2, 15, 25, 28–37, 53, 75, 158 *see also* Gibbon
decolonisation xiv
'denationalisation' 37, 59, 115, 123
Dervish 47
despotism 20–1, 24, 27, 52, 64, 107, 115, 157, 161
druid 75, 79

Edward VII 59
education: xi, 9; classical 9–10, 38, 40, 52, 70, 83, 86, 90, 95, 102, 137; university 9
Egerton, H. E. 94
Egypt 31, 34, 52, 87
Egyptian 116
Eldridge, C. C. 6
Elgar, E. 76
Empire and the Century, The (1905) 23
Englishness, the concept of 3–4, 61–2, 96–7, 159–61
Enlightenment 145, 162

Fens 83
First World War 62, 89, 95, 97, 132
Fletcher, C. 33, 52, 65, 68, 70, 85, 88, 91, 128

Forbes, Duncan 40
Ford, Henry 58, 66
forts *see* Roman forts
France 8, 20, 59, 81–2, 106, 157
Freeman, Philip xiv, 53, 55, 117
French 81, 97, 106
Frere, S. S. 12, 131, 136, 140–3, 146, 148, 151
frontiers, the concept of 37–48, 56–9

Gardiner, S. R. 66
Gaul 40, 43, 64, 67, 98
Geoffrey of Monmouth 124
germanic peoples *see* Anglo-Saxons and Teutons
German 22, 89, 92, 104–6, 113
Germany 22, 30–1, 39, 45, 47, 55, 59, 62, 94, 105, 132, 157–8
Gibbon, Edward, 20, 28–31, 115
Gilgit 47
Grant Duff, Sir M. E. 42
Great Wall of China, The 42
Greece 10, 36, 64, 146
Greek 9, 35–6, 40, 116, 145, 157
Green, G. E. 92
Griffiths, G. 9
Grose-Hodge, H. 100, 106–7

Hadrian 21
Hadrian's Wall 21, 33, 41–4, 47, 57–8
Hamilton, Sir Ian 44, 47
Hanoverians 39–41, 159
Haverfield, Francis: xi-xii, 1–2, 4–5, 12–5, 25, 28–9, 35–8, 42, 44–8, 50, 53–6, 58–9, 62, 88–9, 91, 94–5, 107, 109, 111–34, 136, 138–48, 151–3, 158, 161–2; addresses 14, 28, 35–7, 53, 152
Hellenic images 19
Henderson, B.W. 25, 82
Henty, G. A. 25, 48, 82–4, 90, 92, 94–5, 104, 123
Hobson, J. A. 25
Hogarth, D. G. 35, 49–50
Holy Roman Empire 5
Honourable Society of Cymmrodorion 124
Hoogvelt, A. M. M. 153

House of Commons 80
Hughes, Mary 100, 105–6
Hyde Park 20

Iberia 64, 116 *see also* Spain
Iceni 73, 77–8, 80, 82–3
Illyrians 116
imperial discourse, the concept of 6–11
imperial estates 139
'incorporation' 38, 51, 59
India 7, 15, 22, 26–7, 31, 34, 36, 38, 42–7, 49–51, 54, 57, 61, 65–6, 68, 82, 108, 123, 138, 147–8, 159–60
Indian: Civil Service 54, 106; Independence Movement 147; 'Mutiny' 82
Indus 42
Inns of Court 10
Ireland 63, 126, 128
Irish 4, 49, 65, 71, 148
Iron Age 134, 151
Israel 64
Italian 107, 116–7, 157
Italy 22, 59, 106, 113, 123, 132, 157

Jameson Raid 44
Japan 31
Johnson, Samuel 40, 88

Kashmir 45
Kingsley, Charles, 20, 64, 70
Kipling, R. 25, 33, 43–5, 47, 52, 56–7, 59, 65, 68–70, 85, 88, 91, 108, 128
Koebner, R. 7, 23

Lake District 46, 126
Lancing College 12
Lee, Thomas Ashe 40
Lee-Warner, W. 51
Liberals 6
Lincoln 90
Locke, W. 72
London: 20, 79, 90; clubs 10; County Council 77, 80–1
Lucas, C. P. 25, 28, 34, 45, 47, 49, 53, 93–4, 103–4, 123

Macdonald, G. 124
Macdonald, S. 73, 75
Mackenzie, J. 122
Madras 42
Majeed, Javed 28, 50
Magnus Maximus 43
Marshall, H.E. 65, 70
Mikalachki, J. 74–5
'military district' 126–8, 139, 144, 162
Millett, Martin xii, 142–3, 151
Mills, Elliot 25, 31–3
Mogul Empire 23
Mommsen, Theodor 22, 89, 113–5, 145, 158
Monypenny, W, F. 24, 48
Mussolini, Benito 106–7, 157
Myres, J. N. L. 133

Napoleon III 20, 22, 81, 157
Nauheim 45
Nero 83
Nineveh 7
non-villa settlements 150–1, 155
Normans 43, 63, 70, 72, 89, 92, 94, 97, 103, 105–6, 161
novels: 11, 57, 76; children's novels 11, 57, 72, 82

Officers see Roman officers
O'Neil, Elizabeth 65
Ordnance Survey 40, 104
Orient, The 23
'otherness' the concept of 10, 159
Oxford 35, 42, 45, 53–4, 56, 103, 123
Oxford University: 9, 26, 31, 36, 44, 90, 94; Brasenose College 103; Christ Church 12; New College 12

Parliament 10, 19–20
Parliament Hill Fields 81
Parnesius 43
Pelham, Henry 12, 42, 45
Pertinax 43
Picts 67
Posidonius 40
post-colonial theory xiv, 11 see also colonial discourse theory

pottery see Roman pottery
Prasutagus 79
progress: the concept of 30, 86–7, 121–3, 143–6; critique of 153–4

Reformation 102
Renaissance 9, 19, 74, 124
republicanism 19
resistance, the concept of xi, 121, 133, 136, 144, 156, 161
Rescue archaeology 152
Rhys, J. 90–1
Rice-Holmes, T. 93, 97, 107
Richmond, Sir Ian 12
Rivet, A. L. F. 43, 57, 107–8, 131, 136–44, 146, 148, 151, 164
Roman: army 5, 85; art 148; cities 65, 68, 70, 88, 163; forts 39, 41, 68, 91, 126, 151, 160, 163; officers 65–8; pottery 119, 134, 140; Republic 5, 22, 24; small town 148, 150–1; towns 70, 91, 117, 133, 137, 141, 148, 150–1, 160; villas 65, 68, 90, 117, 133–6, 138–9, 148, 150–2, 160, 163
Romanisation: concept of 4–5, 89, 91, 111–3, 161–2; progressive 122, 144–9, 161–2; 'by osmosis' 143; critique of 143–9, 161–2
Roman Society, The 12, 35–6, 45, 48, 53, 56, 123
Rotherley 134, 141–2
Rothschild, Baron 20
Rough Castle 39
Roy, Major General William 39–40, 56
Royal Titles Bill (1876) 22, 24
Russia 22, 31 see also Soviet Union

Said, Edward xi, xii, 8, 11
Salisbury Plain 134–5
'Salt Hedge' see Customs Hedge'
Samuel, Raphael 3, 96
Sands, P. C. 25, 51–2
Saxons 64, 67, 92–4, 97, 124 see also Anglo-Saxons
Scarborough signal station 98–9
Scarth, H. M. 90–1, 123
Schmidt, H. Dan 7, 23

school: xii, 9, 31; pubic 9; teachers 19, 23
Scotland 39–40, 42, 63, 126, 128, 157
Scots 4, 65, 71, 73, 93, 148, 158–9
Scott, J. M. 146
Second World War 106
Seebohm, Frederic 92
Seeley, J. R. 6, 23–5, 67
Sheppard, J. G. 20, 41, 64, 70
Shipston on Stour 12
Silchester 118–9
small towns *see* Roman small towns
social anthropologists *see* anthropologists
Society of Antiquaries of London, The 39, 81
Society of Antiquaries of Scotland, The 42
Society for Promoting Christian Knowledge, The 90
Society for the Promotion of Roman Studies, The 104 *see also* Roman Society, The
South Africa 31
Soviet Union 7 *see* also Russia
Spain 67 *see also* Iberia
Spurr, David 6, 11
Stobart, J. 25, 33–4, 87–8
Stonehenge 67
Stray, C. 9–10
subaltern, the concept of 10 *see also* Celtic subaltern
Sudan 52
Sydney Grammar School 103
Symonds, R. 9, 55

Tacitus 40, 73–4
Tennyson, A. 76–8, 81
Teutonic origins, concept of 61, 63–5 *see also* Anglo-Saxons and Saxons
Thackeray, F. 65
Theoretical Roman Archaeology Conference xiv

Thomas, Charles 151
Thornycroft, Sir John Isaac 77
Thornycroft, Thomas 77–8, 80–1.
Tiberius 44
Tiffin, H. 9
Times, The 77
Titus 30
Tories 31, 78 *see also* Conservatives
Towns *see* Roman towns
Trevelyan, Marie 77–9, 81, 90
Turkish Empire 20

urban planning 55
USA 7, 31 *see also* America

Vance, Norman 42, 72
Vectis, Isle of Wight 43, 67, 68
Vercingetorix 81–2, 157
Vespasian 30
Victoria, Queen 6, 22, 27, 76, 79, 80–1
villages 133–6, 138–9, 142, 147–8, 151
villas *see* Roman villas
Vinogradoff, P. 93

Wales 63, 65, 119, 125–6
Warner, Marina 81
Watson, Sir William 25, 31
Webster, Graham 80
Webster, Jane 112
Weigall, A. 100, 103–5, 123
Wells, Colin 57
Welsh 4, 47, 63, 65, 71, 77–8, 93, 121, 123–4, 126, 136, 148, 159
Western Isles 40
Westminster Bridge 77
Whittaker, C. 143
Winchester School 12
Windle, Bertram 68, 91, 100, 106
Woodcuts 119–20, 134, 141–2
Wolfe, James 40

York 70